The BBC Proms Pocket Guide to Great Symphonies

Nicholas Kenyon has been Director of the BBC Proms since 1996. He was a music critic for *The New Yorker*, *The Times*, and the *Observer*, and was Controller, BBC Radio 3, from 1992 to 1998, responsible for the award-winning Radio 3 seasons 'Fairest Isle' and 'Sounding the Century'. He wrote the history of the BBC Symphony Orchestra and edited the influential volume *Authenticity and Early Music*. In 2001 he wrote a new edition of his biography of Simon Rattle. He is now Controller, BBC Proms, Live Events and Television Classical Music, and was appointed a CBE in 2001.

D1464826

SACE
£3

in the same series

THE BBC PROMS POCKET GUIDE TO
Great Symphonies

edited by Nicholas Kenyon

faber and faber

First published in 2003
by Faber and Faber Limited
3 Queen Square London WC1N 3AU
Published in the United States by Faber and Faber Inc.
an affiliate of Farrar, Straus and Giroux LLC, New York

Typeset by Faber and Faber Limited
Printed in England by Bookmarque Ltd, Croydon

A CIP record for this book
is available from the British Library

ISBN 0–571–21688–9

10 9 8 7 6 5 4 3 2 1

Contents

List of Contributors

Introduction

This book provides an accessible and authoritative guide to some of the greatest works in the musical repertory: symphonies that have shown their continual power to move and engage audiences, and which have remained central to our listening – to concerts, broadcasts and recordings – over several generations. Tastes change, sometimes very quickly, and our understanding of the canon of great works in the classical repertory also changes, but it is remarkable how some works retain their key place in our tradition because they transcend the conditions of their time. If you want to know more about how the great symphonies were written and what to listen out for as you encounter these remarkable pieces, this is the place to start.

The survival of the symphony is the more remarkable because its death has often been predicted and the challenges to its existence have been intense. Over the last hundred years, in the now-completed twentieth century, musical certainties were questioned as never before, as composers began to explore all manner of new means of expression and forms. Yet the idea of the symphony, which now dates back some 250 years (perhaps not so long in the whole sweep of a millennium of Western musical history) has proved astonishingly resilient and adaptable in the face of changing styles.

Although composers called works symphonies, *symphoniae*, *sinfonia*, long before 1740, the term conveyed only the general meaning of 'sounding together' – as in the grand canzonas of the Venetian Giovanni Gabrieli's *Symphoniae sacrae*, or the fizzy operatic overtures of Handel. I dimly recall encountering – in an academic context rather than a performance – the earliest works to be designated as symphonies in the modern understanding of the word, because they included not only the three fast–slow–fast movements of the operatic sinfonia, but also, for the first time, a minuet as the third movement.

(A movement from one of them, by Georg Matthias Monn, dated 24 May 1740, was included in the well-known *Historical Anthology of Music*.) It is generally agreed that the invention of that four-movement form marks the birth of the modern symphony. Apart from that, there is little agreement, and an ever-widening understanding of what the symphony and its formal characteristics can be.

Traditional surveys of the symphony – I was brought up on the excellent Pelican books edited by Ralph Hill and Robert Simpson – traced a trajectory of the form from the supposedly somewhat primitive inventions of C. P. E. Bach and Haydn (though what extravagant inventiveness and formal variety there is in those two composers' symphonies!) through to what Hill described as the 'tonal monsters of Mahler', somewhat disapproving of their 'deviations from the essential purity of the classical style'. That remark sounds very dated now, in part because so much has happened since Mahler that has radically expanded our idea of what a symphony can be. And its formal boundaries have extended far beyond the codified 'sonata form' beloved of musical analysts, which was supposed to shape at least the first movements of symphonic structures – though as Antony Hopkins points out in another popular guide to the symphony, 'there was no composers' conference in Margate in 1773 at which sonata form was finally ratified . . . it just grew.'

The idea of a single developing line of symphonies, which fits well with the notion of the Western classical tradition in the eighteenth and nineteenth centuries, was balanced around Beethoven and Brahms. It has been undermined, however, by the new approaches to performance styles which gained ground towards the end of the twentieth century. You could, just about, imagine that Haydn and Mozart were part of the same stylistic tradition as Mahler, when performances of their work were confined to a few symphonies played as appetisers at the start of a concert programme. Now, with the rise of period-instrument orchestras devoted to the Baroque and classical repertory, their music, and still more that of

Beethoven, can be seen as the thrilling climax of the previous two hundred years of music-making rather than the embryonic beginnings of the next two hundred years. Because so much is available to us in the age of mass communication and broadcasting, stylistic development is no longer perceived to proceed in a straight line. This can be an advantage: if the traditional idea of a single symphonic line is supplanted by a richer understanding of the variety of traditions in the twentieth century, Elgar's symphonies, for example, no longer need to be seen as pale imitations of a post-Brahmsian style. (It is, incidentally, surely a testament to the strength of the idea of the symphony in the public mind that the completion of Elgar's Third Symphony by Anthony Payne, first heard in 1998, has caught the imagination of the concert world.)

What has happened to the symphony is what has happened to many great inventions of the human mind: it has proved capable of reinvigorating and reinventing itself, because it is fundamentally such a strong idea. In the hands of contemporary composers as diverse as Michael Tippett, Karl Amadeus Hartmann, Hans Werner Henze, Luciano Berio, Witold Lutosławski, Peter Maxwell Davies and Oliver Knussen, the symphony has maintained its ability to contain extensive musical argument in a powerfully expressive form. It is a pity not to be able to include more of those contemporary works and pieces by living composers in this first volume, but we wanted to start with a book of unquestionable classics and then hope to expand outwards.

Why the connection with the BBC Proms? At the Proms, as part of our commitment to a season that is both of the highest artistic quality and available to all, we have had a long tradition of providing the best possible programme notes for all concerts during the season. We have felt for some time that the excellent material that has been provided night after night for audiences at the Royal Albert Hall in London should be able to reach a far greater number of music lovers, and should be given a more permanent form. We were therefore delighted when Faber and Faber was responsive to the idea of a collection of programme notes for some of the central works in the repertory.

The BBC Proms, as the largest festival of orchestral music in the world, provides a fascinating window on changing taste, for the programmes are shaped not just by the whims of planners but by the enthusiasms of conductors, orchestras and above all audiences. And it is revealing how those tastes have changed over the years. Whereas in the first half of the twentieth century the staple diet of the Proms (apart from chunks of Wagner operas and a huge miscellany of solo vocal and lighter orchestral items) was the symphonies of Tchaikovsky, Brahms and Beethoven, in the second half of the century there was a gradual expansion of that core repertory. Beethoven remained important, and was joined by an increasing number of Mozart's symphonies as well as Haydn's. Tchaikovsky, however, is arguably now less popular with conductors and audiences than Shostakovich, whose symphonies have become absolutely central to our post-war experience. Sibelius became popular, then faded after his death, but is now gaining ground again. Mahler achieved huge popularity in the 1960s and is an indispensable part of the Proms repertory, perhaps partly because his music is so well suited to the large arena of the Royal Albert Hall. Another composer similarly well suited to that space is Bruckner, and it is difficult to believe how rarely his music was performed in earlier decades.

The popularity of composers will ebb and flow because different music speaks to us most powerfully at different moments in our history. The confidence of Beethoven was needed at one period, the ambivalence of Mozart at another. The neuroticism of Mahler and the serenity of Bruckner will always find different admirers, but no one will now question the importance of either of them. It is our hope that this book will enable all listeners and concert-goers to find and understand more in these inexhaustibly rich works.

Each note is designed to be consulted and read separately; some repetition is thus inevitable between different notes.

Acknowledgements

Our first thanks go to the many outstanding authors who have allowed their work to be reprinted in this new format. The notes were originally commissioned by BBC Proms Publications, under the editorial guidance first of George Hall, and more recently of Mark Pappenheim, whose expert hands have made an important contribution to the consistency and shape of the notes. My thanks to them, to Mark Pappenheim for his initial thoughts on how this project could work, and especially to Edward Bhesania who has contributed the new composer biographies and helped with the selection and editing of the material. Sarah Breeden, who now runs BBC Proms Publications, has overseen the organization of the project, and her assistant Hannah Rowley has been tireless in her help. At Faber, Belinda Matthews and her team have been both supportive and patient as this book has taken shape alongside the unforgiving deadlines of the BBC Proms season. My thanks to them all.

Nicholas Kenyon
Director, BBC Proms

Ludwig van Beethoven (1770–1827)

Beethoven left his native Bonn in his early twenties for Vienna, where he became established in fashionable circles as a composer, piano virtuoso and improviser of considerable ability. His 'early' works develop the classical models of Haydn and Mozart. As early as 1796, he recognised signs of his impending deafness, and his subsequent suffering and alienation, as well as his creative resolve, were disclosed in his 'Heiligenstadt Testament' of 1802. His 'middle period' was characterised by a broadening of form and an extension of harmonic language which reflects his proto-Romantic expressive tendencies; this period produced the Symphonies Nos 2 to 8, notable piano sonatas, several string quartets and his only opera, *Fidelio*. From 1812 to 1818 he produced little music, but his last years saw the mould-breaking 'Choral' Symphony, and an exploration of increasing profundity in the more intimate genres of the string quartet and piano sonata.

❧ Symphony No. 1 in C major, Op. 21 (1800)

1 Adagio molto – Allegro con brio
2 Andante cantabile con moto
3 Minuet and Trio: Allegro molto e vivace
4 Adagio – Allegro molto e vivace

It is one of the received truths of music history that Beethoven, as the first great composer to approach the symphony with caution, ensured its transformation from something which just happened to be the most substantial form yet devised for orchestral concert music into a vehicle for the expression of personal dramas and philosophies, symbolising the deliverance of composers from their servitude to the princes of church and state. With Beethoven, symphonies ceased to pour off the conveyor belt: each one had to be individual, hand-made, a landmark in the composer's development.

Some such formulation may go some way to explain why Beethoven reached the age of thirty before he completed a symphony, though sketches made five years earlier for a symphony in C have survived, details of which were drawn on for Symphony No. 1, his Op. 21. If the composer had been in the grip of inexorable historical forces which had decreed that his First Symphony should be delayed until he was capable of expressing in it both the revolutionary spirit of the late eighteenth century and the Romantic aspirations of the early nineteenth, it is indeed surprising – and disappointing – that the work, when it came, was not a grander and more dramatic affair. After all, Beethoven had already composed several striking and substantial instrumental works whose character and structure alike had advanced well beyond the still-classical confines of Haydn's late music. Why not then a Symphony No. 1 on the lines of the celebrated Piano Sonata in C minor, Op. 13 (the 'Pathétique'), or of the C minor String Quartet, Op. 18, No. 4? Or, if it had to be in C major, something which profited more obviously from the majestic proportions of the early Piano Sonata, Op. 2, No. 3, or the confident breadth of the C major Piano Concerto No. 1, Op. 15?

Another received historical truth proclaims that a composer tends to be more experimental in chamber or solo instrumental music than when writing for that most conservative of institutions, the orchestra, and neither public nor players expect to be dazzled by a symphony in the way they might be by a concerto. Some people were evidently startled, at the first performance of this work on 2 April 1800, by the bold opening, which uses the slow introduction to discover the main key via some relatively dissonant chords, rather than merely asserting the key to ensure the listener's familiarity with it before the main argument begins. It would be particularly interesting to know whether Beethoven actually began the composition here: the best introductions are often fairly late additions, and it is most probable that the tone of economy and precision which it possesses is the distillation of the character of a work already well on the way to completion.

The evident economy affects the early stages of the main Allegro in two ways: phrases tend to be compressed, ending earlier than expected, while ideas are built by varied repetition of such fundamental shapes as the first three notes of the first subject. The expected contrasts of key and theme are present, but the string accompaniment to the second subject also functions as a development of an element from the first theme. So unity is ensured at a deeper level by making so-called sonata form a continuous play of basic motifs and their transformations.

The second movement disappoints those who would have preferred something on the lines of one of Beethoven's profound early adagios or largos, and it is indeed a distinctly courtly affair; though like the first movement it avoids a succession of predictably regular phrase lengths, and some tensions rise to the surface through the sheer richness of the orchestration. This Andante fits the symphony because of a concentration which is quite consistent with its generally relaxed tone, and after it the impact of the scherzo – the label Minuet in the score, even if ironic, is wholly inaccurate save as an indication of certain formal conventions – is all the greater. This is the most original, forward-looking movement in the symphony, with a Trio section which seems more concerned with texture than theme in the traditional sense.

Yet the finale is no perfunctory gesture to convention, either. Its humour has a characteristically sharp edge, its graces are purposeful, not effete. At the end, the bold outlining of the tonic triad and the abrupt cadences indicate more than relief that a hurdle has been surmounted without disaster. The confidence is explicit, as if the composer sensed that what we now know as the 'Eroica' was only four years off.

© Arnold Whittall

‭ Symphony No. 2 in D major, Op. 36
   (1799–1802)

1   Adagio molto – Allegro con brio
2   Larghetto
3   Scherzo and Trio: Allegro
4   Allegro molto

'It is a crass monster, a hideously writhing wounded dragon that refuses to die and, in the finale, though bleeding, lashes about furiously with its tail.' Astonishing as it must seem to us today, this was how Beethoven's Second Symphony struck a Viennese music critic of the time. Nor was his a lone voice: others found the work strange, too intent on striving for the novel and sensational, too long, too violent, 'grotesque, wild and shrill', and with 'too frequent and too extravagant modulations'. This about a symphony that has long since been cherished as showing young Beethoven (he was thirty-one when he wrote it) not only in energetic high spirits and with original ideas in plenty, but already in full command of techniques of structure, and with instrumentation considerably more advanced in assurance and scale than in his First Symphony of three years earlier. Its overall light-heartedness is the more remarkable in that it was completed in the summer of 1802 in Heiligenstadt (a small suburb outside Vienna), from where, in the same year, he wrote the so-called Heiligenstadt Testament, which recorded his profound depression at realising that his deafness was permanent and was isolating him from society.

As always with Beethoven, the gestation of this symphony had taken time. A sketchbook from the years 1799–1801 reveals his ideas evolving for the first movement along with its introduction: the opening is extensively roughed out, and the rhythm of the second subject adumbrated (though with different notes); a later sketchbook contains, in three drafts, eleven pages relating to the finale. The symphony received its first performance at the Theater an der Wien on 5 April 1803 in a concert which also included the oratorio *Christ on the Mount of Olives*, the C minor Piano Concerto (with the composer as soloist) – both these works new – and the First Symphony. The rehearsal began at eight a.m. and continued until two-thirty p.m., leaving the players exhausted, limp and ill-humoured: the situation was mollified by Prince Lichnowsky sending in baskets of food and wine for the orchestra and singers. It was to him, one of Beethoven's first and staunchest patrons in Vienna (he had housed the composer on his arrival in the city, and accompanied him to Prague in 1796 – as he had accompanied Mozart to Berlin seven years earlier), that the symphony was eventually dedicated: he was already the dedicatee of the Op. 1 piano trios and the Op. 13 'Sonate Pathétique'.

The boldness and grandeur of the 'Eroica' lay only a year ahead, but the Second still belongs stylistically to Beethoven's 'first period' and looks back to the century that had just ended: the modest orchestra includes only two horns (the first is taken up to high C in the Larghetto), and the clarinets are treated very much as junior members of the woodwind group, except during the Larghetto. Like the First Symphony, this begins with an introduction after the Haydn model, but one which, following an imperious summons and a cantabile theme, embarks on modulations more adventurous even than those of his great predecessor. So adventurous, in fact, that at one point it arrives at a unison D minor outburst prophetic of the opening of the Ninth Symphony. The themes of the adjoining main Allegro are, like this, based on the common chord. The four-semiquaver figure of the Allegro's first subject (which initially appears in the bass) is later used as a dramatic element in its own right; the second subject resembles a military march; and there is a vigorous, jubilant coda. In contrast, the Larghetto (whose tempo indication Beethoven qualified by adding the words 'quasi Andante' when making an arrangement of it for piano trio) is warmly lyrical and leisurely, even expansive, being in full sonata form. The two sections of the first subject are each repeated in the Mozartian serenade colour of clarinets and bassoons; the second subject contains three distinct thematic elements.

For the first time in his symphonies, Beethoven called the third movement a Scherzo (though that in the First Symphony is one in all but name, and he had used the term previously in chamber works). It is brief and deceptively simple in texture: what may well have disconcerted his original hearers (in the same way as the numerous stabbing sforzandos in the first movement) are the constant alternations of forte or fortissimo and piano. The innocent-sounding Trio, starting in a pastoral woodwind colour, unexpectedly veers into F sharp major and seems reluctant to return to its 'proper' key: when it does so, the theme is accompanied by a staccato bassoon line, the ensemble effect offering a remarkable foretaste of the trio in the scherzo of the Ninth Symphony. The finale, in rondo-sonata form, is one of boisterous humour, its principal theme a two-note tweak (with which much play is later made) followed by a dismissive growl; between this and a cheerful second subject comes a suave transition passage that is eventually taken up in the lengthy coda, which is twice interrupted by dramatic pauses.

© Lionel Salter

✎ Symphony No. 3 in E flat major, Op. 55 'Eroica' (1803)

1   Allegro con brio
2   Marcia funebre: Adagio assai
3   Scherzo and Trio: Allegro vivace
4   Finale: Allegro molto

To overestimate the significance of the 'Eroica' in the history of symphonic writing is not easy. This is a work with which no earlier symphony can compare, an enormous leap forward that must have left the composers and audiences of its time gasping in its wake. It was not just that it expanded the

physical size of the symphony to hitherto unknown dimensions (though that is important enough); what really broke
the mould was that it imbued symphonic form with a new and
gigantic message, turning it into an artistic and philosophical
statement that transcended any of its previously accepted
functions. For here Beethoven was expressing nothing less
than his abiding faith in mankind's irrepressible capacity for
greatness.

It is well known that the figure with whom he most associated greatness when he wrote the work in 1803 was Napoleon,
the man who at that time seemed to embody the republican
ideals of many of Europe's intellectuals. But Napoleon turned
out to be 'nothing more than an ordinary human being'
(Beethoven's words) when he crowned himself Emperor in
1804, thereby prompting the famously violent expunging of
his name from the title page of the symphony, where he had
been cited as dedicatee. Yet although Beethoven lost faith in
Napoleon, he did not lose faith in Man. Heroism – personal
and idealistic – still held overwhelming significance for him,
and, since we can assume that he did not consider every man
a hero, it seems reasonable to see the hero of the symphony
as being the composer himself. It was with this realisation of
the extra-musical, autobiographical potential of the symphony that the 'Eroica' was to set the ideological tone for the next
hundred years of symphonic writing.

Beethoven's claim to heroic status can hardly be denied.
In 1802 he had suffered the near-suicidal despair and self-
doubt that prompted the so-called Heiligenstadt Testament,
the document in which he laid bare the misgivings brought
on by his encroaching deafness. Yet he had won through
with his creativity unimpaired. This, surely, was an act of
artistic heroism, and the spiritual rebirth it represented is
outlined in the four movements of the 'Eroica': the first a
titanic struggle; the second a tragic funeral march that
seems to offer no hope for the future; the third a joyous
renewal of life; the last a confident and triumphant affirmation of the power of Man.

In the 'Eroica' the familiar is made to sound impressively different; the opening chords are almost startlingly terse, while in its smooth spaciousness the first subject is like no first subject written before. The development is where the struggle really takes place, in a massively long and brutal battle, but the moment of recapitulation is hushed and mysterious: over a quiet anticipatory tremolando from the violins, the suspense grows until one of the horns can wait no longer and creeps in quietly just before the orchestra follows suit. After all this, the movement's long, gently developmental coda is nothing less than a structural necessity.

The second movement – the funeral march – makes large-scale use of what is basically a simple design. The immensely slow, grief-stricken outer sections frame a vainly hopeful major-key 'trio', a solemn double fugue and a cataclysmic orchestral upheaval, each separated from its neighbour by heart-rending fragments of the first theme. There is another long coda, at the end of which, in one of the symphony's most radical gestures, the music literally disintegrates, seemingly incapable of consolation.

But all is not lost. The Scherzo now steals in almost imperceptibly on the woodwind and strings. Only eventually does the rest of the orchestra jubilantly join in the dance, as if until then not sure if it should. The Trio does not do much to calm the celebrations, though it is less frantic, and the repeat of the first section is no mere formal nicety, but a winding-up of the euphoria, with the orchestra at one point almost falling over itself with glee.

The Finale is one movement in which Beethoven did create a new formal design – a unique combination of variation form, passacaglia, free development and rondo. After a noisy orchestral opening, the movement's early progress from stark bass line to dance-like tune and accompaniment is borrowed from an earlier set of piano variations, which took *their* theme from Beethoven's music for the ballet *The Creatures of Prometheus*. That theme proper appears in the third variation, after which developmental procedures begin. A rondo feel is suggested, however, by occasional returns to recognisable versions of the main theme, culminating in a slower section that brings the movement a dignity befitting the heroic theme of the work as a whole. This is then brushed aside as a return of the orchestral introduction sweeps the music into a joyful coda.

The story of the *Prometheus* ballet had concerned a figure who creates two beings with the aid of fire stolen from the gods and then instructs them in human arts and passions. As a representation of the creative artist's role as educator and civilising influence, it could hardly have failed to appeal to Beethoven; by making such direct reference to it, how better could he have concluded this masterly symphonic self-portrait?

© Lindsay Kemp

✆ Symphony No. 4 in B flat major, Op. 60 (1806)

1 Adagio – Allegro vivace
2 Adagio
3 Allegro vivace – Trio: un poco meno allegro
4 Allegro ma non troppo

Partly because of its position in the sequence of Beethoven's nine symphonies – coming after the 'Eroica' and before the equally heroic Fifth and the grand and poetic 'Pastoral' – No. 4 has tended to be misunderstood and underrated. Schumann called it a 'slender Grecian maiden between two Norse giants'. It contained no extra-musical elements to hang discussion on, it had no title and proposed no obvious drama to the listener's heightened attention, and its humour, though charming, could not be regarded as the attribute of a truly profound composition.

Such a view does not stand up to serious examination. The Fourth belongs as centrally to what the American musicologist Joseph Kerman calls 'the Beethovenian symphonic ideal' as its more famous neighbours. Schumann's 'slender maiden' is a tougher, more combative character and by no means wholly concerned with the sunny side of things. The light the music casts owes its brilliant effect to the darkness from which it emerges in the opening pages of the work. For all its lack of big issues, the Fourth contains as much drama as the others, albeit a purely musical drama: a conflict and eventual reconciliation between lyricism and the singing line on the one hand and, on the other, rhythmic insistence, violent accents, and syncopation. In energy it is second to none. You never know when the most carefree theme is going to erupt into volcanic activity. Rhythm – once the almost motionless introduction is passed – is a ubiquitous, irresistible force.

The work also has its long-range thematic connections (where apparently minor events have momentous consequences) and its far-sighted tonal designs. Thus the introduction's dark tunnel is not forgotten after the music has burst from it into the sunlight and high spirits of B flat major: the double basses' low G flat, which became F sharp halfway through the introduction, is remembered in the remotest reaches of the first movement's development section, where a similar modulation takes the music into the dominant of B major. Just at that distant point, the drums enter softly with a roll that pretends to be on A sharp in the key of B but is actually on B flat, the key of the movement. B flat is quietly insisted on, and under its influence the modulation takes place in reverse: F sharp turns back to G flat and then, with a typical Beethoven half-step, slips down to F, the dominant of the home key. While the drums continue rolling, and successive string entries emphasise the notes of the chord of B flat, a long crescendo carries us in one huge surge into the reprise.

The slow movement, with all its deep enchanted lyricism, carries on and even deepens the first movement's tension between melody and rhythm. At its still centre, the clarinet's recall of the opening theme's first four notes is framed by the same insistent rhythmic figure that has shadowed the theme throughout; and at the very end, in a sudden dramatic silence, the drums are heard quietly beating it out.

Rhythm and syncopation are again predominant in the third movement, the first double scherzo and trio in a Beethoven symphony. Though the Trio begins with a gentle, rather rustic oboe tune that seems all quiet playfulness, it generates a crescendo of gargantuan energy, by means of an oscillating figure previously heard as accompaniment to the first group of themes in the opening movement.

The symphonic drama reaches its culmination in the fleet-footed finale. Right from the beginning, moto perpetuo semiquavers alternate with elegant legato phrases, and there is a systematic contrast between airy pianissimo and mock-furious fortissimo. Grand climaxes are built up, only to dissolve in wisps of melody. We hear more of Beethoven's favourite half-steps. And the bassoon is made the butt of the composer's sadistic joking by being required to get its tongue and fingers round the moto perpetuo theme. At last, in the coda, the legato phrases, which have previously been heard in alternation with the moto perpetuo, are combined with it, singing out on violins and woodwind above a grumbling bass. Then, with a last masterful gesture, Beethoven reconciles the two conflicting principles of the symphony; rhythm and melody become one. The moto perpetuo figure is metamorphosed into a smooth theme, in notes twice as long. But the composer emphasises the transformation, and at the same time keeps faith with the humour that has been such a vital feature of the work, by halting the theme three times in its tracks. The violins play the first twelve notes only, stopping comically in mid-air; the bassoon (compensated for its earlier victimisation) is given the next four notes, but again pauses, questioningly; the middle strings carry it on but also stop. Then, in a downward fortissimo rush, the theme is completed at full speed, and a few chords bring the marvellous work to a characteristically brusque conclusion.

© David Cairns

∾ Symphony No. 5 in C minor, Op. 67
   (1807–8)

1   Allegro con brio
2   Andante con moto
3   Allegro –
4   Allegro

When Berlioz's teacher, the French composer Jean-François Le Sueur, first heard Beethoven's Fifth Symphony, he was so disturbed that, on attempting to put on his hat as he left the hall, he was momentarily unable to find his head. Le Sueur would have found echoes of the patriotic songs of the French Revolution and their clarion calls to Liberty, which left such a mark on Beethoven's style – but transfigured and universalised into a musical utterance of unimaginable power.

Almost two centuries later, is it possible to feel anything approaching the emotions of exhilaration, amazement, alarm even, that possessed musicians and music lovers when Beethoven's work was new? Has it not been performed and popularised to death? The Fifth Symphony is the one piece of classical music that almost everybody has heard of, the one most often alluded to and quoted from (think only of the wartime 'Victory V' signal or the 'fate knocking at the door' bell chimes in Kubrick's film of *A Clockwork Orange*). Its musical gestures are of such devastating simplicity and directness that this is hardly surprising. The work's greatness is not in question; but the character of the music is such that even the most innocent ear responds to it instantly. The difficulty is rather to recapture the freshness of that first encounter, to hear the work (and to play it) with ears still alive to the astounding originality and force, the sheer eventfulness, of Beethoven's symphonic drama.

We cannot, of course, expect it to make the same physical impact on us as it made on Beethoven's contemporaries. They had heard nothing remotely like it: nothing like the naked intensity of expression of the first movement which, in those opening unisons, seemed to spring at the audience and seize it by the throat; nothing, in a slow movement, like the martial splendour of the Andante's C major tuttis, nor the scherzo's ghostly menace, contrasted so vividly with the elephantine gambollings of the trio; nothing like the long, dark tunnel from the scherzo to the finale, with its electrifying crescendo culminating in a blaze of sound, which at one of the work's first performances in France is said to have made a veteran of Napoleon's Grande Armée start to his feet and cry, 'L'Empereur!' The sound of trombones, piccolo and contra-bassoon – intruders on the normal Viennese symphony orchestra of the period – set the seal on an experience of which there had been no warning even in the works of Beethoven. The Fifth Symphony was a musical adventure without prece-dent. People's ears and minds still tingled from the shock. The concept of 'Beethoven's Fifth' had not become so familiar as to cover the reality. It was the gateway to a new world.

Since then there have been many symphonies in which composers lay bare their inner struggles, chaos is mastered by the will and conflict resolved in triumph. Resounding final affirmations, dear to Romantic and neo-Romantic symphon-ists, have even given Beethoven's finale a bad name. He him-self parodied it in his Eighth Symphony, as well as greatly expanding it in his Ninth. Yet the Fifth remains unique. It was the first work to use symphonic form as a medium for personal drama; and if we let it, it still speaks to us with an urgency that time has not weakened. Repetition cannot quite exorcise the demons of the scherzo or tame the concentrated fury of the opening Allegro (where tension is created out of the combination of extreme rhythmic insistence and great breadth of melodic phrase). And familiarity only deepens understanding of Beethoven's controlling plan. Everything that happens has a purpose; each movement acquires its full meaning in relation to the whole.

Understood in this way, the C major sections of the Andante – a brief vision of triumph over the enemy within and without – link the movement with the finale; and the reiterated C major of the conclusion of the work becomes not an indulgence but a necessity. The length of the final coda is explained by the grim conflict of the first movement, which is relived in the nightmarish scherzo: anything less emphatic would not suffice. By bringing back the scherzo at the height of the jubilation, Beethoven shows the threat to be still malignantly active. The splendour of the finale, growing from a pinpoint of light till it seems to fill the universe, had apparently banished it for ever; but suddenly everything is put in question again. It is as if the scherzo had not been silenced but had all the time been continuing beneath the surface. It can be overcome only by an even more vehement assertion of C major, which must go on and on until everything else is, for the moment, blotted out.

© David Cairns

❧ Symphony No. 6 in F major, Op. 68, 'Pastoral' (1808)

1   Pleasant, cheerful feelings awakened on arrival in the countryside (Allegro ma non troppo)
2   Scene by the brook (Andante molto moto)
3   Merry gathering of country folk (Allegro) –
4   Thunder. Storm (Allegro) –
5   Shepherd's song: benevolent feelings, combined with thanks to the deity, after the storm (Allegretto)

'No one can love the countryside as much as I do,' Beethoven once said. He was famous for taking walks in all weathers, always armed with a notebook; he spent most summers until his later years outside Vienna, in villages or spa towns from where he could stride straight into the countryside. And his love of the natural world was reflected in his beliefs: although brought up in the Catholic faith, he was an admirer of a book by the Protestant pastor Christian Sturm called *Reflections on the Works of God in the Realm of Nature*, which described the wonders of nature as evidence of the hand of their Creator.

In these attitudes Beethoven was a child of his time (and he was, after all, an exact contemporary of Wordsworth). His teacher Haydn, born in a village, knew all about rural life, but on his visits to England he seems to have been content to admire the view from inside country houses and carriages; and it is even harder to imagine Mozart, a real city boy, enjoying a country ramble. Yet Schubert, a generation younger than Beethoven and a native of the Viennese suburbs, went on long walking holidays and, during one of them, wrote his 'Great' C major Symphony, which has been interpreted as a wordless hymn to God in nature.

However, even if earlier composers did not have a strong feeling for the countryside, they still had a stock of musical ideas to represent it: imitations of rustic instruments, including bagpipes with their drone fifths; and approximations of natural sounds, such as birdsong, running water, wind and thunder. Many of these ideas are to be found in Haydn's pastoral oratorio *The Seasons*, a work that Beethoven knew well – though he is said to have disapproved of some of its more frivolous word-painting.

The same musical types also occur in an earlier, and less exalted, work by the Swabian composer Johann Heinrich Knecht, a 'grand symphony' published around 1784 with the title *Le portrait musical de la nature*. Beethoven may have played this as a young member of the court orchestra in Bonn; if not, he must surely have seen the detailed movement titles in an advertisement in a musical magazine (alongside an announcement of his own earliest publication). They describe a beautiful pastoral landscape, with singing birds and a waterfall, then a storm gathering, breaking out with full force and gradually abating, and after the storm Nature's hymn of thanks to its Creator. The resemblances to the sequence of movement titles in Beethoven's 'Pastoral' Symphony (translated at the head of this note from the versions in his manuscript, rather than those of the first and subsequent editions) are surely too close to be coincidental.

The main difference between Knecht's intentions and Beethoven's is that Beethoven wanted to go beyond the merely pictorial. While he was writing the Sixth Symphony, between February and July or August 1808, he noted on his sketches as a kind of warning to himself: 'All tone painting loses its value if pushed too far in instrumental music.' And when the work had its first performance – at the marathon all-Beethoven concert in Vienna in December 1808 that also included the premieres of the Fifth Symphony and the *Choral Fantasy* – he announced it as 'more the expression of feeling than painting'. This has to be taken with a pinch of salt, when the score includes unambiguous imitations of bird calls, a village band and a thunderstorm. But much of the fascination of the piece lies in the balance it strikes between painting, feeling and symphonic form.

The first two movements are scored for an unusually small orchestra, no more than double woodwind, two horns and strings. The first movement is the complete opposite of its counterpart in the Fifth Symphony, written a little earlier: it is expansive and relaxed whereas its predecessor is intensive and driving. The harmonies are generally simple and slow-moving; the central development section, in which a single motif is repeated over an unchanging chord for many bars at a time, anticipates the vast symphonic paragraphs of Schubert and Bruckner.

The B flat major second movement (hardly a slow movement, with its marking of 'very fast walking pace') is unequivocally pictorial in its depiction of a murmuring brook by the strings (mostly muted, and with two solo cellos), and its woodwind cadenza towards the end representing three birds, identified in the score as nightingale, quail and cuckoo. Again the chord changes are leisurely, though they are not always predictable, especially in the development – surely suggesting the pace of a country walk through changing scenery.

The rest of the symphony consists of three linked movements – an expansion of Beethoven's linking of scherzo and finale in the Fifth Symphony to include a complete intermediate movement. This fourth movement is extraneous to the symphonic scheme in that it is a tone-picture of a storm, in free form and highly unstable in tonality. The orchestra is augmented by two trumpets from the trio of the scherzo onwards, then also in the storm movement by timpani (but no other percussion), piccolo and, towards the end, two trombones (rather than the usual three). The trumpets and trombones remain for the finale.

The first section of the scherzo ('Merry gathering of country folk') is built on quicksilver switches of key between F major and D major; the second section settles firmly in F major for its happy imitation of a village band, in which the oboist is none too sure where the downbeat is, and the bassoonist can manage only three notes. The contrasting trio section is a rough dance in 2/4 time, with changing modal inflections: noting that the melody appears in one of the composer's sketchbooks as early as 1803-4, the Beethoven scholar Barry Cooper suggests that it may have been a transcription of an actual folk dance. The scherzo and trio are repeated complete; then the final reprise of the first section settles into a firm F major, the better to be interrupted by the first rumbling D flats of the coming storm.

While the fourth movement is shaped only by its descriptive intentions, it is not without subtlety in its thematic treatment: notably towards the end, when a figure that has earlier suggested raindrops is stretched into what Barry Cooper sees as a representation of a rainbow – with a momentary resemblance, unusual for Beethoven, to a Protestant chorale. This passage leads into the finale, which with its Allegretto 6/8 metre is, for its time, a uniquely gentle ending to a symphony. It is in a rondo form obscured in its later stages by variations of the main theme; and that theme is itself only one of many variants of an Alpine *ranz des vaches*, or cow-call, which begins the movement on clarinet and horn, and is heard in its simplest form on muted horn at the very end.

Anthony Burton © BBC

∾ Symphony No. 7 in A major, Op. 92
(1811–12)

1   Poco sostenuto – Vivace
2   Allegretto
3   Presto
4   Allegro con brio

In the autumn of 1813 Austrian and Bavarian forces achieved a notable victory over the French at the Battle of Hanau in central Germany, a significant outcome that signalled the beginning of the end of the Napoleonic Wars. It had been a hard-fought battle with heavy casualties on both sides; in Vienna several charity concerts were organised for the benefit of the widows and orphans of Austrian soldiers. Beethoven had always been a willing supporter of charity concerts in Vienna, partly out of genuine goodwill and partly because it enabled him to persuade the management of the theatres to grant him the opportunity to organise his own concerts. On 8 December a concert in the hall of the university, promoted by Johann Nepomuk Maelzel, inventor of the metronome and a friend of Beethoven, included two new works by the composer, his Seventh Symphony and *Wellington's Victory* (now better known as the *Battle Symphony*); the concert was such a success that it was repeated four days later.

In the circumstances, the Viennese could have been forgiven if they had regarded Beethoven's Seventh Symphony, which is certainly jubilant, even euphoric, as another victory symphony. Few would have known that the work had in fact been composed in the period between autumn 1811 and early summer 1812.

In his Fifth Symphony Beethoven had traversed the emotional journey from tragedy to triumph, and in the Sixth he had explored the centuries-old image of the pastoral. Here in the Seventh the self-imposed challenge is once again fundamentally different: the continuous, cumulative celebration of joy. The result is Beethoven's most incessantly energetic symphony, dependent on untiring rhythmic articulation.

The opening Poco sostenuto is not merely a preparatory introduction but an expansive discourse on two main themes, both announced by the oboe. The wide intervals of the first provide the generating power of the introduction; the tuneful progress of the second offers momentary repose. The power of the section allows the following Vivace to begin in a deceptively lightweight manner in a tripping 6/8. Out of this material Beethoven fashions a sonata form of exhilarating buoyancy and vigour, in which, significantly, tutti sections are nearly always marked fortissimo rather than forte.

The critic of the leading German music periodical of the day, the *Allgemeine Musikalische Zeitung*, noted that in the first two performances of the symphony the second-movement Allegretto had to be encored and that it 'enchanted connoisseur and layman' – an indication, perhaps, that the Viennese welcomed the chance to be diverted rather than always being challenged. Certainly its hypnotic rhythms and bleak orchestral colours make it very different from the surrounding movements.

The scherzo returns to the predominant mood of the symphony, utilising what by this stage in Beethoven's career was becoming a trademark of such movements: fast, fleeting phrases in a piano dynamic as well as brusque forte passages. The evocative phrases of the trio section were said by one early Austrian music historian, Abbé Maximilian Stadler, to be based on a pilgrims' hymn from Lower Austria.

To call the last movement athletic would be a colossal understatement, for this athlete has been reared on a diet of steroids. It is not so much the speed of the movement that impresses – the end of Beethoven's *Egmont* overture, for instance, is faster and more excitable – but its muscular prowess. Rushing semiquavers, offbeat accents, repeated-note figures, instruments (particularly violins and horns) playing at the tops of their registers, all contribute to the aggressive vitality. In the concluding pages Beethoven requires his forces to unleash a *fff*, an unprecedented demand in the composer's symphonies.

There is an account by the composer Louis Spohr of the rehearsal for the Seventh Symphony that suggests that Beethoven's increasing deafness certainly moulded the performance, if not the conception, of the work:

> Beethoven had accustomed himself to indicate expression to the orchestra by all manner of peculiar bodily movements. Every time a *sforzando* occurred, he tore his arms, which he had previously crossed upon his breast, with great vehemence asunder. At a piano he crouched down lower and lower as he desired the degree of softness. If a *crescendo* then entered, he gradually rose again and at the entrance of the *forte* jumped into the air. Sometimes, too, he unconsciously shouted to strengthen the *forte* . . . It was obvious that the poor man could no longer hear the *piano* of his music.

© David Wyn Jones

∿ Symphony No. 8 in F major, Op. 93 (1812)

1 Allegro vivace e con brio
2 Allegretto scherzando
3 Tempo di Menuetto
4 Allegro vivace

The summer of 1812 found Beethoven for the second year in succession recuperating in the Bohemian spa town of Teplitz. The previous year he had met a stimulating crowd of friends and fellow intellectuals there, but this time circumstances were rather different. Beethoven was clearly lonely, and going through an acute emotional crisis. On 6 July he wrote his famous letter addressed to his 'Immortal Beloved'; and ten days later he complained to a friend, 'There is not much to be said about Teplitz, few people and among the few nothing extraordinary, wherefore I live alone! alone! alone! alone!'

But within forty-eight hours, someone extraordinary did arrive in town, and the historic meeting between Beethoven and Goethe took place. 'His talent amazed me,' Goethe told the composer Carl Friedrich Zelter. 'Unfortunately he is an utterly untamed personality who is not altogether in the wrong in holding the world to be detestable, but surely does not make it any the more enjoyable either for himself or others by his attitude.'

If Beethoven was in low spirits in Teplitz, his mood could hardly be gauged from the ebullient Eighth Symphony, which he began to sketch out at this time. His sketchbook also contains jottings for concerto projects, and the opening pages of the Eighth Symphony seem actually to have been destined in the first place for a piano concerto.

When, in the summer of 1815, Beethoven wrote to the impresario Johann Peter Salomon asking him to find a London publisher for some of his recent works, he mentioned the Seventh Symphony, which he described as 'one of my most excellent works', and 'a smaller symphony in F major'. It is true that, by comparison with Beethoven's other later symphonies, the dimensions of the Eighth's first three movements are quite modest; but its finale is a piece of epic proportions and – for all the wit embodied in its main subject – one of the composer's most powerful symphonic utterances. Not since the Fifth had he placed the centre of gravity of an entire symphony so firmly in the last movement.

While the Seventh Symphony had begun with the longest of all Beethoven's symphonic slow introductions, the Eighth finds no room for such preliminaries. Beethoven's process of compression becomes apparent almost at once: the assertive opening phrase is followed by a quiet answer on the woodwinds; but instead of providing the expected restatement of the first phrase Beethoven omits it altogether, and jumps forward to what ought by rights to be the answer to the woodwinds' answer. Much later in the movement, at the start of the recapitulation, the procedure of abridgement is carried a stage further. The recapitulation coincides with the climax of the piece, which has the main theme thundered out by cellos and basses while the rest of the orchestra continues its ascent towards the movement's high point. This time, however, even the quiet answering phrase is omitted, and the entire theme is reduced to a mere eight bars.

According to a legend initiated by Beethoven's one-time secretary Anton Schindler, the second movement, with its 'tick-tock' accompaniment on the wind instruments, was based on a canon the composer had provided at a farewell dinner for Johann Nepomuk Maelzel, the inventor of the metronome. The anecdote has, however, been discredited – not least because the canon itself has been shown to be a forgery (almost certainly by Schindler himself). Beethoven's piece has the lightness and grace of a ballet, though the joke which rounds it off is of characteristic gruffness. It is true that the music finishes resolutely on the chord of the home key; but the preceding pages have so firmly established a different key that in its context this miniature conclusion sounds like an excursion within that previous key, and the listener is left with the inescapable feeling that the music remains hanging in mid-air.

That sense of inconclusiveness is in no way lessened by the 'stamping' start of the third movement, back in the symphony's main key of F major. Since the previous movement itself had been scherzo-like in character, Beethoven writes, for the only time in his symphonies, not a scherzo but an old-fashioned minuet. (It is true that the third movement of the Symphony No. 1 is labelled as a minuet, but the music itself has all the hallmarks of a scherzo.) Its trio is a serenade-like piece with prominent parts for the first clarinet and the two horns.

The finale begins with one of Beethoven's favourite conundrums: the sounding of a wholly unexpected 'foreign' note whose function and meaning become clear only much later on. As the hushed main theme dies away, an unexplained C sharp blares forth – whereupon the theme bursts out fortissimo still in the home key, as if to dismiss out of hand what had been no more than a rude interruption. It is not until the start of what is perhaps the most gargantuan coda Beethoven ever wrote that the C sharp succeeds at last in making its mark. Here, the note is hammered out over and over again, with the insistence of the Stone Guest knocking at the door in *Don Giovanni*, and this time it cannot be ignored: with hair-raising effect, the orchestra plunges into the very remote key of F sharp minor, and the home key is not established again without a good deal more hammering. So conscious is Beethoven of the distance traversed, and of the scope of his canvas as a whole, that it takes an overwhelming series of F major chords to bring the work to a satisfactory conclusion.

© Misha Donat

∾ Symphony No. 9 in D minor, Op. 125, 'Choral' (1823–4)

1   Allegro ma non troppo, un poco maestoso
2   Molto vivace – Presto
3   Adagio molto cantabile – Andante moderato
4   Presto – Allegro assai – Alla marcia: Allegro vivace assai – Andante maestoso – Adagio non troppo, ma divoto – Allegro energico, sempre ben marcato – Allegro ma non tanto – Poco Adagio – Poco allegro, stringendo il tempo – Prestissimo

Beethoven's symphony 'with the final chorus on Schiller's "Ode to Joy"' had become a cultural icon within a generation of its premiere and has remained so ever since. Probably no other piece of music has provoked so many flights of critical fancy or had so many interpretations foisted upon it since its premiere, with the composer standing at the conductor's elbow, in Vienna's Kärntnerthor Theatre on 7 May 1824. Beethoven's many supporters in the audience were loudly enthusiastic. There was spontaneous applause at the timpani entry in the scherzo. And either at the end of this movement or at the end of the whole performance – reports are contradictory – Caroline Unger, the contralto soloist, tapped the deaf composer on the shoulder and turned him round so he could see the wild applause.

Not surprisingly, though, the symphony's gigantic scale, elemental power and sheer diversity of material – above all in the finale, with its unprecedented amalgam of instruments, four solo voices and choir – also provoked bewilderment and hostility, especially in England, where it was first heard in March 1825 in a concert given by the Royal Philharmonic Society, which had in fact commissioned the work in 1817. English critics attacked the symphony for its exorbitant length and what they heard as eccentricity, crudeness and arbitrariness. In Vienna Beethoven's enormous prestige ensured a warmer – if not unmixed – critical reception; and while the finale was generally deemed too long and diffuse, several writers were quick to place the symphony, for all its revolutionary originality, within the classical tradition begun by Haydn and Mozart.

At the same time the seeds were sown for the Romantic view of the Ninth Symphony as autobiography. The tragic first movement was interpreted as Beethoven's own heroic grappling with deafness and 'destiny'; the next two movements embodied the composer's quest for joy – through a display of raw, unbridled energy in the scherzo, and through human love in the Adagio; while the finale depicted the euphoric fulfilment of that quest.

Then Wagner got in on the act. For him the symphony, beginning in the void and ending in a corybantic frenzy, was at once a representation of the Creation myth and a revelation that 'every human soul is made for joy'. And, never one to miss a trick when it came to self-promotion, Wagner saw in the finale's 'rejection' of purely instrumental music the prototype of his own aesthetic, whereby music is redeemed through the word 'from its own peculiar element into the realm of *universal art*'.

In the wake of the revolutions of 1848 Beethoven's symphony – thanks again largely to Wagner – became politicised. The '*Millionen*' of the finale were now the millions of free men and women proclaiming the gospel of happiness in a new civilisation. The plausible but unfounded notion took root that Schiller's 'Ode to Joy' (*Freude*) was a veiled 'Ode to Freedom' (*Freiheit*), with the key word altered for reasons of censorship. In Nazi Germany 'all men shall become brothers' was, of course, applied to Aryans alone; and the symphony became a monument to pan-Teutonic culture. Then, when the Berlin Wall fell in 1989, the Ninth Symphony – with the substitution of '*Freiheit*' for '*Freude*' – was the only possible choice to celebrate the overthrow of Communism and the triumph of Western democracy.

Given the symphony's ineluctable progression from darkness to light, and its finale hymning the Enlightenment's belief in mankind's infinite potential for good (Schiller's poem was written in 1785, three decades before Metternich's totalitarian censorship and secret police), such subjective or opportunistic interpretations were inevitable. As for the symphony as autobiography, few would deny that the finale is the most ecstatic expression of Beethoven's ethical idealism and his belief in an all-loving deity (somewhat distorted in most English translations of Schiller's poem, incidentally, which underplay its elements of paganism and humanism in favour of an orthodox Christianity). Even here, though, there seems to be something ironically incongruous in the sudden intrusion of the jaunty, demotic march, complete with 'Turkish' percussion and obscene grunts from the bassoons, after the heaven-storming cries of '*vor Gott*'. And while the remote, modally inflected chant at '*Brüder, über'm Sternenzelt*' ('Brothers, there above the firmament') may be an authentic expression of religious awe – albeit, to some ears, flecked with a sense of doubt and emptiness – the naive, childlike music (with shades of Mozart's *The Magic Flute*) after the soloists' entry at '*Freude, Tochter aus Elysium*' in the coda perhaps suggests a nostalgia for ideals that were irrevocably lost by 1824.

What is irrefutable is the symphony's mighty tonal architecture, founded on the gradual victory of the tonic major over the tonic minor. In the first movement D major is first glimpsed at the beginning of the development, after a return to the nebulous opening has led us to expect a repeat of the exposition. The development itself is actually the least dynamic part of the movement, exploiting fragments of the main theme to whimsical or pathetic ends, and moving at leisure through a narrow spectrum of tonalities. But the catastrophe comes with the recapitulation, which explodes out of nowhere with the main theme fortissimo in D major in its unstable first inversion – 'instead of a distant nebula we see the heavens on fire' was Tovey's characterisation of this apocalyptic moment, where the tonic major, perhaps for the first time in music, becomes an alien, dissonant intrusion. It is almost a relief when D minor is restored; and for the rest of the recapitulation D major is ambiguously shadowed with the minor. The huge coda offers a brief gleam of D major in a famous horn solo – one of the first ideas Beethoven jotted down for the symphony. But it ends in an implacable D minor, with the wind wailing over a chromatic ostinato in the strings – traditionally a metaphor for lamentation and death.

Surprisingly to us, perhaps, early critics heard playfulness, 'roguish comedy' and 'the wildest mischief' in the scherzo, a movement combining a complex sonata structure with extended stretches of fugato. More recent writers have emphasised the music's gargantuan upsurge of cosmic energy after the tragic close of the first movement, though there is also an element of rough burlesque in the timpani disruptions and abrupt metrical manipulations. The luminous pastoral trio introduces an unsullied D major for the first time in the symphony: the first stage in a tonal and spiritual process that will culminate in the orgy of D major at the end of the finale.

In the third movement, action yields to music of profound contemplation and inwardness. As in the slow movements of the Fifth Symphony and the A minor Quartet, Op. 132, the structure is based on the alternation and variation of two themes: a lofty, hymn-like Adagio in B flat (the most important secondary tonality in the first movement), and a warmer, more fluid Andante heard first in D major – another important staging post in the symphony's tonal progression – and then in G major.

The rebarbative 'terror fanfare' (Wagner's description) that launches the finale combines the triads of D minor and B flat major, the most important tonal centres in the symphony so far. Fragments of the previous movements, brushed aside in snatches of recitative, lead to the birth of the 'joy' theme – a melody of quintessential lyric simplicity – and the establishment of D major. This is briefly disrupted by the recurrence of the fanfare, now made still more dissonant. But after the bass soloist liberates the symphony into song, D minor is henceforth banished in a vast, unique structure that marries elements of sonata form (with the 'Turkish' march, significantly in B flat, as the second-subject group and the following orchestral fugue as development), concerto and rondo with a series of nine variations on the 'joy' theme. There is also a suggestion of a four-movement structure: introduction and first movement (to '*und der Cherub steht vor Gott*'); scherzo (the 6/8 'Turkish' march and the following fugue); slow movement, beginning in G major at '*Seid umschlungen, Millionen!*' – the mysterious spiritual core of the movement; and a finale initiated by the double choral fugue combining the '*Seid umschlungen*' subject with the 'joy' theme. Whether or not Beethoven could, by 1824, believe unreservedly in Schiller's vision, the whole movement remains at once a magnificent synthesis of classical formal structures and the most overwhelming expression of affirmative idealism in all music.

Richard Wigmore © BBC

Hector Berlioz (1803–69)

A pupil of Jean-François Le Sueur and Antoine Reicha at the Paris Conservatoire, Berlioz encapsulated the essence of the Romantic artist. Headstrong, with a turbulent emotional life, he was strongly drawn to literature; his music was inspired by Shakespeare (*Romeo and Juliet*, *Beatrice and Benedict*, as well as his overture: *King Lear*); Goethe (*The Damnation of Faust*), and Byron (*Harold in Italy*). His epic opera *The Trojans*, based on Virgil's *Aeneid*, represents the pinnacle of the French grand opera tradition. He was one of the leading conductors of his day and published much vivid musical criticism. Among his writings is a famous and influential treatise on orchestration and an illuminating book of memoirs.

❧ *Symphonie fantastique*, Op. 14 (1830)

1 Rêveries – Passions: Largo – Allegro agitato e appassionato assai
2 A Ball. Valse: Allegro non troppo
3 Scene in the Country: Adagio
4 March to the Scaffold: Allegretto non troppo
5 Dream of a Witches' Sabbath: Larghetto – Allegro

Programme music has had for so long such a bad name that even now we may feel the need to apologise for it; there is still a lingering sense that works 'based on a programme' are inferior to those that are 'pure': the work being promoted must at all costs be cleared of extra-musical associations. Thus a note on Butterworth's orchestral rhapsody *A Shropshire Lad* quotes approvingly Sir Adrian Boult's remark that the work's form 'arises naturally . . . out of its musical and psychological character, not out of a literary programme' – as indeed must be true of all music of lasting value.

In this disapproving climate some commentators were driven to play down the programme of the *Symphonie fantastique* and even to deny that the work had in a fundamental sense anything to do with the composer's infatuation with the Irish Shakespearean actress Harriet Smithson. Berlioz would hardly have agreed. The symphony, he told a friend, would 'depict the course' of his passion for Miss Smithson; his friend would have 'no difficulty in recognising the hero' of his 'Episode in an Artist's Life'. True, it was more than the distillation of his love of one woman. In the words of the lines from Victor Hugo which he copied on the title page of the manuscript score, it stood for 'all I have suffered, all I have attempted . . . the loves, the labours, the bereavements of my youth'. But of the general autobiographical connotations of the symphony there can be no doubt. Berlioz himself saw it in those terms.

There is nothing that requires apology in that. To find musical suggestion in non-musical things is not peculiar to Berlioz. The capacity to do so is one of the distinguishing marks of a composer. Extra-musical ideas provided the impulse for many more works of Beethoven than the 'Pastoral' Symphony. Nor do we experience the 'Pastoral' differently from the way we experience the Beethoven symphonies whose movements do not have titles. The conventional distinction between programme music and music that is 'pure' is artificial and unreal. Any stimulus may get a composer started, and any ideas, avowed or not, may be embedded in the composition. The 'programme' may be explicit, as in the *Symphonie fantastique*, or hidden, as in Berg's *Lyric Suite*. In both cases it is a stage in the creative process; the resulting music, as Beethoven said of the 'Pastoral', is 'expression of feeling rather than painting'. Mahler was saying the same thing when he suppressed the literary titles which he had originally given to his early symphonies: he meant not that those titles did not reflect the intentions behind the music, but that they were no longer necessary. What matters is what comes out of a piece of music, not what goes into it.

Berlioz's own programme note for the *Symphonie fantastique* set out not to describe the music but, as in an opera, to prepare the listener for it by supplying its context. Weber (as Berlioz pointed out in an article on 'Imitation in Music') did not actually depict moonlight in the second act of *Der Freischütz*, nor Rossini the movement of oars in *William Tell*, though they were often credited with doing so. What they did was to create sounds which the listener, being acquainted with the context, accepted as plausible images of these things. The introduction to Berlioz's note stated that the words that followed should be regarded as like 'the spoken text of an opera', serving to introduce the music.

That he should associate symphony and opera and see symphonic music in dramatic terms should not surprise us. The musical culture in which he was brought up was predominantly operatic. During the first years of his apprenticeship the Paris Opéra was his chief haunt, and the works of Gluck and Gluck's successors – Spontini, Méhul, Salieri, Sacchini – were his main musical diet. A symphonic tradition scarcely existed in France at that time. And Berlioz's teacher Le Sueur had imbued him with the notion that the symphony was a lesser form of music: abstract, decorative, essentially non-dramatic.

The discovery of Beethoven's music at the Conservatoire Concerts in 1828 changed all that. It did not weaken his allegiance to dramatic music; rather, it widened his whole concept of it to include the symphonic. Beethoven's symphonies – above all Nos 3, 5, 6 and 9 – taught Berlioz that there could be a drama of instruments as well as of the voice and the characters on a stage. They showed him what a profound and subtle medium the language of instruments could be for reflecting the innermost experiences of the soul, and how freely the musical material could be treated, within a disciplined framework, in the service of the dramatic idea. At the end of the funeral march of the 'Eroica', for instance, the melody literally broke into fragments, disintegrated, so as to convey in the most direct and vivid way an image of death.

The fragmentation of the love theme in the final section of the tomb scene of Berlioz's *Romeo and Juliet* symphony demonstrates the same principle. Similarly, in the slow movement of the *Symphonie fantastique*, the gradual slackening of rhythmic pulse just after the central climax was inspired by the conclusion of Florestan's aria in *Fidelio*, where a comparable physical and emotional effect was achieved by the same means. Both passages exhibit a dramatic, extra-musical approach to musical language.

With all its innovations (including its handling of the symphony orchestra and its introduction of instruments, textures and rhythms new to symphonic music), the symphony springs from Berlioz's perception of Beethoven. Its melodic style, based on what Wilfrid Mellers calls 'a long-breathed melodic line harking back to classical opera', may show the influence of Berlioz's first mentors, Gluck and Spontini, but it is 'subjected to Beethoven's technique of thematic generation and transformation'. The symphony that was presented to the world in December 1830 was, to Berlioz, a logical consequence of the revelatory events two and a half years earlier in the same hall. It was addressed to the same eager young public and performed by many of the same players, under the same conductor, Habeneck. Certainly it was typical of Berlioz's freedom of spirit that his first major orchestral work should comprise a mixture of genres analogous to what the Romantic dramatists were attempting, after the example of Shakespeare, and that in the process he should override the normal categories of symphonic discourse and create his own idiosyncratic, heterodox version of classical sonata form in response to the demands of the musical drama. Yet he saw himself as simply carrying on from Beethoven, in whose symphonies 'a poetic idea, active at every moment', was embodied in a self-sufficient musical form.

Continuing the work of the composer of the 'Pastoral' and the Fifth, he could use intense personal experience, and movement titles, to bring music's inherent expressivity further into the open, and at the same time widen its frame of reference and blur more than ever the distinction between 'absolute music' and music that is associated (as most music has been since the beginning of time) with words or with an identifiable human situation. All sorts of extra-musical ideas could go into the composition, and yet music remained sovereign. It could describe the course, from dream to nightmare, of one man's idealistic, hopeless love for a distant beloved, and still be 'expression of feeling rather than painting'.

The words of the literary programme offered to those first Conservatoire audiences give the context of the work; they introduce the 'instrumental drama' (to quote Berlioz's prefatory note), whose 'outline, lacking the assistance of speech, needs to be explained in advance'. It is not they that hold the symphony together and make it a timeless record of the ardours and torments of the young imagination. The music does that.

The five movements may be summed up as follows:

1 *Rêveries – Passions*. Slow introductory section (Largo): sadness and imagined happiness, creating out of the state of yearning an image of the ideal woman, represented by the *idée fixe*, an extended, asymmetrically phrased melodic span of forty bars, heard at first (at the outset of the Allegro) virtually unaccompanied, then gradually integrated into the full orchestra. The melody, in its alternate exaltation and dejection, its fevers and calms, forms the argument of the main (Allegro) part of the movement. At the end, like a storm that has blown itself out, it comes to rest on a series of solemn chords.

2 *A Ball*, at which the beloved is present. Waltz, at first dream-like, then glittering, finally garish. Middle section with the *idée fixe* assimilated to the rhythm of the dance.

3 *Scene in the Country*. A shepherd (cor anglais) pipes a melancholy song, answered from afar by another (oboe). The main theme is a long, serene melody, with similarities of outline to the *idée fixe* and, like it, presented as a bare monody

and then in progressively fuller orchestral textures. Pastoral scene, disturbed by the imagined presence of the beloved. Agitated climax, precipitated by the *idée fixe*, which later takes on a more tranquil air (without its characteristic sighing fourth). At the end, dusk and distant thunder; the first shepherd now pipes alone. Drums and solo horn prepare for the opening of:

4 *March to the Scaffold*. The dreams of the first three movements are intensified into nightmare; the full forces are deployed for the first time in the work: massive brass, percussion, prominent (and grotesque) writing for the bassoons. The *idée fixe* appears at the end, pianissimo on solo clarinet, abruptly truncated by a guillotine stroke of the whole orchestra.

5 *Dream of a Witches' Sabbath*. Strange mewings, muffled explosions, distant cries. The executed lover witnesses his own funeral. The beloved melody, now a lewd distortion of itself on E flat clarinet, joins the revels. *Dies irae*, parody of the church's ritual of the dead. Witches' round dance. The climax, after a protracted crescendo, combines round dance and *Dies irae* in a tour de force of rhythmic and orchestral virtuosity.

© David Cairns

Johannes Brahms (1833–97)

Often seen as a classicist inhabiting the Romantic era, Brahms worked mainly in the established forms – concerto, sonata, symphony – rather than developing new ones, like the tone poems of Liszt or the grandiose music dramas of Wagner. From an early age Brahms was forced to earn money for his family by playing the piano in Hamburg's seedy sailors' taverns. In 1853 a concert tour brought him famously into contact with Schumann, who publicly declared the young composer a genius. The *German Requiem* (1868) and *Hungarian Dances* (1868–80) increased his reputation and his *Variations on the St Anthony Chorale* (1873) attracted attention ahead of his First Symphony (1876). He wrote much choral music (he conducted both the Singakademie and the Singverein in Vienna), and led a revival of interest in Renaissance and Baroque music. He also wrote over two hundred songs and much chamber and piano music, but no opera. Late in life he wrote a trio, a quintet and two sonatas inspired by the clarinettist Richard Mühlfeld, which figure among his finest achievements in chamber music.

❧ Symphony No. 1 in C minor, Op. 68
(*c.* 1862–77)

1 Un poco sostenuto – Allegro
2 Andante sostenuto
3 Un poco allegretto e grazioso
4 Adagio – Più Andante – Allegro non troppo, ma con brio

When the twenty-year-old Brahms presented himself at Robert Schumann's house in Düsseldorf in autumn 1853, he set momentous events in train. Shaken by the almost unknown young man's gifts as composer and pianist, Schumann publicly hailed Brahms in Germany's *Neue Zeitschrift für Musik* as 'the chosen one', who, 'fated to give ideal expression to the times', would 'not gain his mastery by gradual stages, but rather spring like Minerva from the head of Jove'. Instantly Brahms was the focus of public curiosity – and scepticism. Schumann urged him to essay the largest musical forms at once, notably the symphony. But three months later Schumann was confined to a mental asylum, and Brahms was left patronless. His sense of duty made him protector of Schumann's wife Clara and their seven children; soon he and Clara were deeply in love.

Already, spurred by the same feelings of obligation, Brahms had begun an ambitious and stormy symphony in D minor. It was perhaps beyond his current powers: he never managed to complete it, though one movement was reworked into the First Piano Concerto and the 'slow scherzo', ten years later, into the *German Requiem* – both pieces partly conceived as memorials for Schumann. After abandoning this D minor work, Brahms was in no rush to fulfil Schumann's prophecy that he would be the age's leading symphonist. His official Symphony No. 1, in C minor, was begun in the early 1860s, but not until 1876 did Brahms complete it and feel confident in releasing it to the world.

In fact, Brahms was pre-eminently the kind of composer who needed to 'gain his mastery by gradual stages'. No composer had a more highly developed historical sense: to write a symphony was to take on the classical form par excellence, suffused with tradition and authority by Haydn, Mozart, Schubert, Schumann and, supremely, Beethoven. 'You don't know what it's like,' Brahms once wrote to the conductor Hermann Levi, 'always to hear that giant marching along behind me.' He knew that any symphony of his would immediately be judged by the very highest standards, and found wanting on the slightest excuse.

Brahms probably first saw the C minor symphony as a whole design in 1868, for that year he sent Clara Schumann a birthday greeting inscribed with the 'Alpine horn' theme we encounter in the symphony's finale, which perhaps stands for the voice of Nature. Many personal associations came to be woven into the work's fabric, including the musical motif Schumann had used to signify Clara herself. Yet like much of Brahms's most original music, the Symphony No. 1 not only expresses his individualism but also engages in a dialogue with the masters of the past.

Above all, Beethoven. We're often told that the first audiences thought the great, broad C major tune in Brahms's finale resembled the 'Ode to Joy' tune in the finale of Beethoven's Ninth Symphony, and that Brahms would dismiss the comment with a snorted 'Any ass can see that!' The point is that the resemblance is precise and deliberate – Brahms's tune is modelled on Beethoven's, bar for bar – to point up the entirely different orientation of Brahms's finale.

There are other Beethovenian references. The scherzo-like 6/8 motion of Brahms's first movement, the tense and troubled introduction to the finale, both recall Beethoven's Fifth Symphony. C minor, the 'fate' key of Beethoven's Fifth, had much occupied Brahms in the years before completing his First. He had 'gained mastery' over the other great Beethovenian form, the string quartet, with his own First Quartet in C minor; and he had completed the tragic, restless Piano Quartet in C minor. Perhaps most significant was his choral setting of Hölderlin's *Song of Destiny*, contrasting the bliss of the gods on their mountain tops with the suffering of blindly striving mankind below, in a symphonic structure which represents humanity by C minor but ends in C major with a return to the music of the gods. The imagery of heights and depths, verbally explicit in the choral work, seems to be echoed in the symphony: there are mountains to be climbed, against enormous odds, and the summit is only reached when we hear the Alphorn in the finale. (Brahms's birthday message to Clara put a scrap of verse to the horn call: 'High on the mountain, deep in the vale I greet you, a thousandfold.')

Passionate melody simultaneously aspires and falls in the symphony's tense, brooding Un poco sostenuto introduction, which outlines in slow motion the principal elements the first movement will discuss (and which did not exist in the 1862 draft). It is underlined by throbbing timpani heartbeats, pinning the music to the 'fateful' C minor tonality like a mountaineer spreadeagled on a sheer cliff. The ensuing Allegro is grim and savagely energetic. Despite its impressive size and sonata outline it has, as mentioned, a pronounced scherzo character. Brahms makes considerable play with its lively dancing rhythms, but in a spirit of continual struggle, working up to a veritable fusillade of blows before the movement's end.

Brahms followed Schumann's lead in casting his symphony's inner movements as lighter inventions of intermezzo character, and the E major Andante, though intensely poetic (and in a key unusually distant from the first movement) is essentially lyrical in expression. The prominent violin solo in its closing stages may well have been suggested by the Romanze of Schumann's Symphony No. 4, but far transcends the model. There is no real scherzo: the first movement has usurped much of that role, and there follows instead a relaxed and delicate Allegretto in A flat, in a smoothly flowing 2/4 time, with a more song-like and impassioned 6/8 trio in B major, which reappears during the tranquil evanescence of the final bars.

These first three movements, despite their fully symphonic scale, throw the weight of expectation, and thus the fulcrum of the structure, onto the finale, which by its vast scope and vigour resolves all the tensions raised (but not dissipated) by the first movement. A feverish and troubled C minor introduction reawakens those tensions with tremendous force. The gloom is suddenly pierced by Brahms's 'Alpine' horn theme, which appears – in one of the nineteenth century's classic orchestral inspirations – atop a shimmering cloudscape of string tremolandi. An ecclesiastical-sounding chorale on trombones then prepares for the C major 'joy' theme, and the movement's splendid energies are finally unleashed in a sonata exposition full of striking ideas and rhythmic drive. The 'joy' theme returns to start off an equally strenuous development, but this progressively transforms the elements of the 'joy' theme into the 'Alphorn' one, which is actually substituted for the main subject at the start of the recapitulation. Nature, it seems, has triumphed over Beethovenian will – and in an exalted and triumphant coda it is the trombone chorale that has the last, decisive word.

© Malcolm MacDonald

∾ Symphony No. 2 in D major, Op. 73 (1877)

1 Allegro non troppo
2 Adagio non troppo
3 Allegretto grazioso (Quasi Andantino)
4 Allegro con spirito

Brahms wrote his Second Symphony in the summer of 1877; it was premiered on 30 December that year in Vienna, under the baton of the young Hans Richter, and was an immediate popular success. The swift and painless delivery of such a large work is all the more surprising when we reflect that Brahms had laboured on his First Symphony, completed only the previous September, for at least fourteen years. On his own admission he had been intimidated by the hallowed reputation of this grandest of all instrumental forms, and by the need to produce a work of the highest possible quality and seriousness. But when he achieved the C minor First Symphony, hailed by some as 'Beethoven's Tenth', a psychological barrier must have been breached, enabling him to embark at once on a second essay in the form.

If Brahms in the C minor was settling accounts with Beethoven (with deliberate allusions to, and personal remodellings of, his Fifth and Ninth symphonies), then in the D major Second he could be much more himself, and attempt a wholly 'Brahmsian' symphonic ideal, less dramatic and more lyrical. In fact No. 2 has traditionally been considered the most genial of Brahms's four; in his own time it was sometimes dubbed his 'Pastoral' or even his 'Viennese' symphony. The first of those epithets is undoubtedly correct: the contemplation of nature is patently one of the work's underlying themes. Romantic nature symbolism (in horn calls, trilling bird-like flutes or clarinets, and so on) suffuses the score, in a very rich and sometimes dark harmonic context.

Before the premiere Brahms amused himself by warning his friends how unrelievedly gloomy the result would be: 'The score must appear with a black border,' he told his publisher Simrock. Commentators have tended to regard this as an example of his odd sense of humour; but perhaps he deliberately overstated the case so that, in their relief when the symphony proved not at all funereal, even close friends should ignore the profoundly elegiac strain that does in fact run through the first two movements. For some personal sense of grief or deep melancholy does indeed shadow these portions of the work, though there is no mistaking the third movement's spirit of delight or the triumphant, liberated mood of the finale.

The first movement's leisurely unwinding of long, graceful, even waltz-like themes is plainly influenced by Schubert rather than Beethoven. Yet Brahms's motivic thinking reaches wide and deep. The three-note figure, D–C sharp–D, which the cellos announce in the first bar, is a germinal motif that is used in countless ways throughout the symphony. But the expansive first subject is soon interrupted by a mysterious timpani roll and a figure of three solemn chords from trombones and tuba. (This is the only Brahms symphony to include a tuba.) The sombre, archaic quality of this idea casts long shadows, reaching through the broad and song-like second subject into the development, where the anxiety underlying so much beauty manifests itself in agitated contrapuntal exploration of apparently innocent materials. A steady increase in tension climaxes in a stark, even lugubrious canonic outburst for trombones. Though the recapitulation returns us to apparent pastoral bliss, in the coda a lyrical horn solo opens up a fervently elegiac string passage (which Brahms in his copy of the score heavily underlined as the movement's expressive goal). Finally a witty scherzando-style dissolution of the opening three-note figure leads into the final bars of very unusual harmonic colouring – a combination of dominant and plagal cadence whose dissonance is somewhat concealed by the scoring.

The conductor Vincenz Lachner (younger brother of Schubert's friend Franz Lachner) wrote to Brahms objecting to the trombone and tuba passage at the beginning, the trombone canon in the recapitulation, and these dissonant cadential bars. Brahms wrote back (in an unusually revealing letter, only published relatively recently) thanking him for his 'perceptive and understanding words . . . the first that I have heard about that work'. He refused to change the passages, confessing 'that I am, by the by, a severely melancholic person; black wings are constantly flapping above us . . .'

The melancholic tendencies seem to increase in the Adagio, which has the character of a meditation in the darkest part of a forest. Its lamenting, descending cello theme, with a soulful bassoon countermelody ascending against it, gives way to increasingly gnarled and knotted contrapuntal developments in solemn neo-Baroque style. The bass instruments turn the three-note motif into a mournful howl before the movement climaxes in almost funereal solemnity.

The mood finally lightens with the Allegretto, a typical example of the delicate intermezzo movement with which Brahms (until his last symphony) tended to replace the more conventional and rumbustious scherzo. Lightly scored and deftly tuneful, it is a kind of pastoral serenade, with a hint of the dance. Its charming main theme is heard three times, and twice interrupted by ebullient, fast variations of itself.

Rumbustiousness is reserved for the finale, which, after an introduction of quiet, mysterious excitement, bursts out in a dazzling display of confident D major. This is probably the most athletic and festive movement Brahms ever wrote (the vigorous neo-Handelian figuration derives from his big and now neglected choral work, the *Triumphlied*). Its brimming current of sheer orchestral power flows seamlessly (with a swooping clarinet solo) into the full-hearted song of the second subject. Even here, shadow and chill invade the music towards the end of the development, but it is only a passing cloud bank, the better to reveal the exultant blaze of recapitulation and coda. Towards the end, trombones and tuba turn the second subject into a hymn-like chant; and the trombones, after all, clinch the entire work with their triumphant blast of D major.

© Malcolm MacDonald

∾ Symphony No. 3 in F major, Op. 90 (1883)

1 Allegro con brio
2 Andante
3 Poco Allegretto
4 Allegro

Though Schumann had predicted that Brahms would write great symphonies, Brahms, inhibited by the legacy of Beethoven, did not complete his First until long after Schumann had died. After that, Brahms wrote his remaining three symphonies quite quickly – the radiant D major following within a year of the First's unveiling. Two grandiose concertos followed – Brahms's one and only for violin, then his second for piano, which he himself played many times. (Even in the 1880s, when his reputation as a major composer was assured, Brahms still did a lot of performing.) The Fourth Symphony crowned Brahms's symphonic output, in 1885, in a spirit of noble resignation and transcendent grandeur.

How does the Third fit into this picture? For a start, it is Brahms's shortest symphony. But although it cannot be characterised as neatly as the others – as 'pastoral' or 'tragic' – it is far from being a lesser sibling in need of special pleading. On the contrary, it was an immediate success after its premiere in

Vienna on 2 December 1883, and has always been a favourite with distinguished musicians – Elgar was one of its particular admirers.

For all his reverence for Beethoven, and despite his unusually wide-ranging knowledge of earlier composers such as Bach, Couperin and Handel, Brahms really formed his musical dialect from a mixture of Schumann and Schubert. Fond reminiscences of both composers permeate Brahms's entire output, transformed by his own passionate and complex personality. The Third Symphony is one example; it was inspired by a visit Brahms made to the Rhine in the late spring of 1883. Schumann's Third Symphony had also been inspired by the Rhine, thirty-three years earlier, and the opening of Brahms's first subject shares exactly the same plunging rhythm as the start of Schumann's 'Rhenish' Symphony. It is cued in by three chords – F major, F minor, and again major – which recall the way Schubert hovers between major and minor at the opening of his great String Quintet in C. The tops of those chords outline an ascending line from F to A flat to the F above, when the violins burst in. In many performances, if the horns and trumpets are too loud, you do not hear the outline clearly, but even if that happens, the motif permeates the whole first movement, often transposed, and Brahms underlines its importance by giving it to a solo horn, in a quiet moment of anticipation, just before the recapitulation.

According to Brahms's biographer, Max Kalbeck, who knew the composer well, F–A–F was his personal cipher, standing for '*Frei aber froh*' (Free but happy), with the major–minor equivocation, A or A flat, expressing ambivalence. Just at the time Brahms was working on the symphony, he struck up a close friendship with a young singer called Hermine Spies, whom he accompanied in recitals and for whom he also wrote songs. Was he free and was he happy? The quiet recollection of the first theme at the end of the first movement and, again, in a contented, snoozing calm at the end of the whole symphony, have prompted some people to describe the work as Brahms taking stock of his life. He was now fifty.

In the first movement, the muscular effort of the first theme is offset by the suave, curvaceous melodies that follow, while the development is a mercifully brief passage through stormy, choppy waters. The second movement is calm but not very slow. It begins as a simple, tranquil chorale for woodwind and horns, with only short, approving echoes from the strings. When the chorale is decorated, becoming graceful and arborescent, Brahms begins to sound like Dvořák (usually it was the other way round). But then comes a quiet, cautiously padding idea that seems to anticipate danger; instead, sweet and pleasant phrases are exchanged between strings and woodwind before a decorated return to the chorale, and something Brahms could not resist, a brief show of fighting spirit.

The second movement has been a sort of interlude, in C major, though that cautiously padding idea is going to return later. The most confiding movement of the symphony is the third, in C minor, with one of Brahms's most amorous melodies introduced by the cellos against lapping triplets in the upper strings. The middle section is hardly melodic at all, but built on accented grace notes, or appoggiaturas.

Now for drama, prepared at the start of the finale by a stealthy theme on bassoons and strings, in bare octaves. The cautiously padding idea from the second movement reappears, hushed, then suddenly the whole orchestra springs to life with those incisive short–long rhythms, separated by rests, that Brahms made so much his own. The second subject, first heard on the cellos and horn, is relatively consoling, as it needs to be when there is so much tension to come. But it is the stealthy first theme that undergoes all sorts of unexpected transformations, including a mournful, ironed-out appearance on muted violas, before a gentle retrospective rumination brings Brahms's most concise symphony to a close.

© Adrian Jack

∾ Symphony No. 4 in E minor, Op. 98
(1884–5)

1 Allegro non troppo
2 Andante moderato
3 Allegro giocoso
4 Allegro energico e passionato

Brahms's last symphony confused and dismayed his admirers when they first heard it tried over in an arrangement for two pianos. The critic Hanslick felt he was 'being beaten over the head by two terribly clever men'. Brahms's biographer Max Kalbeck advised the composer to throw the scherzo in the waste-paper basket, and publish the finale as a separate work. Even his close friends Clara Schumann and Elisabeth von Herzogenberg found the work terribly severe – though the latter, after close study at the piano, soon realised it was a master-piece. Brahms was disappointed in their reactions, but changed nothing for the first performance, which he conducted on 27 October 1885 at Meiningen. Immediately afterwards the Meiningen Orchestra took the new symphony on tour, and it began to be recognised at its true, and remarkable, worth.

The Fourth Symphony in fact represents Brahms's supreme achievement in orchestral music: the most impressive result of his lifelong struggle to revivify the strict musical architecture of the Baroque and infuse it with the supercharged passion of the Romantic era in which he lived. Though it was composed during the summers of 1884–5 in the Austrian village of Mürzzuschlag, Brahms had been pondering the most remark-able movement, the finale, for some years. About 1880, at the Berlin home of the conductor Siegfried Ochs, Brahms had discussed the church cantatas of J. S. Bach with a more famous maestro, Hans von Bülow. During the conversation Brahms played the final chorus of Cantata No. 150 (*Nach Dir, Herr, verlanget mich*) on the piano – a chorus Bach had written in the form of a chaconne: continuous variations on a ground bass theme. (Bach's cantata was still unpublished; the manuscript

Brahms played from, given him by the Bach scholar Philipp Spitta, still exists.) 'What would you think', he asked von Bülow, 'of a symphonic movement written on this theme some day? But it's too heavy, too plain. It would have to be chromatically altered in some way.'

And so it happened: in the finale of Symphony No. 4, Brahms revived the ancient form of passacaglia (a more elaborate form of chaconne, whose theme can appear in any register, not just the bass) with incalculable consequences for symphonists who came after him, from Alexander Zemlinsky to Alexander Goehr. The finale theme, derived from Bach's cantata bass, is modified in rhythm and gains a single chromatic degree, an A sharp, which vastly increases its drama and permits Brahms to employ the full resources of late-nineteenth-century harmony. This inspired marriage of the contemporary and the archaic is reflected throughout the symphony, in which epic tragedy and melodic lyricism find their most powerful – and most quintessentially Brahmsian – expression in the composer's entire output.

The clouded and troubled first movement already contains the seeds of the finale. The almost matter-of-fact beauty of its opening subject, its deliberate motion, vibrantly ambiguous harmony and, most of all, its intricate architecture (the long-spanned, eloquent themes develop out of the smallest motifs and intervals) all foreshadow elements to be developed in all four movements, and which come to full fruition in the last. The second subject begins with fanfares and passes to a glorious, impassioned cello theme. After an eventful development of these themes, the recapitulation starts in a passage of profoundest mystery: the first notes of the opening theme appear enshrouded by nebulous, swirling string writing. From this enigmatic withdrawal the music gathers force and splendour all the way to an ending of tragic vehemence.

The gorgeous slow movement, which opens with a Romantic horn call, continually plays off the austere colouring of the ancient, ecclesiastical Phrygian mode (the opening theme, for woodwind and pizzicato strings) against the ardent warmth of a fully developed E major (the great singing tune of the second subject, first heard on cellos). This creates a deep-hued harmonic colouring and an intensely elegiac atmosphere which, after the tension and eventual assuagement of the development section, culminates and closes in a wonderful glow of autumnal melancholy.

The C major third movement – the last to be written, and the only true symphonic scherzo that Brahms composed – disperses these sombre shadows with an intoxicating physical energy and rhythmic urge. Even the appearance of the triangle (rare in Brahms) merely serves to burnish the steely brightness of mood. This is an amazingly concentrated sonata structure with a lengthy coda that accumulates enormous impetus over a long, pulsing dominant pedal in the timpani, finally unleashing its full force in the choleric and exultant final bars.

The passacaglia finale consists of the theme derived from Bach (announced by the brass), thirty variations and a coda: a tightly woven sequence, almost entirely confined to E minor. The individual eight-bar variations group themselves into large paragraphs to give a semblance of sonata shape. There is no need to detail each one, especially as the sense of continuous, irresistible flow of ideas is undoubtedly the most important aspect of the movement. Any listener, however, can recognise the infinite pathos of the central turn to the major key, with the eloquent, imploring flute solo of Variation 12, closely followed by two slow, funereal variations in sarabande rhythm, with mysterious trombones.

The theme bursts out afresh in E minor to signal the second half of the movement, where Brahms applies ever-increasing pressure to his subject, to disclose its infinite latent possibilities. At last it escapes its E minor confinement into the thrilling modulations of the coda, which crowns the symphony with an outburst of magnificent, wintry resolve. The theme is still defiantly growing and reshaping itself, even as it is terminated by the final cadence.

Benjamin Britten (1913–76)

Born in Suffolk on 22 November 1913 (propitiously, the feast day of St Cecilia, patron saint of music) Britten began piano lessons aged five, composing songs for his mother by the age of ten. At thirteen he began composition studies with Frank Bridge before entering the Royal College of Music in 1930. His documentary scores for the GPO (General Post Office) Film Unit brought him into collaboration with W. H. Auden, a liberating force; in 1937 he not only attracted international attention with his *Variations on a Theme of Frank Bridge* at the Salzburg Festival, but also met the tenor Peter Pears, who would become his lifelong partner and an influential interpreter of his work. Britten revitalised English opera with his first stage triumph *Peter Grimes* (1945), launching the Aldeburgh Festival three years later. He performed often as a conductor and pianist, and though he wrote a significant number of chamber and choral works (among them three string quartets, and the *War Requiem*, 1961) it is principally for his vocal and especially operatic output that he is remembered.

❧ *Sinfonia da Requiem*, Op. 20 (1939)

1 Lacrymosa (Andante ben misurato) –
2 Dies irae (Allegro con fuoco) –
3 Requiem aeternam (Andante molto tranquillo)

Britten's only purely orchestral symphony was commissioned by the Japanese government, just after the outbreak of the Second World War, for the celebrations in 1940 of the 2,600th anniversary of the Japanese Empire. But, by the time of the proposed premiere, the political alignments which Pearl Harbor would soon render absolute were already clear. The chief musical tribute to the Mikado came instead from the septuagenarian Richard Strauss; Britten's score was rejected, on the grounds that it did not 'express felicitations', was specifically Christian in its reference and of 'melancholy tone'.

It is hard to disagree with these comments, yet the composer had outlined his programmatic ground plan to the Japanese at an early stage of the negotiations. What he did not reveal emerges in a letter to his sister, describing the *Sinfonia da Requiem* as combining 'my ideas on war and a memorial for Mum and Pop'. Much later, Britten was to fuse Japanese and Christian sources in his three 'church parables', but the fusion ignited here is of personal mourning with an outrage bordering on despair at the cataclysm that was beginning to engulf the world.

The three movements, which are played continuously, create a powerful emotional cycle, underlined by the titles taken from the Mass for the Dead. Yet the inexorable momentum coexists with an obsessive concentration on that pitch, D, which launches the work so explosively. Pulling against the march background to which this subsides, the cellos unfold a threnody, coloured by semitonal tensions. A reiterated bassoon figure becomes the accompaniment to a balefully undulating saxophone theme before the first idea returns as a tutti.

What follows retains syncopations (muted trumpets) and melodic germs from this, but acquires a 'second subject' character from the confrontation between major and minor chords in low and high orchestral sonorities. A development of the saxophone theme mounts urgently towards the achievement of a new tonal focus, the pitch B, celebrated by a cymbal clash. But the initial D minor fatalistically reimposes itself (trombones) for a frenzied recapitulation of the second subject. The thunderous march beats return, on an A that cadences to D with a recall of the first subject – a moment made incandescent by the addition of the second subject's chords (in the brass), creating constant clashes of major and minor between the two elements.

From these unresolved tensions the music subsides into another, as an eerily fluttering flute rhythm, set askew to the muted trumpets, begins the central dance of death. Manic activity from every corner of the orchestra takes on a more directed menace when the initial rhythm hammers out that familiar D. For its Last Trumpet, this *Dies irae* offers a whooping tarantella; it culminates in the projection of a strident chord, reiterated as accompaniment in the trio section. This central stage of the cycle points back to the first movement's threnody (now wailed by the saxophone) and forward to the finale's refrain (here a sardonic brass rhythm). The scherzo's da capo reaches a shattering climax with the dominating rhythm, founded on D, and detonations of this pitch become the only certainty in the tearing apart of the orchestral fabric that signifies the ultimate descent into chaos.

Yet if this is the young Britten's protest against war, he offers a symbol of hope too, for it is out of the scherzo's dying reverberations that harp and bass clarinet fashion the revolving bass of *Requiem aeternam*. The shape first snickered by the brass in the trio now floats on three flutes, in a D major made achingly bright by clashes of adjacent pitches; the horns add a lullaby refrain. But the liturgy's 'eternal rest' can only be longed for, and in an aspiring central paragraph the first movement's threnody is expanded by the strings into a visionary (and very Mahlerian) climax. The return of the flutes' theme is recessional, but the embers flare in an intense melodic curve before the last D of all is reached.

© Peter Evans

Anton Bruckner (1824–96)

Bruckner's path to recognition was a slow and arduous one. Born in Upper Austria in 1824, he was expected to become a schoolteacher, but began his career as an organ teacher at the Church of St Florian, where he had earlier been a choral scholar. In 1856 he became organist at nearby Linz Cathedral, and seven years later was deeply and lastingly affected by Wagner's *Tannhäuser*. Until this time his compositions centred on sacred music – he was devoutly religious throughout his life – but in 1866 he produced his First Symphony. It was only with the premiere of his Seventh (1884), by which time he had reached sixty, that Bruckner first gained public recognition. In 1891, to his great delight, he became the first musician to be honoured with a doctorate. from the University of Vienna. Even today, Bruckner's symphonies divide both experts and music lovers. His detractors talk of bombast, empty rhetoric and uninspired thematic material; while his supporters admire his grand architectural scale and spiritual radiance.

∾ Symphony No. 4 in E flat major, 'Romantic' (1874–80)

1   Bewegt, nicht zu schnell [Lively, not too fast]
2   Andante, quasi Allegretto
3   Scherzo: Bewegt [Lively] – Trio: Nicht zu schnell. Keinesfalls schleppend [Not too fast. But not dragging]
4   Finale: Bewegt, doch nicht zu schnell [Lively, but not too fast]

It isn't easy to see why Bruckner should have singled out his Fourth Symphony as the 'Romantic'. All Bruckner's symphonies are clearly products of the Romantic era, however much they may owe to the music of Palestrina and Bach or to the architecture of the medieval and baroque cathedrals in which Bruckner (a superb organist and a devout Roman Catholic) worked and prayed. When it first appeared, the Fourth Symphony was provided with a naively descriptive programme (dawn over a medieval town, processions of knights, hunting scenes, etc.). In fact Bruckner may have had little – if anything – to do with this; or if he had, it could have been because his arm was twisted by over-zealous friends, anxious to help the still largely unconverted musical public get to grips with a long, complex and highly original new work.

But the music does have an extraordinary power to evoke moods or mental pictures. The opening – solo horn calls sounding above quietly shimmering string tremolandi – is one of the most magical beginnings to a symphony in the entire repertoire. As the high woodwind take up this theme, in counterpoint with the horn, one may hear echoes of the once-famous Gounod–Bach 'Ave Maria', composed fifteen years before Bruckner began work on the Fourth Symphony in 1874. This beginning also reflects Bruckner's new-found confidence as a symphonist. From the initial horn theme, through the long crescendo to the arrival of the second main theme, fortissimo, on heavy brass, the music flows forward like a great river. At no point does this movement let us down. Bruckner may allow himself frequent pauses for breath or reflection, but the steady momentum continues. The horn theme returns twice in its original form: at the start of the recapitulation (embellished by a touchingly simple counter-melody on flute), and the very end of the movement, where it sounds out thrillingly on all four horns in unison.

The slow movement is something of a departure from the Brucknerian norm. Instead of profound, lyrical meditation, it seems to have more of the character of a funeral march. Although the tempo marking, Andante, quasi Allegretto, suggests a fairly mobile pace, the underlying pulse is slow, the musical landscape spacious. The composer Hugh Wood compared this movement tellingly to a big Central European forest – the kind of very un-English woodland where it's possible to see vast distances between the trunks of high-arching trees. No matter how fast you walk, the distant prospect remains more or less the same – as though one had hardly moved at all. This feeling of immense shadowy space is enhanced by the second theme: violas singing long, calm phrases through quiet pizzicato string chords. There are moments of almost mesmerising stillness, in which solo woodwinds and horns call to each other like birdsong. Eventually this movement builds to a magnificent climax – one of the few passages in the Fourth Symphony which directly recalls Bruckner's idol Wagner. But the splendour soon fades, and we are left with the march rhythm on timpani, and lamenting phrases on horn, viola and clarinet.

In the Scherzo the long-forgotten programme for once makes a kind of sense: the horn and trumpet fanfares do suggest 'hunting' scenes. But there is something cosmic about this music, as though the horses were careering across the skies rather than pounding the earth. In contrast, the central Trio section is a delicious example of the cosy, rustic Bruckner: a lazily contented *Ländler* (the country cousin of the Viennese waltz) introduced by oboe and clarinet. In his younger days, before he moved to Vienna, Bruckner had augmented his meagre teacher's income by playing in village bands, and the experience left a deep imprint on his symphonic style.

After the Trio, the Scherzo is heard again. Then begins the longest and most exploratory of the four movements, the Finale. Bruckner told how the main theme came to him in a dream, played by a friend, the conductor Ignaz Dorn, who had encouraged Bruckner in his enthusiasm for Wagner. 'Dorn appeared to me . . . and said, "The first three movements of the Romantic (Fourth) Symphony are ready, and we'll soon find the theme for the fourth. Go to the piano and play it for me." I was so excited I woke up, leaped out of bed and wrote the theme down, just as I'd heard it from him.' If by this Bruckner means the elemental unison theme for full orchestra that enters in full at the height of the first crescendo, it's not surprising he was so excited. Interestingly, this theme is one of the few things that remains essentially unchanged in the two major revisions Bruckner made of this movement.

Arriving at the eventual form of the Finale caused Bruckner a lot of trouble, and there is evidence that he wasn't satisfied even after he'd completed the second revision (1880). Commentators have tended to agree with him: although there are splendid ideas, there are also passages in which Bruckner momentarily seems to lose his way. Patience is ultimately rewarded, however. The final long crescendo, beginning in minor-key darkness with the first theme sounding quietly through shimmering strings, is one of Bruckner's most thrilling symphonic summations, ending in a blaze of major-key glory.

© Stephen Johnson

∾ Symphony No. 5 in B flat major (1875–6)

1 Introduction: Adagio – Allegro
2 Adagio: Sehr langsam [Very slow]
3 Scherzo: Molto vivace (Schnell) [Quick] – Trio: Im gleichen Tempo [At the same tempo]
4 Finale: Adagio – Allegro moderato

Bruckner was fifty-two when he completed his Fifth Symphony in 1876. By the time of his death, twenty years later, he had not heard a note of the music, for he was too ill to attend a performance given in 1894. This was in a version that involved massive cuts and reorchestration, and it was this version that was published in 1896. A further forty years had to pass before Bruckner's original score was performed and published.

For many years the disparity between Bruckner's towering achievement and his unassuming personality led to misunderstanding. The image of a 'naive' and 'childlike' composer led even perceptive musicians to assume that there was no intellectual shaping power behind the music, that his massive symphonies relied on a sort of inspired improvisation, where glorious passages of orchestral grandeur occurred from time to time in the midst of shapeless ramblings. The seventy-five-minute span of the Fifth Symphony is in fact meticulously organised. Every theme in this symphony is motivically related, and the rhythmic relationships are just as all-pervasive. The close-knit web of connections between the themes is such that, towards the end of the Finale, we have the feeling that everything we have previously heard is present in the background, contributing to the grand summation.

Instead of the unmeasured tremolo or quiet ostinato figures that open Bruckner's other symphonies, the Fifth begins with a steady pizzicato bass over which the upper strings weave a solemn counterpoint. The music moves towards the dominant key and then pauses. At this point the most natural thing would be a big statement in B flat. What happens instead is a burst of sound from the full orchestra in the unexpected key of G flat major. Another pause. The brass answer with a chorale-like phrase tending towards A major. The two phrases are repeated, this time moving from B flat to E major; the tempo quickens and then broadens out again for an orchestral tutti in A major. This entire introduction could well be the preparation for a movement in D minor; and when the principal Allegro theme appears, played by violas and cellos beneath high violin tremolos, it only touches on B flat before moving away from it.

No symphony before this had ever been so elusive about its tonic key. Bruckner's conception is evolutionary, a searching for a stability that is effectively reached only in the movement's coda; and even there, the predominance of the major over the minor mode is far from being a foregone conclusion. Minor-key inflections are characteristic of the movement as a whole. The main subsidiary theme – a hushed pizzicato string chorale, reminiscent in texture of the introduction – appears first in F minor, and is later recapitulated in G minor. A third theme, more expansive than its concise predecessors, is the only theme to be regularly associated with the major mode.

Pizzicato strings again open the D minor Adagio, playing a slow, processional figure. On this is superimposed a forlorn oboe theme whose duple time, conflicting with the strings' triple time, adds to its fragility. A second section begins with a C major theme in the strings, as warm and rich as the oboe theme is bleak. The two sections alternate in an ABABA pattern, at each appearance accruing more beautiful and inventive decoration. The last appearance of the A section – the oboe theme now played by the full woodwind section against a wonderful background of string traceries – sounds at first as though it will build up to the sort of great sequential climax found in the Adagios of the Seventh, Eighth and Ninth Symphonies; but Bruckner refrains from a monumental climax here, and the music dies away quietly, with a change from D minor to D major at the very end.

The Scherzo shares not only the key of the Adagio – D minor turning to D major at the end – but also its thematic material. The pizzicato opening of the Adagio reappears – much speeded up and played by bowed strings, but each note is the same. Above it comes a spectral, descending woodwind theme. This has barely been stated when, with a slackening of tempo, a bucolic, *Ländler*-like music comes from the strings. There is power, even violence, in the stamping dance figures; changes of tempo and phrase length constantly subvert any comforting sense of regularity; offbeat accents, unexpected entries and strange-sounding instrumental combinations reveal a Bruckner far more knowing and aware of contradiction than many people would expect. The Trio, quiet and restrained apart from a single fortissimo outburst, is less disruptive; but its good humour is tinged with nostalgia and even a sense of mystery.

The instability of the first movement, the absence of a big climax in the Adagio and the dislocations of the Scherzo have all implicitly pushed the balance of the symphony towards the Finale. The movement begins in retrospection. We hear again the very opening of the symphony – a literal quotation, apart from the seemingly incongruous detail of a downward octave leap on a solo clarinet. In the ensuing pause this figure is extended: the downward leap curls into an upward leap. The theme of the first movement's Allegro reappears, and then the opening of the Adagio, both followed by the clarinet figure. This device of recalling the themes of previous movements derives from the finale of Beethoven's Ninth Symphony, but whereas Beethoven rejects his themes in the search for something new, Bruckner's purpose is to bring them back to mind, to allow them to take their place in the final synthesis.

The Allegro moderato is launched by cellos and basses, who take up the clarinet figure of the introduction and turn it into a vigorous, marching fugue subject. When this comes to rest in the dominant key, a new, more lyrical and expansive theme in D flat major is begun by the violins over a running pizzicato bass. So far, these passages could be the first and second subjects of an orthodox sonata form; but after a big tutti pervaded by the octave leaps of the fugue subject, a change comes over the movement. The music dies away over a soft drum roll, and then there blazes forth a magnificent brass chorale, answered softly by the strings.

The chorale leaves in its wake a passage of quiet reflection, and then its theme is taken by the violas in a calm but purposeful fugue. It is at this point that Bruckner begins to tie together all the strands of his symphony. From now on the momentum increases, the fugal textures begin to absorb all the significant themes and motifs, and there is a gradual but implacable movement to establish, convincingly and unambiguously, the B flat major tonic. When at last the coda is reached, with the brass chorale dominating the orchestra, the sense of finality and achievement is masterly.

© Andrew Huth

∾ Symphony No. 7 in E major (1881–3)

1 Allegro moderato
2 Adagio: Sehr feierlich und sehr langsam [Very solemn and very slow]
3 Scherzo: Sehr schnell [Very quick] – Trio: Etwas langsamer [Somewhat slower]
4 Finale: Bewegt, doch nicht zu schnell [With movement, but not too fast]

Much of the effect of Bruckner's writing lies in his use of the most basic elements of music and the constant tension between departure and return, between the exploration of remote areas of experience and the rediscovery of simplicity. Nothing better illustrates this than the opening of the Seventh Symphony. A long, arching theme emerges from the hushed opening violin tremolo in the golden colours of cellos and horn, a pure E major arpeggio, 'nature music' recalling that most elemental of nineteenth-century musical images, the prelude to Wagner's *Das Rheingold*.

As the theme continues, the harmonic tension increases; the melody rises and falls, phrased with vocal expressiveness. From its high point it gently sinks back into its initial E major for a sonorous counterstatement from the full orchestra. This arching melody is a microcosm of Bruckner's musical language: expressive chromatic harmony set against an unambiguous statement of tonality, an original world of tone colour, and a flexibility of rhythm and phrasing which sounds almost improvised, but is in fact controlled by a master architect.

The symphony's themes are protean. They can be transformed by the simplest of means, and their continuations and combinations show Bruckner's supreme contrapuntal skills. There is no passage in this symphony with anything like a conventional fugal texture, but almost every theme is subjected at one time or another to the devices of canon, augmentation, diminution and, above all, inversion. From whatever angle the themes are seen, and in whatever shape they appear, they are always instantly recognisable, but always subtly different.

If ever a musical idea was inseparable from its instrumental colouring, it is the opening of the Adagio. For the first time Bruckner introduces into the symphony orchestra two pairs of Wagner tubas – those instruments devised by Wagner to bridge the gap in tone quality between the horns and trombones. This quartet of rich, dark-toned instruments, supported by the lower strings, stamps the music with an unmistakably elegiac character. The first section of the movement consists of a sustained procession of solemn phrases, welded into a huge melodic span. The second of these phrases, a rising figure for strings alone, also appears in Bruckner's contemporaneous setting of the *Te Deum* at the words '*non confundar in aeternum*' ('let me never be confounded').

In broad outline, the Adagio has the form ABABA; the B section quickens the tempo slightly, changes from quadruple to triple time, and assumes a more flowing, pastoral style of lyricism. The third appearance of the A section brings back the awesome sound of the Wagner tubas with lower strings, but this time with the addition of eloquent rising figures in the violins. Here is the very heart of the symphony. A vast, slow and implacable progression drives towards a climax on a remote and unexpected chord of C major (with G in the bass) as the '*non confundar*' motif proudly blazes out.

Richard Wagner had for many years been Bruckner's musical idol, and this Adagio was drafted at the time when Wagner's health was failing. On 13 February 1883 he died in Venice. The news reached Bruckner as he was about to compose the coda to the movement, which remains as Bruckner's memorial 'to the memory of the late, deeply beloved and immortal Master'.

Bruckner's scherzo movements all have in common a sense of driving, cumulative power, an almost pagan delight in physical energy. The Scherzo of the Seventh Symphony is virtually monothematic, dominated by a clarion trumpet call and its two pendants: the tense repeated string figure which precedes it, and the more relaxed falling figure which follows it. The slower Trio section is a moment of stillness, the only passage in the symphony where Bruckner allows some respite from the constant movement towards or away from climactic points: it exists in its own world, an island of peace in the middle of the Scherzo's turbulence.

For all its powerful energy, the symphony's Finale has a more relaxed character than the earlier movements. The principal theme, characterised by a sharply dotted rhythm, is closely related to that of the first movement (a relationship that is made overt in the coda). A second theme takes the form of a smoothly modulating chorale, scored for violins and violas over pizzicato cellos and basses. There is a strong reminiscence of the '*non confundar*' motif from the Adagio, and here too the Wagner tubas reappear – no longer elegiac as in the Adagio, but adding warmly expressive colour to the music.

This Finale does not aim for a grand synthesis of all the work's elements, such as we find in the Fifth and Eighth Symphonies. It is as though Bruckner feels that in expressive terms nothing need be added to the splendour of the first movement, the deep grief of the Adagio or the forcefulness of the Scherzo: what we have instead is a completion of the picture, a rounding-off in which the symphony's progress comes to rest with a return to its tonic E major, now powerfully enhanced by the lyrical wealth, glowing orchestral colour and range of emotional experience which have been uncovered in its course.

The Seventh Symphony was the first of Bruckner's works to bring him anything more than local success. Even before it was completed, Bruckner's pupils Josef Schalk and Franz Zottmann had given a public performance on two pianos of the first movement and Scherzo, and it was Schalk who persuaded Arthur Nikisch to conduct the first performance in Leipzig on 30 December 1884. The symphony made a deep impression, and a second performance under Hermann Levi in Munich was even more successful. The first British performance, under Hans Richter, took place in 1887.

© Andrew Huth

∾ Symphony No. 8 in C minor (1884–7, rev. 1887–90; 1890 version, ed. Nowak)

1 Allegro moderato
2 Scherzo: Allegro moderato – Trio: Langsam [Slow]
3 Adagio: Feierlich langsam; doch nicht schleppend [Solemn and slow, but not dragging]
4 Finale: Feierlich, nicht schnell [Solemn, not fast]

After a performance of Bruckner's Eighth Symphony many listeners may ask themselves whether what they've just heard is the greatest symphony ever written. Even if they would normally dismiss such a question as naive, the impact of the work is such as to make it difficult to feel that any other symphonist – even one whose name also begins with a 'B' – has succeeded in building an edifice at once so substantial and so immediately appealing to the emotions. Yet qualification is, of course, inevitable, for this is one particular kind of symphony: its modes of construction and expression are expansive. Other symphonists, from Haydn to Sibelius, have worked more naturally in terms of compression. Haydn was quite capable of using the same basic theme twice within a movement in two different keys, while Sibelius completed his cycle of seven symphonies in the 1920s with a work which, while not exactly short, concentrates its contrasts and evolutionary processes within a single-movement span.

Bruckner is the last composer from whom we would expect such economy, and long movements need strong contrasts, on most – if not all – levels, if the demonstration of what ultimately makes them cohere is not to seem tiresomely obvious and protracted. So Bruckner is rightly spoken of as following on from the larger symphonic designs of Beethoven and Schubert, though he never took the Mahlerian step of expanding his tonal schemes to end in a different key from that established at the start: in this respect, however emotionally satisfying it may be, the Symphony No. 9 *is* Bruckner's 'Unfinished'.

The Eighth was begun in a rare spirit of confidence, for at the end of 1884, when Bruckner was already sixty, he had at last achieved genuine public success with the first performance of his Symphony No. 7 in Leipzig. He worked on the Eighth for almost three years, until September 1887, then offered the score to Hermann Levi, the great conductor who had worked with Wagner on the first performances of *Parsifal* earlier in the decade. Yet Levi was totally unable to comprehend a new symphony so different from the Seventh, and his rejection of it not only propelled Bruckner into a serious nervous crisis but led to a confusing process of revision which has left permanent doubts as to what the composer's final intentions were. Between 1887–90 he made substantial alterations to all four movements; cuts, rescorings and recompositions which would take many pages to discuss in detail. In general, however, the process can be described as a dual one: first, enriching the orchestral sound by increasing the original woodwind from double to triple, and doubling the number of horns from four to eight; second, concentrating the musical argument by cuts, while also giving it a distinctly more serious character by eliminating the fortissimo ending of the first movement and writing a new central section for the Scherzo. In its revised form the first movement offers a more effective contrast to the Finale, and the symphony as a whole gains in dramatic tension and emotional breadth. But there are still two editions, apart from the original, for conductors to choose from: one by Leopold Nowak, which claims to represent Bruckner's final intentions in 1890, and one by Robert Haas, which restores some of the passages from the original version in the Adagio and Finale. This note concerns the Nowak edition.

The large-scale tonal unity of Bruckner's symphonic structures is explicit, but the diversity within the work will, naturally, be more evident to the listener who doesn't already know it well. As far as the thematic material is concerned, it is the contrast of shape, colour, rhythm and mood which matters most, even though there is enough of a common basis for elements from the themes of all four movements to be superimposed in a grand unifying gesture at the very end. Some sophisticated ears may identify the steadily climbing steps of the first subject as providing a basic shape for most subsequent ideas; they may even perform such feats as relating the first three notes of that first-movement theme to those of the Adagio's main theme. Yet it is the extraordinary consistency of style, rather than mere motivic likenesses, which gives all the material such arresting immediacy, and the superb control of structure which ensures the inexorable inevitability with which the symphonic potential of the material is realised. The obvious and extended points of repose within the faster movements are important and necessary, not least because Bruckner is working with a much more explicit relationship between thematic process and tonal structure than did his idol Wagner in his music dramas. The Wagnerian (or Wotan-like) mood of heroic renunciation is closest in the Eighth at the end of the Adagio, where the Wagner tubas reinforce with their melancholy richness that D flat major which is the nearest thing in the *Ring* cycle to a central key. How different, though, is Bruckner's distillation of thematic variety and harmonic unity into a simple descending scale in the first violins from Wagner's glowing cadence at the end of *Götterdämmerung*, where the violins reach upwards in a gesture at once conclusive and aspiring.

Here Bruckner achieves a profound repose, and this resolution of spiritual conflict seems to have exorcised both the pessimistic tension of the first movement and the simpler physical exuberance of the Scherzo, offset though this is by the more ambivalent mood of the Trio. In order not to be redundant, therefore, the Finale has to argue the case for renewed action: it has to intensify, not merely recapitulate. Above all, assuming that a soft, grim ending like that of the first movement is impossible, it has to achieve a grandly asserted apotheosis which is positively convincing, not emptily rhetorical. How a man as timid and indecisive as Bruckner could produce this supremely confident music is perhaps no longer a mystery to a psychologically sophisticated age. But it is not necessary to summon up any extra-musical ideas to affirm that Bruckner's genius for balancing contrasts and unities to generate so profound a progressive structure places him with the greatest masters, and in this work his own greatness and originality are unchallengeable.

© Arnold Whittall

∾ Symphony No. 9 in D minor (1887–96)

1 Feierlich, misterioso [Solemn, mysterious]
2 Scherzo: Bewegt, lebhaft [With lively movement] –
   Trio: Schnell [Fast]
3 Adagio: Langsam, feierlich [Slow, solemn]

Like a number of other great works left incomplete at their respective composers' deaths – notably Mozart's Requiem and Mahler's Tenth Symphony – Anton Bruckner's last symphony has come to be seen as a valedictory testament. There is, however, no reason for supposing that Bruckner had any such idea in his mind when he began to sketch the work in August 1887, just two days after completing the original version of the Eighth Symphony. With the first performance of Symphony No. 7 in December 1884 he had at last achieved something more than local renown, and although he never lost his painful shyness and humility, he had come in his mid-sixties to enjoy a measure of respect and a sense of his own worth that had been sadly lacking in most earlier periods of his life.

Unfortunately, Bruckner's hard-won confidence was shattered two months later when the conductor Hermann Levi, who had premiered Wagner's *Parsifal* in 1882, declined to accept the Eighth Symphony for performance, confessing himself bewildered by it. Work on the Ninth Symphony was interrupted by a thorough recomposition of the Eighth, and then by revisions of the First, Second and Third Symphonies in turn. It was not until the autumn of 1894 that the first three movements of the Ninth were ready in full score, and by then Bruckner's health had begun to deteriorate alarmingly. He worked on the finale until the day of his death on 11 October 1896. There are some two hundred pages of drafts and sketches, many fully scored, but the uncertain quality of the material, the lack of direction of many passages and even the appearance of the handwriting (often shaky to the point of illegibility) show only too clearly the effects of the physical and mental illnesses that darkened the last two years of his life. Various attempts have recently been made to prepare performing versions of this material, but none of them can claim the slightest authority. It is not simply a question of filling in textures or providing connecting passages: Bruckner had set himself a Herculean task, and it is clear that he never reached the stage where he could see the shape of the finale as a whole. There are no sketches for a coda.

Bruckner's completed symphonies, whether in major or minor keys, all end with such affirmative visions of glory that this single exception is bound to leave a disturbing impression. There are passages of darkness and conflict in the earlier symphonies, even tragedy in the Eighth, but these negative elements had always been held under control and absorbed into a symphonic argument that eventually culminated, in every finale, in a triumphant establishment of the tonic key. Not only does the unfinished Ninth lack such a finale, but the passages of agonised chromaticism, the battering, dissonant climaxes that appear in each of the three completed movements, introduce a vivid expression of pain and spiritual anguish that had nowhere before been heard in Bruckner's music.

The work opens with a hushed tremolo in the strings: a gesture familiar from earlier Bruckner symphonies, and ultimately derived from Beethoven's Ninth. Against this tremolo,

fragments of themes gradually materialise, as if looming out
of the darkness; and eventually this procession culminates in
a massive D minor statement in octaves for the full orchestra.
This is not, as one might at first think, a slow introduction, but
the first stage of a huge organic process which establishes a
timescale broad even by Bruckner's standards. In the Ninth
Symphony Bruckner's highly original approach to sonata
form reached a stage where the functions of development and
restatement are so often fused together that it is no longer
helpful to think in terms of the conventional division of a
movement into exposition, development and recapitulation
sections. The basic principles of sonata form, however, are
exploited with great subtlety. In this monumental first movement, built up out of paragraphs each lasting several minutes,
it is the long-range contrasts of tonality and expressive character that carry the music forward. There are many quiet
passages, but few moments of genuine repose. Even the
orchestral climaxes, formidable as they are, mark not so much
areas of achievement as moments that increase the overall
tension by revealing further directions in which the argument
might develop. Few pages in symphonic music can match the
thunderous power of this first movement's ending, but it is
deliberately inconclusive. The entire orchestra batters away
on the notes D and A – an empty fifth, without any clear def-
inition of major or minor – and in the following silence we
feel that the drama has only been suspended for a moment.

The Scherzo begins in a strange harmonic half-light, with
a rhythmic idea played by oboes and clarinets, joined by
pizzicato strings. It leads to a fortissimo reassertion of D
minor, but a D minor treated with a boldness that looks forward to the harmonic disintegration of Mahler and even early
Schoenberg. The raw, unprepared dissonances and the eerie
orchestral textures are very far from the open-air celebrations
of physical movement found in other Bruckner scherzos. The
Trio is the part of the symphony where we would normally
expect a measure of relaxation, perhaps a still point of pastoral meditation. There is certainly contrast in the Trio of the

Ninth Symphony, but no relaxation whatever: it is, unusually, in a faster tempo than the Scherzo, and slips into the remote key of F sharp major. For all the delicacy of the orchestral writing, there is a sinister, anxious quality about this part of the symphony.

When he eventually realised that he would never live to complete the Ninth Symphony, Bruckner came to think of the Adagio as his 'farewell to life'. Like most of his previous slow movements, it is based on the alternation of two groups of themes. The first, opening with wide, arching leaps, seems to strive towards resolution; but the moments of glorious beauty that frequently emerge are soon swallowed up again in darkness. There is a sense of desolate questing, which owes much to the fact that no clear tonic key is ever established. The second group, beginning with an expansive violin melody in A flat major, promises greater stability. It is with the recapitulation of this theme in the long-withheld tonic of E major that Bruckner starts to build the movement's climax. With the appearance of a noble chorale played by the brass choir, he might now be expected to create a powerful sequential progression towards a moment of visionary illumination such as had transfigured the Adagios of the Seventh and Eighth symphonies. Instead, the movement's tortured opening figure is hurled out by the brass and the climax erupts, against all expectations, in a hideous dissonance. It is as if all the negative elements in the symphony had been distilled into a single chord.

We must assume that Bruckner intended his finale to transcend this grim vision. As it is, the Adagio's coda is deeply peaceful, but following what has occurred it cannot be considered a peace either of certainty or of resignation. Because the Ninth Symphony is incomplete, Bruckner's battle is neither won nor lost; but the three surviving movements tell us clearly enough the terms on which it is being fought, and what is at stake.

© Andrew Huth

Aaron Copland (1900–90)

Very much a child of the twentieth century, Copland left the musical conservativism of his native New York in 1921 to study with Nadia Boulanger in Paris. There, influenced by the rhythmic complexity of Stravinsky, he wrote his ambitious ballet *Grohg* and returned to the USA in 1924 with a commission from Boulanger for an organ symphony (later rescored as the First Symphony). After Koussevitzky premiered Copland's jazzy *Music for the Theatre* and Piano Concerto in Boston, the composer adopted a simpler style during the 1930s that led to the wide appeal of his three ballet suites on American subjects, *Billy the Kid*, *Rodeo* and *Appalachian Spring*, as well as the patriotic *Lincoln Portrait* and *Fanfare for the Common Man*. He produced three film scores for Hollywood, and in 1950 wrote a Clarinet Concerto for jazz clarinettist Benny Goodman. In the 1950s and 1960s he once again attempted to become a progressive, but he gave up composing in the 1970s. He was a huge influence on the formation of a distinctive American music, not only through his compositions, but also as a writer, educator, administrator and supporter of younger composers.

∾ Symphony No. 3 (1944–6)

1 Molto moderato – with simple expression
2 Allegro molto
3 Andantino quasi allegretto –
4 Molto deliberato (Fanfare) – Allegro risoluto

In the mid-1940s Aaron Copland was at the height of his powers. In a number of works, but especially in his three great ballet scores, he had forged a musical language which was recognisably American and appealed to a wide audience, but which involved no compromise of his natural inclination towards clarity of form, texture and thematic processes. The time was ripe for a symphony which would sum up this phase of his career, in the same way that the early Symphony for organ and orchestra (later reworked without organ as Symphony No. 1) had rounded off his period of study with Nadia Boulanger, and the *Short Symphony* (No. 2) had represented his 'constructivist' period of the early 1930s. A commission from Serge Koussevitzky, Copland's champion since the mid-1920s, provided the opportunity; and the Third Symphony, begun in 1944, was completed in time for its first performances by Koussevitzky with his Boston Symphony Orchestra in October 1946.

The symphony is conceived on a large scale: it is Copland's longest concert orchestral work, and it is scored for a big orchestra, with a woodwind section including piccolo, cor anglais, E flat and bass clarinets and contrabassoon, four trumpets in the brass section, a substantial array of percussion, piano, celesta, and a pair of harps. Small groups of instruments are frequently deployed in chamber-music textures of considerable delicacy; but the full orchestra gives weight to climaxes of great rhetorical force. A strain of public declamation is a recurring (and perhaps quintessentially American) feature of Copland's music; and he once said that in this work he was 'certainly reaching for the grand gesture'. The grandest gesture of all is the incorporation into the finale of his now famous *Fanfare for the Common Man* of 1942. But while its principal statement acts as a focal point for the work's rhetoric, launching the most substantial of the four movements, the fanfare also provides the focus for the work in a more subtle way: its intervals, especially the rising fourth and fifth of its first phrase, permeate the thematic material of the entire symphony.

The formal layout of the work is far from traditional. The broad E major first movement is in the nature of a prelude, in one of Copland's characteristic arch forms – though with its two massive climaxes it is decidedly a triumphal arch. The second movement is a more conventional scherzo and trio, but with a much-altered restatement of the scherzo, and a coda including the grandiose return of the trio melody. The third movement is a free-flowing sequence of episodes growing out of a simple flute theme, framed by an introduction and coda based on an idea from the first movement. It leads straight into the finale, in which an introduction derived from the *Fanfare* precedes an energetic Allegro risoluto, and the conventional recapitulation is replaced by an extended coda which gathers in many different ideas – including the opening theme of the whole work – on its way to a powerful D major peroration.

© Anthony Burton

Antonín Dvořák (1841–1904)

It was Brahms who recognised Dvořák's talent when, around 1875, he recommended the Czech composer to his own publisher, Simrock. Born in a village north of Prague in 1841, Dvořák worked as a viola player at the Provisional Theatre, then as an organist. The success of tours in the 1880s led to wider recognition, and his appointment in 1891 as director of the newly founded National Conservatory of Music in New York. During his three years in America he was influenced by Negro and indigenous music, composing the 'New World' Symphony and the 'American' Quartet, Op. 96. But the pull of his homeland, whose folk music and pastoral beauty were reflected strongly in his music, was great: he returned to a post at the Prague National Conservatory, later becoming director. He never achieved the success of his older compatriot Smetana in the field of opera, but wrote three concertos (for violin, cello and piano), some fine string quartets, and established the Czech oratorio with his *Stabat mater* in 1883. He is best known for his symphonies and his sets of *Slavonic Dances*, originally written for piano duet, then arranged for orchestra.

～ Symphony No. 7 in D minor, Op. 70 (1884–5)

1 Allegro maestoso
2 Poco adagio
3 Scherzo: Vivace – Poco meno mosso – Vivace
4 Finale: Allegro

The 'English' Symphony is a nickname that used to be given to Dvořák's Eighth, because it was published in Britain. But the sobriquet belongs by rights to the Seventh, which has on the manuscript the inscription 'composed for the Philharmonic

Society in London'. The Royal Philharmonic Society, as it is now, invited Dvořák to write a new symphony during his triumphant second visit to England, in the summer of 1884, at the same time electing him an honorary member. Dvořák composed the work between December that year and the following March, and conducted the first performance at St James's Hall on 22 April 1885. Shortly afterwards, he wrote to a friend that the English audiences had again welcomed him 'heartily and demonstratively', and that the symphony had been 'immensely successful'. Bernard Shaw, then getting into his stride as a music critic, opined that the symphony 'seems to be the expression of the composer's happy and romantic vein; but the happiness and romance are of a serious Northern sort'.

Shaw meant 'Northern' merely as the opposite of 'Mediterranean'; but he may have hit on a distinctive feature of a work that owed a good deal to Dvořák's North German-born mentor and friend Johannes Brahms. On a visit to Brahms in the autumn of 1883, Dvořák had been impressed by the senior composer's strongly argued Third Symphony. And on a later occasion Brahms had said to Dvořák about the latter's projected new symphony, in relation to its sunny predecessor, No. 6 in D major, 'I imagine your symphony will be quite unlike this one' – a remark that had left Dvořák determined not to let his friend down. Meanwhile, Dvořák was, it seems, wrestling with his conscience about whether he should break with his Czech background and settle in Vienna, perhaps even write an opera in German. The result of this confluence of Brahmsian influence and personal crisis is that the Seventh is the darkest of Dvořák's nine symphonies, the most concerned with symphonic argument, and by far the most consistently powerful.

The opening of the first movement, much worked over by Dvořák in his sketches, establishes the predominant mood, with its dark colouring and muttered melody, and, as early as its eighth bar, the first of the symphony's many dramatic, pivotal diminished-seventh chords. The contrast between the dark chromaticism of the opening and the gentle diatonic lyricism of the B flat major second subject is one that recurs throughout the work. A tightly controlled development section leads to a much-truncated recapitulation, beginning with the first subject played *fff* by the full orchestra; the original muttered version is reserved for the coda.

The slow movement begins with a lyrical theme in a cloudless F major; but this is disrupted by an anguished minor-mode episode, with dropping diminished sevenths in the first violins and cellos, followed by a richly consoling horn melody. The central development, based largely on the horn theme, is dramatic and intricate, and the calm simplicity of the opening is not recaptured until the very end of the movement.

The Scherzo has a captivating double-stranded principal melody, with cross-rhythms reminiscent of the Bohemian dance called the *furiant*, and a melodic echo of the second-subject group of the first movement. But the minor mode imparts a touch of melancholy; the trio section, with its murmuring semitone trills, is distinctly uneasy; and the coda introduces a sorrowing viola melody before the forceful conclusion.

The Finale brings no relaxation of the drama. Most of its argument grows out of the opening idea of the in-tempo introduction, a rising octave and a falling semitone; this is later expanded in rocketing triplets to form the first subject proper. As in the first movement, there is a contrasting second subject of diatonic major-key lyricism, and a development section that builds up tension until the recapitulation is launched with explosive force. The second subject seems at one point to be sweeping the work towards an unexpectedly happy ending, in the manner of a Weber overture; but finally another version of the rising-octave figure leads through granite-like chords to a hard-won major-key resolution.

Anthony Burton © BBC

∾ Symphony No. 8 in G major, Op. 88
(1889)

1 Allegro con brio
2 Adagio
3 Allegretto grazioso
4 Allegro ma non troppo

Dvořák wrote the last but one of his nine symphonies between late August and early November 1889, mostly in the peaceful surroundings of his country cottage at Vysoká, in southern Bohemia. It was first performed, under his own direction, in Prague the following February, and eventually published – after a protracted dispute between Dvořák and his regular publisher Simrock over payment for his larger works – by Novello of London. This led to it being nick-named for many years the 'English' Symphony: hardly an epithet it was entitled to, when its predecessor had actually been commissioned by the Philharmonic Society in London and first performed there; but the English connection was reinforced when Dvořák conducted the work (as well as his *Stabat mater*) in Cambridge in June 1891, on the eve of the ceremony at which he received an honorary degree.

The new symphony marked a change in Dvořák's attitude to the form, following the generally traditional construction (and strongly Brahmsian colouring) of Nos 6 and 7. This time, he said, he wanted to write a work 'different from the other symphonies, with individual thoughts worked out in a new way'. The German scholar Hartmut Schick has suggested that one source of these new ideas may have been Tchaikovsky's Fifth Symphony, which Dvořák had heard the composer conduct in Prague in November 1888, only weeks after its premiere: he cites similarities in the themes, formal procedures and orchestral writing of the two works, and suggests that Tchaikovsky's use of a unifying motto theme is par-alleled by Dvořák's use of march rhythms in three of the four movements. But if one were looking for another precedent for the opening theme of the first movement, for example, one might find it in the colouring, modality and initial rhythm of the melody which begins the 1840 overture *Echoes of Ossian* by the Dane Niels Gade, a work well known in Europe in the mid-nineteenth century. The truth of the matter is surely that, while open to these and other influences, Dvořák was instinctively drawn towards 'making new', and could no more repeat accepted forms without variation than he could write out a repetition of a theme without adding some new touch of melody, harmony or scoring.

The most strikingly original movement, in formal terms, is the first. Since the symphony is announced as being in G major, the G minor tonality of the opening melody should immediately proclaim it as introductory; and that impression should be confirmed when the melody returns in a self-contained paragraph at the end of the exposition section, marked 'Un poco meno mosso' (a little slower) – which has led many conductors to hold back the tempo at the start as well. And yet the ideas which follow this melody in the opening section are much more fragmented and harmonically unstable: a chirpy flute theme beginning with a rising major triad peters out after a few bars, and its return later for full orchestra is equally brief; an apparently assertive hymn-like theme proves similarly elusive. Moreover, the initial melody contributes a significant phrase to the argument of the development section; it returns at the end of the development section on the trumpets, riding a rather Tchaikovskian storm, in its original key; and this last appearance is followed by a recapitulation which is a highly compressed version of the exposition, holding back the tempo for the chirpy flute theme (now initially on cor anglais, the instrument's only three bars in the whole work), and leaving out the hymn-like theme altogether. Since the 'introductory' melody behaves in so many ways like a first subject, is it then the true first subject? In a sense, the answer is unimportant: as Jan Smaczny has written, 'a dogmatic interpretation of sonata form in this movement simply will not do'. What is important is the ambiguity implied by the question, which keeps the attentive listener really listening, unsure even on repeated hearings (especially of different interpretations) exactly what is going on and how it all fits together.

The slow movement is hardly any more predictable. Alec Robertson, in his vintage 'Master Musicians' study of Dvořák, wrote that 'it could stand as a miniature tone poem of Czech village life described by a highly sensitive man', and heard in it not only bird calls and 'the village band, cimbalom and all', but also 'a touch of pain'. A more scholastic writer might view it as a study of the way in which one tiny idea, a four-note rising scale landing on a downbeat, together with its simplified inversion, a falling fourth, can generate an entire, varied movement. As in the first movement, the opening is deceptive: the strings begin in E flat major but settle into C minor; the woodwind bird calls are in C major, though the clarinets' responses are tinged with the minor; the anguished repetition of the opening paragraph is in C minor; the march of the village band, full and busy in texture, is in a cloudless C major. The second half of the movement is a much varied restatement of the first, never straying far from C major or minor, but developing the opening idea to an even more intense climax before the return of the march, now with even fuller textures. After a last cry of pain, the ending lies with the bird calls and the falling fourths.

The third movement is a lilting G minor waltz – or perhaps, like Dvořák's well-known Slavonic Dance Op. 72 No. 2, which has the same tempo marking, a Lachian *starodávny*. The major-key trio has a melody salvaged from an aria in the composer's early one-act opera *The Stubborn Lovers*. After a literal repetition of the main section, there is a coda in which this melody is speeded up into a brisk 2/4 Molto vivace, alternately playful and riotous.

The finale is basically a set of variations, on a cello theme (much revised in Dvořák's sketches) which begins with the rising triad of the flute theme in the first movement, and continues with a turning figure from the introductory trumpet fanfare. But Dvořák subverts the predictability of the variation scheme with elements of ternary and sonata forms. Variation 2 is an energetic tutti version of the first half only of the theme, at a faster tempo; and it returns after Variation 3, giving rise to a transitional passage on the strings in octaves. This leads into an independent march-like section in C minor, which is in turn followed by a short development, incorporating not only phrases from the theme of the variations but also the trumpet fanfare. After this, the return of the theme in almost its original form takes on an element of recapitulation; but the subsequent variations are simple and increasingly gentle, finally getting becalmed on repetitions of the rising triad and the turning figure. Another reprise of Variation 2 comes to the rescue, acting as a springboard for an exhilarating, and accelerating, coda.

© Anthony Burton

∾ Symphony No. 9 in E minor, Op. 95, 'From the New World' (1893)

1   Adagio – Allegro molto
2   Largo
3   Scherzo: Molto vivace
4   Allegro con fuoco

'The new American school of music must strike its roots deeply into its own soil,' Dvořák wrote in a letter to the *New York Herald* on 25 May 1893, adding in a later paragraph that 'the country is full of melody, original, sympathetic and varying in mood, colour and character to suit every phase of composition'. He was writing, not simply as an internationally famous composer whose own music had grown out of his native Czech soil, but as director of the National Conservatory of Music in New York, a post he held for three seasons from the autumn of 1892 to the summer of 1895. The Conservatory had been founded by its patron Mrs Jeannette Thurber specifically to foster a 'new American school of music'; it ran on idealistic lines, offering free tuition to talented students who could not afford its fees, and (unlike most colleges at the time) encouraging the admission of women and black students. And what makes Dvořák's letter especially significant is that it was written the day after he had put the finishing touches, following four months of labour, to the last of his nine symphonies – a work which seemed designed to embody the aspirations of the Conservatory in music, showing American composers, and in particular his own students, the way to finding a national voice. It was with this in mind that, some months after its completion but before its first performance, he gave it the title of 'From the New World'.

In describing America as 'full of melody', Dvořák did not mean to suggest that composers should make use of real folk tunes, any more than he had done in writing his *Slavonic Dances*; and there is no sign that he quoted any existing melodies in his model American symphony. Instead, he absorbed some of the feeling of the spirituals sung to him by his black student Harry T. Burleigh; and he was clearly aware of the 'plantation songs' of the successful white composer Stephen Foster. But at the same time he seems to have seized on features of these songs – syncopated rhythms, the pentatonic scale, the flattened seventh in minor modes – which were common to folk music in many countries, including his own.

As for Native American music, it seems unlikely that it could have contributed much to the symphony: Dvořák probably did not hear 'Indian' musicians until his visit to the Czech community in Spillville, Iowa, in the summer of 1893, after he had completed the work. But Native American culture, albeit at one remove, did find its way into the score. Dvořák told a newspaper interviewer that the slow movement of the symphony was a study for a 'cantata or opera' which he planned to write on Longfellow's epic poem *Hiawatha*, a conflation of various Native American legends, and that its Scherzo was suggested by a scene in the same poem 'where the Indians dance'. In two articles, the American scholar Michael Beckerman has linked the slow movement to the homeward journey of Hiawatha with his bride Minnehaha and Minnehaha's forest funeral, and found close parallels between the Scherzo and the scene of Pau-Pau-Keewis's increasingly frenzied dance at Hiawatha's wedding feast.

Dvořák's comments on the American origins of his symphony appeared in a New York newspaper interview on the eve of its premiere, given in Carnegie Hall in December 1893 under the direction of the leading Wagnerian conductor Anton Seidl. No doubt they contributed to the enthusiasm with which the work was received. Every movement was applauded; and at the end, Dvořák reported delightedly to his publisher Simrock that 'the people clapped so much I had to thank them from the box like a king!' European performances soon followed, with similar success, and before long the work had attained the status which it still holds today, as one of the most popular of all symphonies.

The first movement of the 'New World' Symphony begins with a dramatic slow introduction, featuring syncopated rhythms right from the start, and anticipating the striding first theme of the main Allegro. This is followed in the exposition section of the Allegro by two more gentle ideas; there is a stormy development section, and then an unorthodox recapitulation, in which the second and third themes are brought back in the remote keys of G sharp minor and A flat major. (Both are given to the second flute, treated as usual by Dvořák as a low-register specialist.) The movement ends with the first theme at its most assertive.

The slow movement, the famous Largo, begins with a solemn sequence of wind chords leading from E major to establish D flat major, in which key the cor anglais makes its first appearance in the work with a memorable spiritual-like melody. There is a middle section in C sharp minor which alternates between two contrasting ideas, both of which grow out of three-note scales – the first descending, the second ascending. A transitional episode, perhaps suggesting a forest dawn chorus, swiftly builds up to a climax, at which the first theme of the first movement is recalled. The cor anglais melody returns, with the strings reduced in numbers until only a trio of soloists is left; and the solemn chord sequence leads to a quiet ending.

The third movement has an unusually complex structure, with a song-like E major middle section to the main Scherzo as well as a lilting, somewhat Schubertian trio in C major. The first theme of the Allegro reappears twice more here, in the transition from scherzo to trio and in the coda.

However, it is the last movement that is the most thoroughgoing exercise in cyclic integration. After the in-tempo introduction, the declamatory first theme grows out of the three-note scale of the middle section of the slow movement; and at the start of the development section that three-note figure is reduced to its simplest form. The remainder of the development ignores the more lyrical second-subject group, instead drawing on the 'spiritual' theme of the slow movement, a little figure from the Scherzo and, inevitably, the first theme of the Allegro. And after the recapitulation, which begins with no more than a brief, reflective statement of the first subject at a slower tempo, the coda adds a thrilling reappearance of the introductory chord sequence of the Largo to the retrospective mix – before ending with a fiery final tutti and an unexpectedly valedictory last chord.

© Anthony Burton

Edward Elgar (1857–1934)

Elgar rose from humble beginnings (his father was a piano tuner and organist) to become Britain's leading composer: he was knighted in 1904, awarded the Order of Merit in 1911 and became Master of the King's Musick in 1924. Born in Worcester, he failed in his early attempt to establish himself in London, though his reputation grew steadily during the 1890s. The *Enigma Variations* of 1899 first brought him to national attention, followed closely by his darkly imaginative *Dream of Gerontius* (1900). He was over fifty when he produced his First Symphony, the first of his large-scale orchestral works, which was followed by the Violin Concerto, the Second Symphony and the Cello Concerto. After the death of his wife in 1920 he lost his will to compose, though in 1932 the BBC commissioned his Third Symphony. Elgar left 130 pages of sketches for the symphony at his death, which were elaborated by the British composer Anthony Payne. Fittingly, the completed work was finally premiered by the BBC Symphony Orchestra in 1998.

❧ Symphony No. 1 in A flat major, Op. 55 (1907–8)

1　Andante. Nobilmente e semplice – Allegro
2　Allegro molto –
3　Adagio
4　Lento – Allegro

'I hold that the symphony without a programme is the highest development of art.' With these words, spoken in a University of Birmingham lecture in December 1905, Elgar declared himself as adhering to the Brahmsian tradition of the abstract symphony, already thought moribund by many, rather than allying himself with Richard Strauss, the modern master of the symphonic poem. Yet it was to be some time before his words bore fruit in music; because the first of Elgar's two completed symphonies was not even begun until the summer of 1907, and was finished more than a year later, shortly before its first performance, given by the Hallé Orchestra in Manchester in December 1908.

Admittedly, we do know that he had been at work on a symphony much earlier, in 1901, and that it was to have been dedicated to the Hallé's conductor, Hans Richter, as was the First Symphony when it finally appeared. But it is hardly likely that the earlier work could have had much to do with the later, since it was to have been based on the life of the military hero General Gordon – a concept far from the abstract symphony postulated in the Birmingham lecture. Indeed, Elgar specifically said to one friend that the First was not the Gordon symphony, and he told another: 'There is no programme beyond a wide experience of human life with a great charity (love) and a *massive* hope in the future.'

What then, in purely musical terms, is Elgar's First Symphony 'about'? The oddest story that we have concerning the piece came from Adrian Boult, who was told that it was written after somebody had bet Elgar that he could not write a symphony in two keys at once. And yet, strange though it is, the anecdote rings true. This 'Symphony in A flat' has a first Allegro which is clearly in the remote key of D minor, turning in the development section to the even more remote key of D major, but with an introduction and final section in A flat major. It has a scherzo in F sharp minor with a trio in B flat major, both keys occupying a kind of middle ground between the two opposing tonalities of A flat and D; and a slow movement which comes down firmly on the side of D, this time major. And then it has a finale with a slow introduction once more in D minor, and a main Allegro which begins in the same key, and turns to A flat major again only towards the end. On the page, all this may seem just so much algebra. But as part of an expressive (which is not to say a programmatic) scheme, it comes off beautifully: how much more massive that 'hope in the future' seems when the symphony ends in a key which, while satisfactorily rounding off the work as a whole, also opens up new vistas in its immediate surroundings.

Elgar's First is also, like all great symphonies (consciously or unconsciously), 'about' unity. This manifests itself on various levels. Within movements, many of Elgar's profusion of melodies and motifs turn out to be subtly interrelated; they come, in Elgar's own metaphor, 'from the same oven'. Between movements, too, there are connections: the most notable example of this is that the first four bars of the theme of the slow third movement use exactly the same notes as the first two bars of the theme of the preceding scherzo. Given this close correspondence, it is small wonder that the two movements are also linked by being played without a break.

Over and above everything else, though, there is Elgar's use of his motto theme, the long, 'noble and simple' melody of the slow introduction. This takes its place in the general scheme of interrelationships, and its opening phrase in particular can be traced in more than one melody in later movements. It also appears, in incomplete but clearly recognisable form, in the development section of the first movement; in the introduction to the finale, where it forms part of a patchwork of ideas from various movements; and in the development section of the finale, where its kinship to the march-like second subject of that movement is uncovered. But its principal appearances are its three full statements, which constitute the three mighty pillars of the symphony's structure, and which – by no coincidence – correspond to the three appearances of the home key of A flat. The first is the sonorous introduction; the second is at the end of the first movement, where the melody gradually creeps into the texture, is briefly affirmed, and then dies away again; and the last comes just before the end of the work, where the motto appears, marked 'Grandioso (poco largamente)', in full orchestral splendour.

Finally, this symphony could be said to be 'about' the orchestra. Elgar was a professional orchestral violinist for some time and a conductor of considerable experience, and had at least a working knowledge of several wind and string instruments; he always felt more at home with orchestral players than with other members of the musical profession – he even dedicated his *Cockaigne* overture 'to my many friends, the members of British orchestras'. So he scored the symphony with inside knowledge, with the utmost skill and with love. And it shows: both to players – who find their parts sometimes taxing but always rewarding to play – and to audiences, who are better placed to judge the overall effect.

It would be useless to start drawing attention to details, because the secret of Elgar's scoring lies in a mass of details, above all in the way he picks out through instrumental doubling just the one or two crucial notes in a phrase. But in general terms one can point to the clarity of even the most densely packed passages of development in the outer movements; the lightness of touch of the second movement, with its trio which Elgar once asked an orchestra to play 'like something you hear down by the river'; the depth of tone of the serene slow movement, achieved through carefully calculated subdivisions of the string sections and restrained reinforcement from the wind; and, not least, the grandiloquence – but never bombast – of the final return of the motto theme and the work's conclusion.

In the same lecture series as that in which he espoused the cause of the abstract symphony, Elgar referred to the modern symphony orchestra as 'the mighty engine, the vehicle of the highest form of art known to the world'. As the First Symphony shows, there was no greater master of that engine than Edward Elgar.

© Anthony Burton

ᴄᴠ Symphony No. 2 in E flat, Op. 63
(1903–11)

1   Allegro vivace e nobilmente
2   Larghetto
3   Rondo: Presto
4   Moderato e maestoso

After the triumph of his First Symphony in 1908, Elgar composed his Violin Concerto, which Kreisler performed on 10 November 1910, to high acclaim. The following month Elgar began sustained work on his Second Symphony, and conducted it with the Queen's Hall Orchestra on 24 May 1911 in the London Musical Festival. He dedicated it to 'the Memory of His late Majesty King Edward VII'. On the score he wrote the first lines of Shelley's 'Song':

> Rarely, rarely comest thou,
> Spirit of Delight!

Commentators used to disagree as to whether the absence or presence of delight was the more potent influence, and wonder how to link the quotation with the monarch's death. Now, more is known about the work's history. All the same, Elgar used words to protect his feelings as often as to convey them. His was not a simple personality, and at its most characteristic his music does not aspire to pure expression, but to a complex of emotions – rich, ambivalent, even conflicting – that is truly Romantic.

In 1903–4 he had wintered in northern Italy at Alassio. When his piano arrived, he improvised the opening theme of the Second Symphony's last movement. Another last-movement idea is strikingly like part of *In the South*, the concert overture (subtitled 'Alassio') which he was then composing: when he was old, Elgar told Barbirolli that this was the germ of the whole movement. The interesting point is that it comes in the middle of the development; which confirms Elgar's unorthodox way of composing. From the autumn of

1905 dates the last movement's second theme; he headed this 'Hans himself!' so it may have been intended for the First Symphony, dedicated to the conductor Hans Richter.

In April 1909 the Elgars stayed at Careggi above Florence. There, 'in *glorious* weather, the world bathed in sunshine, the air scented with flowers', he sketched part of the first movement. Then they went on to Venice. Elgar saw the sombre magnificence of San Marco, and in the Piazza he noted down the rhythm of some strolling musicians who took a 'grave satisfaction in the broken accent' of what they played. Later he said that the openings of the Larghetto and of the Rondo represented the 'contrast between the interior of St Mark's and the sunlit and lively Piazza outside'.

Home again in Hereford in June, it was down to work on the Violin Concerto. Not until October did Elgar look at the Italian and older sketches, when he 'was quite inspired with Sym 2'. Some of the old sketches may have been from the 'General Gordon' symphony that Elgar talked of before 1900, but had come to nothing beyond a few sketches.

In spring 1910 Alice Stuart-Wortley and her family were staying at Tintagel, of romantic Arthurian legend; Elgar, touring the West Country, visited them and saw the 'austere yet lyrical beauty' of the place. Mrs Stuart-Wortley was the daughter of the painter Millais, the wife of a Conservative Member of Parliament; she was a good amateur pianist, and a beautiful, cultivated woman. She had become Elgar's creative muse, and persuaded him to complete the Violin Concerto when he was despondent. He associated the lyrical theme in the Second Symphony's Scherzo (cue 106) with her. No specific theme can be linked with Tintagel, though Elgar dated the score 'Venice– Tintagel 1910–1911'.

Back in his rented London flat, Elgar played what 'Dorabella' (Dora Penny, subject of the tenth of the *Enigma Variations*) recalled as a slow movement for his Second Symphony – 'the sound of a funeral march'. This was before Edward VII died on 6 May 1910. Elgar had been honoured by him, dined with him, composed the *Coronation Ode* (1902) for him. He offered to produce a march for the funeral, but there was not time for rehearsal. It used to be supposed that the Larghetto was inspired by the king's death, but clearly much of it was composed before. When Elgar first played it to his wife, she heard a 'lament for King Edward and dear Rodey in it, and all human feeling'. Alfred Rodewald was a Liverpool businessman and amateur musician, dedicatee of the *Pomp and Circumstance* March No. 1. He had died in November 1903 and Elgar, who arrived just too late to see him alive, had walked the streets distraught. He composed at that time a sketch for a passage of creeping chromatics that appears (cue 74) in the Second Symphony's Larghetto.

On 29 January 1911 Elgar wrote to Alice Stuart-Wortley: 'I have recorded last year in the first movement to which I put the last note in the score a moment ago and I must tell you this: I have worked at fever heat and the thing is tremendous in energy.' In March he gave her some sketches and the draft score 'of the (your) symphony'. Later he told her, 'I have written out my soul' in the Violin Concerto, the Second Symphony and *The Music Makers*; 'in these three works I have shewn myself.'

Elgar told his publisher that 'the spirit of the whole work is intended to be high & pure joy: there are retrospective passages of sadness but the whole of the sorrow is smoothed out & ennobled in the last movement, which ends in a calm &, *I hope & intend, elevated* mood'. All Shelley's poem may be read, he said, though neither poem nor music wholly illustrate or elucidate each other. He told the critic Ernest Newman: 'My attitude toward the poem, or rather to the "Spirit of Delight", was an attempt to give the reticent Spirit a hint (with sad enough retrospective) as to what we would like to have!'

So many memories, such rich associations, went into this music. But what inner history led Elgar to Shelley, and to choose so ambiguous a clue? His private turmoils, his extremes of elation and morbid despair, are at the heart of this music, transfigured by the power of his imagination so that his emotional experience becomes universal.

It is a long symphony. It had to be, to contain his prodigality: it would take several dozen music examples to chart the
music's course. Also it needs, literally, the passage of time, for
themes are recalled in later movements, not as direct quotations, nor to strengthen the structure, but as if the composer
were reliving a remembered emotion. Elgar needed length as
a novelist sometimes does, to uncover the significance of the
past by looking back through subsequent experience ('with
sad enough retrospective'). His key relationships, too, need
time and space. He had absorbed the extended tonality of
Liszt and Wagner, and this, together with his mobile basses
and his habit of thinking in sequences, make it often more
accurate to say that a theme is in a tonal region rather than in
a key.

The first movement breaks from a unison into a mettle-
some long paragraph of which the third bar (the descent from
the crest of the climax) may be the 'Spirit of Delight' figure.
The profuse ideas are related by the plunge and soar of their
outlines, and by the swinging 12/8 metre. All is valiant, energetic, splendid; throughout the symphony, most of the positive, assured themes have a prominent melodic perfect fifth.
But a harmonic progression based on an augmented fourth
carries seeds of introspection and apprehension, for the exuberant vitality is often undermined by desolation and self-
doubt. As the development begins, confidence falters; there
are glimpses of wraiths and anxieties. In the middle comes a
long cello tune, weird and disturbing – 'a sort of malign influence wandering thro' the summer night in the garden', Elgar
called it – though its potential is not realised until the Rondo.

After the raw nerve-endings of the first movement, the
grief of the Larghetto is the more powerful for being formally contained. The main theme is heard above a muffled processional tread; when it comes back, a solo oboe twines
lamenting triplets round it. Twice accumulated feeling wells
up thrillingly into simple major diatonic climaxes. Just before
the end, the 'Spirit of Delight' seems a wan memory of lost
happiness.

The Rondo-scherzo theme drives impatiently across the bar lines, with steep dynamics. The repeats of it, and the lyrical episodes, all attract fragments of countersubjects, so nothing is clear-cut. Then the movement settles grimly onto a tonic pedal and gathers itself together for an utterance of the 'malign' theme from the first movement – a desperate suffocating passage. Elgar told orchestras to think of 'a man in a high fever . . . that dreadful beating that goes on in the brain – it seems to drive out every coherent thought'. Spirit of delight, indeed! He associated this with lines from Tennyson's 'Maud':

> Dead, long dead,
> Long dead.
> And my heart is a handful of dust
> And the wheels go over my head . . .

A healthy pride marks the E flat finale. The development opens with vigorous fugatos, but the return to the first theme is poetic, by way of a melancholy C minor. After the sumptuous, rhetorical sequences towards the end, the mood relaxes to welcome the 'Spirit of Delight'. But here is no triumph, no certainty, but a courageous and compassionate reconciliation of the extremes of this great work.

The first performance did not attract a full Queen's Hall, and Elgar missed the note of warmth in the applause. 'What's the matter with them, Billy?' he asked the orchestra's leader. 'They sit there like a lot of stuffed pigs.' Perhaps the word 'delight' had led people to expect a brighter note; the black passages were disconcerting. In some ways the audience's sober reaction was a true one to a work that demands a thoughtful appraisal rather than carefree excitement. It is, as Elgar agreed, the 'passionate pilgrimage of a soul'.

© Diana McVeagh

∾ The Sketches for Symphony No. 3,
elaborated by Anthony Payne

1 Allegro molto maestoso
2 Scherzo: Allegretto
3 Adagio solenne
4 Allegro

In all Elgar's published output there is nothing quite like his sketch for the opening of this symphony: brazen fifths and octaves, grinding in contrary motion, building in sequence to an imposing march rhythm, underlined by timpani. The basic motif derives from a sketch for the unfinished oratorio, *The Last Judgement*. But here that idea is transformed: an odd, distinctly un-Elgarian-looking figure becomes a theme that fairly erupts with potential energy, capable of setting a huge, sweeping musical paragraph in motion. A little later, after Elgar's beautifully engineered transition, comes the second main theme: tender, lilting, in Elgar's best 'feminine' vein. Apparently the inspiration was a young admirer, the violinist Vera Hockman (the initials 'V. H.' stand next to the theme in one sketch).

This 'exposition' section (completed in short score by Elgar) is repeated. Then the development is inaugurated by the opening 'Last Judgement' motif in combination with two new themes: a calm, chordal figure for strings and, later, an energetically striding motif for horns. After a powerful climax, a march section follows in B flat minor (martial music plays a significant part in both outer movements). The recapitulation is relatively straightforward – though Elgar indicated some glorious deviations from the expected course (e.g. the sudden hush after the return of the first theme). The coda assembles all the main ideas and builds to a triumphant C major conclusion, based on the original march rhythm.

In some of Elgar's sketches the second movement is labelled 'In place of Scherzo'. At first glance this is relatively familiar territory: Elgar the wistful miniaturist, the supremely

gifted salon composer. But at the same time there is something elusive about the movement, in spirit and in form
(though this is the clearest and most extensively planned
movement in the sketches). The opening theme – a gently
airborne dance tune (the tambourine is clearly indicated by
Elgar!) – recurs in something like rondo fashion, at one point
threatening a return of the first movement's martial style; but
at the end it seems simply to evaporate into thin air.

Like the Larghetto of the Second Symphony, the slow
movement of the Third probes dark emotions: grief, terror,
aching nostalgia – though where the earlier movement tends
to objectify these feelings (principally through the image of
the funeral march, a symbol of collective mourning), the
Third Symphony's Adagio solenne suggests, to this writer at
least, something more acutely personal. Elgar wrote that the
opening bars of this movement would 'open some vast bronze
doors into something strangely unfamiliar'. The harmonies
of the introductory figure, and of the elegiac first theme,
may not be unfamiliar in terms of the early 1930s, but they
certainly feel strange here: disturbing harmonic twists and
dislocations, agonised chromaticism. A warmly consoling
second theme brings respite, but not for long. The recapitulation intensifies the dark side of the main theme and its
poignant introductory figure – at one point there is a magnificent climax based on a sketch that Elgar marked 'cumulative
crescendo'. At the end the introductory figure's quiet,
anguished questioning is left unanswered, as Elgar clearly
intended.

After this, the finale returns to the first movement's heroic
vein: a fanfare, surging string figures, a martial main theme
with a singing 'subsidiary' tune that clearly ought to carry
Elgar's favourite marking, 'nobilmente', and a glorious 12/8
climactic passage with chiming strings and swaggering brass.
In contrast to the first movement, the finale's 'second subject'
section offers no lyrical consolation. Instead one follows the
gradual and dramatic emergence of a full-throated tune from
a few scraps of motif. The development introduces another

theme from Elgar's sketches – one of those peculiarly Elgarian sequential tunes that makes one want to join in and sing (or at least discreetly hum along). The broad, exciting crescendo leading to the recapitulation is Anthony Payne's invention, but it was Elgar who indicated the surprise swerve to A minor at the return of the main theme. He left no indication, however, as to how the symphony would have ended. But during a sleepless night in an American hotel, Payne was suddenly struck by the notion that the finale's martial main theme could be made into a huge, rhythmically repeating crescendo–diminuendo – like the extraordinary movement 'The Wagon Passes' from Elgar's *Nursery Suite*. Thus the military music has the last say, marching eventually into silence.

© Stephen Johnson

César Franck (1822–90)

Franck showed early signs of a promising pianistic career, studying at the conservatoire in his home town of Liège and undertaking a concert tour of Belgium at the age of twelve. In 1835 his family moved to Paris where Franck entered the Conservatoire. He wrote a number of piano pieces, including a concerto; an oratorio, *Ruth*, was premiered in 1846. He married in 1848, and took a number of teaching and organist posts before becoming organist at St Clotilde in 1858. Here, according to his pupil d'Indy, he would 'stir up the fires of his genius in admirable improvisations'. Franck was appointed organ professor at the Paris Conservatoire in 1872, which finally brought him recognition after a series of disappointingly received works. Most of the works for which Franck is now remembered were composed after this appointment, and the majority of these – the *Prelude, Chorale and Fugue* for piano, the *Symphonic Variations* for piano and orchestra, the Violin Sonata and the Symphony in D minor – were written in his last six years.

∾ Symphony in D minor (1886–8)

1 Lento – Allegro non troppo
2 Allegretto
3 Allegro non troppo

Some scepticism about the value of French symphonies is understandable from those French composers – like Debussy and Boulez – who have avoided writing them. Yet even the sceptics have found things to admire in works such as Berlioz's *Symphonie fantastique* and Messiaen's *Turangalîla Symphony*, which prosper by challenging – if not totally contradicting – Teutonic orthodoxies. The usual reason for doubting the success of César Franck's Symphony in D minor has therefore been the assumption that it seeks, ineffectively, to enshrine and even to sanctify those orthodoxies. Yet it can equally well be claimed that Franck – belying Gounod's alleged jibe that the work was 'the affirmation of incompetence pushed to dogmatic lengths' – was fully aware of what writing an effective symphony in the late 1880s could involve. After all, this was the era of Bruckner and the young Mahler, as well as of Brahms and Dvořák: a time when even Germanic composers were allowing symphonies to be larger and looser than tradition decreed. It was also a time when the quality of thematic ideas mattered more than the construction of tightly controlled forms, and it may well be that Debussy's reaction to Franck's effort – 'I should prefer less four-square structure. But what smart ideas!' – expresses the view that Franck had succeeded in what mattered.

This symphony is a late work by a late developer, written between 1886 and 1888, at the end of a composing career that had only begun to blossom with the Piano Quintet, completed when Franck was fifty-seven, in 1879. The music is distinctive, yet it also creates many associations, and its originality and ambition stem from the extent to which it brings into contact two quite separate symphonic principles: the dynamic, Beethovenian progress from doubt to certainty, darkness to light; and the more discursive, Lisztian technique of presenting different versions of basic ideas in ever-changing lights, the ideas recurring cyclically in such a way that the music both circulates and advances. The main results of bringing these principles together is to create a large-scale design in which contrasts of mood, texture and tonality feature more prominently than they do in more classical symphonic music, from Haydn to Brahms. And it is the ability to enhance contrast without losing all impetus and all sense of forward movement that links Franck to the likes of Bruckner and Mahler. They were greater than he, no doubt – after all, they made rather more extensive contributions to the symphonic genre – and they were very different in style: but similarities of aim and principle remain.

The relative flexibility of form in Franck's composition is evident in the conflation of 'slow' movement and scherzo, so that the symphony has three movements rather than four. And Franck also emphasises the contrast in the first movement between what is less a slow introduction and a fast first subject than slow and fast versions of the first subject. Here the Beethovenian association is strong, since Franck's theme has a 'must it be?' shape recalling the questing curve of the first idea in Beethoven's last string quartet. In Franck's case the answer to the question is provided by the first movement's main contrasting theme, a narrow-intervalled but warmly expressive idea that has become known as the 'Faith' motive: faith replaces doubt, major tonality replaces minor, and the programme of the whole work is encapsulated in the first movement's exposition. Otherwise the movement's form is straightforward, with the arrival of the recapitulation especially effective in setting slow and fast versions of the first theme in radically different tonal areas. This is a skilful way of preparing the movement's arrival in its – and the whole symphony's – goal tonality of D major.

The contrasts in the central (not literally 'slow') movement are not as great as they might have been if reflective and scherzo-like elements had been given radically different tempos: but an unmistakable polarity is achieved through texture and tonality. First, the stately, sombre unfolding of the cor anglais melody and its more flowing continuation; second, after the shortened restatement of the cor anglais tune, the more dance-like yet shadowy scherzo material. It is precisely because Franck eventually superimposes these two ideas that the movement achieves its effect, as a well-proportioned character piece in which the elements of lyric reflection and scherzo interact, neither losing its identity, in attractive, expressive counterpoint.

The main theme of the finale may not be as elegantly shaped as that of Franck's *Symphonic Variations* or the last movement of the Violin Sonata, but it has a syncopated vivacity well suited to the context. There is a substantial, strongly contrasted subsidiary theme, and this is followed by the first clear evidence of the work's cyclic principles, the return of the second movement's cor anglais tune. After this both finale themes are fully developed, and a recapitulation is efficiently prepared, the harmonic issue kept in doubt by the avoidance of strongly defined cadences. After the first theme has been restated, a fully orchestrated version of the cor anglais theme usurps the role of the original second subject, and is placed so that its minor tonality answers the first theme's major tonality in the most dramatic manner. The stage is therefore set for the return of the first movement's 'Faith' motive to heal the breach, and the final stages of the symphony pursue the consequences of this process. After the restrained recall of the 'Faith' motive the first movement's first theme reappears, transformed into affirmative major harmony, and Franck makes aurally clear the links between this, the 'Faith' motive and the finale's own main theme, in a cogent and exciting conclusion.

© Arnold Whittall

Roy Harris (1898–1979)

Along with Copland, Roy Harris was a major influence in creating a distinctively American musical identity. Born in Oklahoma, he moved to California with his family at an early age. Here, after a stint as a farmer, he studied composition with Arthur Farwell, before leaving to study in Paris with Nadia Boulanger. In Paris he studied the music of Bach, Beethoven, Lassus and Palestrina, and returned to the USA with a Concerto for piano, clarinet and string quartet (1927). He rose to fame in America through the success of his Symphony No. 3. From 1932 to 1940 he taught at New York's Juilliard School – the first of a string of prestigious lectureships and composer residencies at American institutions. He wrote fifteen symphonies in total, including the *Folksong Symphony* (No. 4), but none equalled the success of the Third.

∾ Symphony No. 3, In One Movement (1938–9)

Roy Harris has often been described as the most distinctively American of all American composers. This may partly be due to sentimentality over his pioneer origins: he was born (on Abraham Lincoln's birthday) in a log cabin in Lincoln County, Oklahoma, of a Scottish–Irish settler family. But there is all the same a grain of truth in the idea. Although, like Aaron Copland, he studied in Paris in the 1920s with Nadia Boulanger, his music has little of the Gallic finish acquired by most of her pupils; instead it retains a rugged, occasionally almost clumsy, highly individual quality of its own. And although he chose to write mostly in the forms of the Germanic tradition, above all in his series of fifteen symphonies, he filled them with melodies which, while rarely quoting any actual borrowed material, have their roots deep in American folk song and Protestant hymnody. All this goes some way towards explaining the acclamation, and perhaps also the relief, with which Harris's Third Symphony was greeted at its first performance in Boston in 1939; the conductor, Serge Koussevitzky, called it 'the first great symphony by an American composer'. For many years afterwards it was the most frequently performed American symphonic work; and certainly its epic strength and expressive power justify its continued inclusion in the international repertoire.

Formally, Harris's Third is that rare thing, a one-movement symphony which generates its own shape, rather than varying and conflating the traditional first-movement form and four-movement plan. (Its most obvious model in this respect is Sibelius's Seventh.) There is very little of the standard procedure of statement and recapitulation, or indeed of the contrast of opposing elements. Harris relies instead on a process of continuous organic growth, a prolonged spinning out of melodic lines which bear at least a family resemblance to one another – the principal unifying factor being the triad, often with alternating major and minor thirds, though here without any hint of jazz feeling. The composer identified five principal sections in the work. Section I (in G major, but increasingly modal and unstable) is 'Tragic', featuring low string sonorities, and culminating in an long, expressive melody at the first entry of the violins. Section II is 'Lyric', and introduces the woodwind, in Harris's characteristic block-like scoring. Section III is 'Pastoral': against an increasingly busy polytonal string background, solo woodwind and brass produce a seemingly endless succession of variants of the triadic material. The climactic Section IV (in a firm D major) is 'Dramatic': in fugal texture, it is based partly on material from Section II, but mostly on a bold, straightforward five-bar subject. Finally, Section V (which resolves eventually into G minor) is identified as 'Dramatic–Tragic': its first part includes a sonorous restatement of the violin melody from Section I; its second develops material from Sections I and II over a timpani pedal, until the unyielding chordal conclusion.

© Anthony Burton

Joseph Haydn (1732–1809)

Haydn trained in the choir of St Stephen's Cathedral in Vienna, and in 1757 became Kapellmeister to the Morzin family. In 1761 he landed a position at the court of the wealthy Esterházy family. During his many years in the family's employment, Haydn claimed he was exposed to little external musical influence, but the position allowed him scope to write anything from dances to full-scale operas, and 'forced me to become original'. One of the first composers to develop the string quartet (of which he produced sixty-eight), he also extended the form and expressive range of the symphony – writing no fewer than 106. He composed a number of dramatic works and was released from the Esterházy court – in 1790, in his late fifties – in order to visit London. He enjoyed two highly successful visits, composing his twelve 'London' symphonies, and produced two great oratorios – *The Creation* (1798) and *The Seasons* (1801) – as well as his six late masses for the Esterházy family.

∾ Symphony No. 45 in F sharp minor, 'Farewell' (1772)

1 Allegro assai
2 Adagio
3 Minuet and Trio: Allegretto
4 Finale: Presto – Adagio

On 10 January 1772 Ludwig Peter von Rahier, the Estates Director of the Esterházy court, wrote to the Prince: 'I have today caused the high order of the 8th inst., whereby neither wives nor children of the musicians (excepting Mesdames Haydn, Fribert, Dichtler, Cellini and Tomasini) are to be allowed to be seen at Eszterháza, to be read word by word to all the musicians; and none of them said they would not agree

to the terms of the high order.' Eszterháza was the new summer palace of the Esterházy family, and, because in 1772
Prince Esterházy had engaged a large theatre troupe, there
was insufficient accommodation in the palace for the families
of most of the court musicians. They did not share Prince
Nikolaus's enthusiasm for the remote summer palace, and
by October, when there was still no sign of a return to
Eisenstadt, lack of enthusiasm had turned to disaffection.
Griesinger, Haydn's earliest biographer, takes up the story:

> Haydn had the notion of writing a symphony (which is
> known under the title of 'Farewell' symphony) in which
> one instrument after the other is silent. The symphony
> was performed as soon as possible in front of the Prince,
> and each of the musicians was instructed, as soon as his
> part was finished, to blow out his candle and to leave with
> his instrument under his arm. The Prince and the com-
> pany understood the point of this action at once, and the
> next day came the order to leave Eszterháza.

Born of typical diplomacy, Haydn's form of 'industrial
action' was highly original. Likewise the symphony itself,
which remains – even if one did not know the circumstances
of its composition – a strikingly individual work, wonderfully
assured in its pace and in its transition from one mood to the
next. The first movement is in Haydn's most agitated minor-
key vein of the time, with a wide-ranging first subject, a consistently nervous accompaniment and, later, disquieting
accentuations and contrasts of dynamic. The key itself, F
sharp minor, is unprecedented in the genre of the symphony,
and – equally novel – the exposition does not move to the relative major but to the dominant minor. This means that the
radiant sound of the major key (A major) is delayed until the
beginning of the development section, where it is complemented by the first fortissimo marking in the movement.
  Most of the slow movement is played by strings alone (with
violins muted), conjuring up that peculiar mixture of lyricism
and inscrutability typical of the composer at this stage in his

career. The Minuet turns to F sharp major for the first time in the symphony, but with a curt 'wrong' note in the third bar of the main theme, and an overriding unwillingness, as shown by the concluding pianissimo phrases, to allow the major to become too assertive.

Initially, the Finale returns to the restless mood of the first movement, now exaggerated by the faster pace. Some twelve bars short of its expected conclusion the movement is halted – not abruptly, but in a manner that suggests that something important is to ensue. The music turns to A major and a slow tempo but, unlike the previous slow movement, the orchestration is now luxurious and the lyricism warm and tender. Beginning with the first oboe and second horn, instruments gradually drop out of the texture. The movement moves to F sharp major and ends with two solo violins, pianissimo: a complete resolution of the musical tensions of the symphony, as well as of the strife that had instigated its composition.

© David Wyn Jones

∾ Symphony No. 49 in F minor, 'La passione' (1768)

1 Adagio
2 Allegro di molto
3 Minuet and Trio
4 Finale: Presto

Of Haydn's 106 symphonies, most of the first eighty or so were composed to be performed at court, initially that of his first patron Count Morzin in Bohemia, thereafter in the palaces of his longer-term employers, the Esterházy princes. For all their unprecedented intellectual rigour and endless ingenuity, the generally amiable nature of most of these works reflects this polite function, in which they served principally as entertainment. But instrumental music was also performed in church in Haydn's time. The best-known examples today are probably Mozart's so-called 'Epistle' sonatas and Haydn's profound and moving set of orchestral slow movements, *The Seven Last Words of Our Saviour on the Cross*, composed for Cadiz Cathedral in 1787. Symphonies could also find their way into the service, however, and it seems likely that Haydn's Symphony No. 49 is such a work. Indeed, its title – as well as its serious nature – may well indicate that it was first heard in a church somewhere one Good Friday.

Composed in 1768, 'La passione' is also the last symphony Haydn wrote using the format known as the *sinfonia da chiesa* (literally 'church symphony', though the term is less an indication of its function than an analogy with the form of the Baroque *sonata da chiesa*, which it resembles). In this type of symphony, the customary movement scheme of fast–slow–minuet–fast is altered by swapping round the first two movements. This is more than a cosmetic change; it allows the composer to write a weightier slow movement than if he had stuck to the normal design, and then to follow it with a faster and more nervously energetic quick one.

In the case of 'La passione', the first movement is a dark and brooding Adagio with an appropriately sombre and penitential feel to it, and the second an urgent Allegro di molto full of the wide melodic leaps and restless syncopations characteristic of many Austrian symphonies of the late 1760s and early 1770s, a style known today by the term *Sturm und Drang* ('storm and stress'). The Minuet relaxes the atmosphere, especially when high horns shine a cool light on its major-key Trio, but the Finale brings a return to the fiery mood of the second movement.

It is sometimes easy to assume that audiences in Haydn's day only liked music that was cheerful and easy on the ear, yet if the number of surviving contemporary manuscript copies and prints of 'La passione' is anything to go by, the power and emotional concentration of this masterly little symphony were enough to make it one of Haydn's most admired compositions.

© Lindsay Kemp

∾ Symphony No. 88 in G major (?1787)

1 Adagio – Allegro
2 Largo
3 Minuet and Trio: Allegretto
4 Finale: Allegro con spirito

When Haydn came to write his eighty-eighth symphony, probably in 1787, he was fresh from composing a sequence of six symphonies, intended for performance in Paris, that represented a blossoming of his symphonic style. The new work was one of a pair written for the celebrated Viennese violinist Johann Tost, former leader of the court orchestra at Eszterháza, where Haydn was employed. It was for Tost also that he was shortly to write no fewer than twelve string quartets; the three each of Opp. 54 and 55, and the six of Op. 64. The new work fulfilled every expectation that its predecessors had generated. It is one of Haydn's most brilliant, concise and witty pieces. Its building blocks, as often with this composer, are deceptively simple – short rhythmic cells, straightforward tunes – but Haydn's great gift is in manipulating them, fulfilling and confounding our expectations, blithely mixing intellect and naivety, and, not least, colouring his music with the deftest instrumentation.

As with many symphonies of this period, the first movement begins with a slow introduction, nothing like as grand as Beethoven's tended to be, but a firm enough call to order nonetheless. It stems from the two initial imposing chords that are followed by a reply of three chords, the first of the three short, as if a particularly grand Baroque sarabande. The formula here is conversational – statement and response – though something more continuous is promised. A close on the dominant D is followed by the almost apologetic opening of the first idea of the main, fast, body of the movement, played by strings alone. It needs reiterating more confidently, and Haydn duly obliges. A florid accompanimental bass figure assumes some importance, leading to the second theme, in the dominant key of D, and close enough to the first to define the movement as monothematic. This figure plays an equal part with the theme in the development section, which shows off Haydn's harmonic daring at its best as the music leaps delightedly from one harmonic region to another. And when the recapitulation comes it is not a bland restatement but a subtle variation of what has gone before.

The slow movement, in D, is one of Haydn's very best, a set of variations each separated by a small, but sometimes dramatic, transitional episode. It opens with the theme played by solo cello and oboe in octaves, a lovely sound to which the strings reply tenderly. For the first variation Haydn supplies a delicate string pizzicato accompaniment. For the second the accompaniment is characterised by slurred groups of two notes, also in the strings. A more extended connecting passage than hitherto leads to a dramatic surprise: four chords, played fortissimo, using the trumpets and timpani that Haydn, prior to this point in the work, had held in reserve. The outburst signals a key change for the ensuing variation, to A major. The return to the home key includes some deliciously ornate string figurations before another version of the dramatic interlude takes the music to D minor; and the chords make a third and final appearance after the next variation, in F and A, to bring the music to its home key again. In this movement Haydn's instrumental palette is stunningly rich and varied; no wonder Brahms admired it.

Its successor, the Minuet and Trio, is all rustic innocence, brash, apparently unlearned, with comically self-important, deliberately misplaced timpani rolls, though in reality this music is as carefully planned and as harmonically varied as everything else in the work. The Trio deliberately breaks the rules with its droning hurdy-gurdy-like open fifths, giving a glimpse of the folk music of Hungary.

Although the Finale increases the pace, Haydn maintains, initially at least, the earthy honesty of the Minuet. This time flutes and bassoons playing in unison make a distinctive contribution to the music's colour. Time and again the innocent main theme returns after some learned build-up, a teasing reminder for us to keep our feet on the ground, or perhaps simply an assertion that all that is complex comes from that which is essentially simple.

© Stephen Pettitt

∾ Symphony No. 96 in D major, 'Miracle' (1791)

1 Adagio – Allegro
2 Andante
3 Minuet and Trio: Allegretto
4 Finale: Vivace assai

'I am Salomon of London, and have come to fetch you. Tomorrow we will arrange an accord.' With this blunt proposal the violinist and impresario Johann Peter Salomon achieved in 1790 an ambition he had cherished for several years, namely to attract Haydn to England to take part in one of his concert series. Self-important though Salomon's words may sound, their significance is not to be underestimated. For nearly two decades, Haydn had been Europe's most respected composer: his music had sold so well in print that publishers had found it possible to market almost anything with his name on it (without having to trouble themselves unduly about whether it was actually by him or not); and in London and Paris, the two major centres of public concert-giving, hardly an evening of orchestral music had gone by without a symphony by him appearing somewhere on the programme. Yet Haydn had never travelled beyond the borders of Austria and Hungary. His employment with the princely Esterházy family had tied him to the court at Eisenstadt and Eszterháza for nearly thirty years, and although in 1779 the terms of his contract were relaxed so that he was at least able to respond to commissions from abroad, he still felt unable to answer the many invitations he received for what today we would call 'personal appearances'.

'Would it not be an achievement equal to a pilgrimage, for some aspiring youths to rescue him from his fortune and transplant him to Great Britain?' wondered the *Gazetteer & New Daily Advertiser* in 1785. If not an entirely practical proposition, it was surely symptomatic of the frustration the situation was causing to music lovers throughout Europe.

Haydn's circumstances had changed just prior to Salomon's visit, however. Prince Nikolaus Esterházy, his appreciative patron, had died, and his expensive court musical establishment had been swiftly disbanded by his successor. Haydn was kept on as Kapellmeister, but only in a titular capacity, and all of a sudden, at the age of fifty-eight, he was practically a free agent. It was this development that enabled Salomon to realise his dream (triumphing over a variety of rivals as he did so); the two men left Vienna in December 1790, and arrived at Dover on New Year's Day 1791.

The visit – the first of two Haydn was to make to London during the 1790s – lasted for a year and a half, and in the course of it the composer was fêted in a way that he surely could never have dreamed of back in Eszterháza. The impressions of this wheelwright's son on being introduced to royalty and accepted into the houses of the nobility, on being the focus of attention of the daily press and on being made a Doctor of Music by Oxford University can only be guessed (though he did say of the last that he felt silly in his gown). But what is clear is that the experience of his two visits to England had a beneficial and rejuvenating effect on his creative powers that was to fuel his work not only while he was there, but for the next ten years as well.

Central to Haydn's compositional activities in England were the twelve symphonies (Nos 93–104) that he wrote for Salomon's orchestral concerts in the Hanover Square Rooms. The symphony was the form for which he was best known by concert-goers all over Europe. A few years before, he had composed six fine examples (Nos 82–7) to a commission from a concert society in Paris, and these had become well known in London. Now, too, a symphony was to provide the main feature of every concert. The first one took place in March 1791, still too early for Haydn to go straight in with a newly composed work (an old one was performed instead), so it was not until a few weeks later that London heard the first of the group of symphonies that was to bear its name, No. 96 in D major.

It was a symphony well tailored to its surroundings. Like Paris, London boasted larger orchestras than Haydn was accustomed to writing for, and as well as taking the opportunity to include parts for trumpets, drums and (for the first time) two flutes, the composer served up a work whose exhilarating breadth and playful scoring could hardly have failed to make a hit with his eager public. They were characteristics that would inform all of Haydn's 'London' symphonies, and the English loved them.

Like almost all of Haydn's late symphonies, No. 96 begins with a teasing slow introduction, short but still taking in a weighty move to the minor. The vigorous Allegro which follows also contains some typically Haydnesque moments, including a false recapitulation of the main theme in the 'wrong' key of G major (heralded by a two-bar silence), and a real recapitulation which immediately heads off in unexpected directions. The joy in orchestral sound evident in this movement is likewise indulged in the middle two, though here the concern seems to be more with the abilities of individual players and the contrast which their delicate colourings offer to the stronger pronouncements of the full band. The work then ends with a deliciously fleeting rondo Finale, once again making witty play of quick-changing orchestral textures.

The event which gave this work its nickname – a lucky escape enjoyed by members of the audience when a chandelier crashed to the floor – actually occurred at another time during the performance of another symphony. But to those Londoners who were at the premiere of this fresh and delightful piece, the appearance of Haydn in their midst must have seemed a miracle indeed.

© Lindsay Kemp

∾ Symphony No. 99 in E flat major (1793)

1 Adagio – Vivace assai
2 Adagio
3 Minuet and Trio: Allegretto
4 Finale: Vivace

One of the ironies of Haydn's long career was that, despite his music achieving universal recognition, the composer himself did not travel beyond his native Austria and its dominions until he was fifty-eight years old. His position as Kapellmeister at the Esterházy court made it inconceivable that he should be given time off to travel; instead, his daily life revolved around composition, together with the supervision of two opera houses and an orchestra of some fifteen to twenty players. In many ways this nose-to-the-grindstone existence suited Haydn's temperament – as he himself said, 'I was forced to become original' – but it should not be thought that the composer was out of touch with musical life beyond the confines of the Esterházy court. On the contrary, during the 1780s Haydn had contacts with individuals, musical organisations and publishers throughout Europe, and was able to nurture and profit from his increasing popularity.

London played a pivotal role in Haydn's wider career. From 1790 onwards its concert life surpassed even that of Paris, and many of the characteristics of modern concerts were now present: admission tickets, printed programmes (though without notes on the works), press reports and a consistent body of instrumentalists – the 'symphony' orchestra. But there was one crucial difference: all the music in London's concerts was avant-garde, with at least one premiere per concert. In the 1780s it was Haydn's symphonies, imported by enterprising publishers or sold directly by the composer, that dominated concert life. As early as 1782 there were reports that the composer himself was to visit London, but for eight years nothing came of these rumours. Then, suddenly, in September 1790 Prince Nikolaus Esterházy died, and Haydn, for the first time in over thirty years, became the master of his own time. Johann Peter Salomon, one of the leading violinists in London, travelled to Vienna and signed a contract with Haydn enabling him to spend four of the next five years in England as the dominant figure in London's musical life.

There were two visits, the first in 1791–2, the second in 1794–5. During the first visit Haydn's latest symphonies, all specially composed for 'Mr Salomon's Concert Hanover Square', dominated musical life in the capital and Haydn became a celebrity. While finding London immensely exhilarating, Haydn also found it tiring and draining, so it was with some relief that he journeyed home to Austria in July 1792. He had promised to return, however, and in the comparative solitude of Eisenstadt and Vienna he was able to recharge his batteries and prepare new works for his second London visit. Six quartets were written (Opp. 71 and 74), the whole of Symphony No. 99, and portions of Nos 100 and 101. The seventh of what were eventually to be twelve symphonies composed for London, No. 99 was first performed at the opening concert of Salomon's 1794 series, on 10 February.

In many ways this symphony is the most neglected of the 'London' symphonies, partly, no doubt, because it lacks that single identifiable feature – a gimmick almost – that encouraged nicknames for many of its companions ('Surprise' for No. 94, 'Military' for No. 100 and 'Clock' for No. 101). But Haydn was incapable of producing a dull symphony and the work contains several individual features, less ostentatious than in other works but no less effective. It is the first symphony by Haydn to include clarinets, and their sound adds a distinctive weight to the wind section, even if their sparing use as solo instruments suggests that Haydn was unsure of the instrument's capabilities or – more likely – the expertise of his London players.

Like eleven of the twelve 'London' symphonies, No. 99 opens with a slow introduction, its full sonorities designed to offset the lightweight beginning of the ensuing Vivace assai.

But the harmonic ambition of the slow introduction anticipates that of the work as a whole; it finishes on a held unison G, the dominant of C minor, and requires a gentle but resonant wind chord to redirect the music to the home key of E flat. The Vivace is an object lesson in how the lightweight can be made to generate enormous power; both its main themes are apparently casual, but in the central development section, in particular, they yield paragraphs of great energy and intensity.

The slow movement is another first. Building on the harmonic ambition of the beginning of the symphony, it is set in G major – a contrast of sonorities without precedent in Haydn's symphonies. Allied to a simple frankness of melodic expression and resourceful orchestration that exploits solo wind instruments (but not clarinets), it is one of the most eloquent and powerful slow movements in the 'London' symphonies.

The Minuet returns the music to a more forthright mood, with a particularly charming Trio section in another third-related key, C major; the repeated single note that links the two sections is something Schubert was often to employ and which he, in turn, passed on to Dvořák.

The Finale is a sonata-rondo: a catchy main theme alternating with contrasting sections, the first incorporating passages for solo wind (including clarinets) and the second finding some unexpected contrapuntal rigour in the main theme.

The premiere of Symphony No. 99 was yet another success for Haydn, with the first movement being encored. The *Sun*, a newspaper which unlike its modern namesake was dedicated to encouraging wonder through prose rather than pictures, reported that: 'The grand instrumental trial of last night was a New Overture [symphony] by HAYDN, a composition of the most exquisite kind, rich, fanciful, bold and impressive.'

© David Wyn Jones

∾ Symphony No. 100 in G major, 'Military' (1794)

1 Adagio – Allegro
2 Allegretto
3 Minuet and Trio: Moderato
4 Finale: Presto

Although Haydn clearly felt great affection for the Esterházy family, he more than once remarked that the happiest days of his life had been spent in London. Certainly London played a crucial role in promoting Haydn to a position of international fame, and in that sense the city can claim to have been of greater importance than Vienna, which by and large was content to reflect the composer's achievement rather than enhance it. Haydn's music was known in this country from the 1760s onwards, but it was during the 1780s that he acquired unrivalled fame when publishers competed for his latest music and concert organisations played his music ceaselessly. As early as 1783 there were attempts to persuade Haydn to visit London to compose symphonies and an opera, but his extensive duties at the Esterházy court prevented him from accepting these invitations. Then, in September 1790, Prince Nikolaus I died after a short illness. His successor, Prince Anton, did not share his father's enthusiasm for music and disbanded the court's musical retinue, except for Haydn and the leader, Luigi Tomasini. The London impresario and violinist Johann Peter Salomon heard the news, rushed to Vienna and secured a deal with Haydn, duly announced in the London newspaper *The World* on 28 December.

Haydn was to be the presiding figure in a concert series organised by Salomon, for which he would compose new symphonies; he also agreed to write a new opera for London, though in the event the work (*L'anima del filosofo*) was never played. Haydn was in the British capital for four concert seasons (1791, 1792, 1794 and 1795). Given the amount of expectation that surrounded the visits, they could easily have turned out to have been disappointing. Instead, Haydn and his public entered upon one of the most fascinating and intense creative relationships in the history of music. His twelve 'London' symphonies at first gained the confidence of the public, before expanding expressive horizons in ever more delightful, challenging and fulfilling ways. Commentators on the musical scene repeatedly thought that Haydn's inspiration would dry up – 'I am afraid he must soon get to the bottom of his genius-box', as one person put it – but were constantly amazed at the composer's powers of invention.

Symphony No. 100 was first performed in the eighth of 'Mr Salomon's Concerts' in 1794, held on 31 March; the concert also included a symphony by Pleyel, a string quartet by Haydn, a concerto by Viotti, and two arias sung by 'Mr Fischer' (Ludwig Fischer, the bass who had created the role of Osmin in Mozart's *Die Entführung aus dem Serail* twelve years earlier). The symphony has the same ground plan as most of the 'London' symphonies – slow introduction, argumentative first movement, tuneful slow movement, dance movement and excitable finale – but the detail is typically innovative. The introduction moves from polite formality, through unease, to something approaching the sinister, while the principal theme of the Allegro is chirpily scored for high woodwind alone. For the slow movement Haydn reuses a march-like movement from a notturno written in the previous decade for the King of Naples, retaining the predominantly wind scoring. If Haydn's audience, by now well accustomed to the composer's teasing humour, thought this beginning suspiciously lightweight, they would have been astonished at the later entry of a battery of percussion instruments. Charming at first, they gradually darken the atmosphere until the music culminates in a solo trumpet fanfare. The movement has always exercised its power, but for Haydn's audience in London in 1794 it must have been overwhelming. The newspapers were full of accounts of the latest atrocities in France, where the Reign of Terror was at its peak. Many French aristocrats had fled to London, and

England had joined Austria, Holland and Spain in the war against France. Clearly Haydn intended to evoke the terrifying sound of the battle. That he succeeded in a sensational way is suggested by the report of one journalist commenting on the second performance of the symphony on 9 April:

> Another new Symphony, by Haydn, was performed for the second time; and the middle movement was again received with absolute shouts of applause. Encore! Encore! Encore! resounded from every seat: the Ladies themselves could not forbear. It is the advancing to battle; and the march of men, the sounding of the charge, the thundering of the onset, the clash of arms, the groans of the wounded, and what may well be called the hellish roar of the war increase to a climax of horrid sublimity! which, if others can conceive, he alone can execute; at least he alone hitherto has effected these wonders.

After this frisson of excitement Haydn returns to the customary elegance of the Minuet, its assertive phrases carefully undermined by some sliding chromaticism in the passage that prepares for the return of the main theme. Musical events move at a brisk pace in the Finale, with material presented and discussed with the skill and audacity of a master conjuror who has the audience totally in his control. Were these last two movements intended as a diversion from the concerns of the slow movement? Or was Haydn attempting something more, a vision of hope as the military instruments are absorbed into the prevailing mood?

© David Wyn Jones

∾ Symphony No. 101 in D major, 'Clock' (1793–4)

1 Adagio – Presto
2 Andante
3 Minuet and Trio: Allegretto
4 Finale: Vivace

Haydn's 'Clock' Symphony was first performed on 3 March 1794 at 'Mr Salomon's Concert' in Hanover Square. Salomon was the violinist and impresario who had invited Haydn to London to be, in modern jargon, composer in residence at his subscription concerts. Haydn's first visit in 1791–2 had confirmed his status in the eyes of the English public as the greatest living composer. Salomon would have liked Haydn to have been available for the 1793 season, but Haydn's employer in Austria, Prince Anton Esterházy, required the family Kapellmeister at home. During the seventeen months that separated the two visits Haydn was able to ponder his success in London and plan for its furtherance. Symphonies, again, were to form the main element of the concerts and in Vienna Haydn composed the whole of No. 99 and portions of Nos 100 and 101 in readiness for the return visit.

At the time Haydn was also involved in the comparatively mundane task of composing music for a mechanical organ built by the monk and Esterházy librarian, Pater Joseph Niemecz. Haydn arranged some existing compositions as well as writing some new ones. One of the pieces he gave Niemecz was a D major Minuet that also appears as the third movement of Symphony No. 101. It is impossible to state with confidence which version came first, but for the symphony Haydn added a Trio section with a delightfully stubborn accompaniment that, at first, refuses to change harmony when the solo flute suggests that it should. Niemecz's mechanical organs often formed the base of large clocks and were sometimes activated by the mechanism (hence the rather misleading term 'musical clock'), and it was probably the association between the minuet and the mechanism that prompted the famous slow movement of the symphony, where the accompaniment imitates the ticking of a clock. Haydn knew that his London audience would be delighted by this feature and complemented it, in his usual fashion in the Salomon symphonies, with a sinister interlude in the minor key in a forte dynamic.

Connoisseurs in Haydn's audience in Hanover Square on 3 March 1794 would have recognised how typically economical the composer was with his material in these middle movements; everything grows naturally out of their respective openings. This combination of easy approachability and intellectual rigour is to be found, too, in the outer movements. The symphony opens with a slow introduction of great portent before moving to the joyous Presto, and even the Finale is a typically entertaining rondo that manages, without ever threatening its appeal, to present the last appearance of the main theme as a four-part fugue, pianissimo.

© David Wyn Jones

∾ Symphony No. 103 in E flat major, 'Drumroll' (1795)

1 Adagio – Allegro con spirito
2 Andante più tosto Allegretto
3 Minuet and Trio
4 Finale: Allegro con spirito

As Europe's leading musical figure, Haydn had been invited in 1791 to be the resident composer at the Hanover Square Concert series, organised by Johann Peter Salomon. In the twelve symphonies which he wrote for London during his two visits in the 1790s, Haydn expanded the expressive boundaries of the form in ever more imaginative ways, laying the foundation for Beethoven's symphonic career and, it may be said, the whole of the subsequent symphonic tradition.

Public concerts in London were held between January and May of each year, an exhausting period for Haydn during which he had to rehearse, make last-minute adjustments and direct his works. In summer and autumn Haydn was able to recharge his batteries, plan for the following season and compose some of the principal works. Haydn's first three seasons were spent as resident composer at the Hanover Square Concert, but in 1795, because of financial uncertainty brought on by unbelievably savage events in France, Salomon joined forces with the management of the King's Theatre in the Haymarket to promote the 'Opera Concert'. The concerts were held in a newly built room at the back of the theatre.

Symphony No. 103 was first performed on 2 March at the fourth concert of the new series. It can justly be regarded as one of Haydn's most sensationally inventive works. Listeners were immediately captivated, if not unnerved, by the unusual beginning. Following an atmospheric timpani roll, cellos, basses and bassoons play a sustained thematic line in the depths of the orchestra. No symphony by Haydn (or, indeed, Mozart) had ever begun in this sinister way, and to emphasise its originality the composer follows this scoring with the exact opposite, violins only with no bass notes. The introduction seems to prepare for an Allegro in a minor key, but when it arrives it is a spirited 6/8 movement in E flat major. These extreme contrasts of mood characterise the progress of the rest of the movement. In the development section Haydn has the bizarre idea of playing the beginning of the introduction in the prevailing Allegro tempo; even more shockingly, towards the end of the movement he brings the music to a halt in order to quote the drum roll and the ensuing slow music once more.

After the driving energy of the first movement the Andante is more static, a set of variations on two alternating themes, one in the minor and one in the major, with the second theme itself being based on the contours of the first. The formal alternation of mood that this structure produces is broken in the coda which first inclines to the dramatic before ending in a positive C major.

The home key of the symphony, E flat major, is reasserted with great aplomb at the beginning of the Minuet; the Trio section is in a soft dynamic throughout, quiet enough for the listener to catch Haydn's rather reticent use of clarinets. The Finale is a tour de force of thematic and harmonic argument that is fully the equal of (but not the same as) that of Mozart's 'Jupiter' Symphony. Its thematic source is the cliché heard right at the beginning, a phrase that Haydn had written for horns in his orchestral works hundreds of times, and his players sounded thousands of times; out of this and other related scraps of material the composer produces paragraphs of great tension and fire.

As usual Haydn's new symphony was enthusiastically received by the audience and by the newspapers. The *Morning Chronicle* remarked that it 'had continual strokes of genius, both in air and harmony', while the *Sun* noted its 'fine mixture of grandeur and fancy'.

© David Wyn Jones

∾ Symphony No. 104 in D major, 'London' (1795)

1 Adagio – Allegro
2 Andante
3 Minuet: Allegro
4 Finale: Spiritoso

The autograph score of Haydn's 'London' symphony carries the annotation 'The 12th which I have composed in England'. Haydn had been invited to London in 1791 to be resident composer at the Salomon subscription concerts, and during the first two seasons he composed six symphonies, Nos 93–8; he returned in 1794 for a further two seasons and composed his last six symphonies, Nos 99–104, including the 'Military', the 'Clock', the 'Drumroll' and the so-called 'London' symphony. Near the end of every concert season, in April and May, the principal composers and performers were traditionally allotted benefit concerts for which their colleagues gave their services for nothing and the beneficiary received the profits. For Haydn's benefit concert on 4 May 1795, the composer provided two new works, the concert aria 'Scena di Berenice', and what was to be his last symphony. In a notebook containing his impressions of English life the composer remarked: 'The whole company was thoroughly pleased and so was I. I made four thousand Gulden on this evening. Such a thing is possible only in England.'

The 'London' symphony may not be about London, but it is certainly Haydn's response to a stimulating urban environment; it is music that, by turn, entertains, startles and enlightens. In 1795 the composer was writing for an orchestra of over sixty players, twenty more than in previous seasons and over twice the size of the Esterházy court orchestra. Haydn clearly revelled in the varied sonorities of this large orchestra, his scoring ranging from delicately coloured woodwind writing to fortissimo passages that leap from the page. His slow movements, especially, were frequently encored, no doubt because the public was enthralled by the contrast between easy tunefulness, projected by a reduced orchestra, and the impassioned declamation of the full orchestra with trumpets and drums.

Connoisseurs of musical science (to use an eighteenth-century term) noticed how economical the composer was in his use of material. The contrasting section in the slow movement employs the same subject matter as the main section, and the two outer movements are exhaustive discourses on their respective principal themes. Indeed, the thematic material of the whole symphony is bound together by the common use of the interval of a fifth, first declaimed majestically by the full orchestra in the Adagio introduction. As well as admiring Haydn's rhetoric and eloquence his public also marvelled at his control over harmonic digression; in the slow movement, when the main section returns, the theme leads magically away from the home key of G major (complemented by a crescendo and diminuendo) to the furthest possible point away from that key, the harmonic cul-de-sac of D flat major; a couple of exploratory phrases in the woodwind redirect the music back towards G major.

Although Haydn's last symphony is in no sense valedictory – it has that same life-enhancing confidence as No. 1 composed nearly forty years earlier – London audiences, and perhaps Haydn too, felt that the genre could not be developed further. The *Morning Chronicle* of 6 May 1795 remarked 'that for fifty years to come Musical Composers would be little better than imitators of Haydn; and would do little more than pour water on his leaves'.

© David Wyn Jones

Gustav Mahler (1860–1911)

More than any composer since Beethoven, Mahler radically altered the course of symphonic form, broadening its scale and instrumentation, imbuing it with vast emotional range and incorporating autobiographical references. Born in Bohemia, he went to study in Vienna, aged fifteen, before developing a conducting career in a succession of opera theatres. In 1897 he became Kapellmeister at the Vienna Court Opera, converting from Judaism to Catholicism in order to do so. The demands of his conducting commitments left only the summers for composing, when he would retreat to the mountains and lakes. He was heavily drawn to the folk-like poetry collection *Des Knaben Wunderhorn* (The Youth's Magic Horn, 1808), writing over twenty 'Wunderhorn' songs and incorporating its texts into his Symphonies Nos 2–4. Five of his siblings died in infancy, as did his own elder daughter – lending further poignancy to his *Kindertotenlieder* (Songs on the Death of Children, 1904). He worked in New York at the Metropolitan Opera and Philharmonic Orchestra, but fell victim to heart disease: he died before completing his tenth numbered symphony, soon after the bitter discovery of his wife Alma's affair with the architect Walter Gropius.

❧ Symphony No. 1 in D major, (1884–8, rev. 1893–6)

1 Langsam, schleppend – Immer sehr gemächlich [Slow, held back – Always very leisurely]
2 Kräftig bewegt, doch nicht zu schnell – Trio. Recht gemächlich [Moving strongly, but not too fast – Trio: leisurely]
3 Feierlich und gemessen, ohne zu schleppen – Sehr einfach und schlicht wie eine Volksweise [Solemn and

measured, without dragging – Very simple, like a folk
melody]

4   Stürmisch bewegt – Sehr gesangvoll [Tempestuously –
Very melodious]

Mahler began his First Symphony in 1884, and struggled
with it for several years before finishing it off in a burst of creative energy early in 1888. Its difficult genesis was reflected in
the problems he had in deciding on its final shape, and indeed
its final title. For the first performance in Budapest in 1889,
he called it a 'Symphonic Poem in two parts', implying a literary programme, but giving no details. At this stage the
work had five movements.

When Mahler conducted further performances in Hamburg
and Weimar, he called the work *Titan*, after the novel completed in 1803 by the German writer Jean Paul (Friedrich
Richter). He also supplied the following description of the
music, based on it:

Part 1: 'From the Days of Youth'

1   'Spring and no end to it'
    The introduction describes the awakening of nature and
    early dawn.

2   'Bluminenkapitel' [Flower chapter]. (Andante)

3   'Set with full sails' (Scherzo)

Part 2: 'Commedia humana'

4   'Shipwrecked'. A funeral march 'in the manner of Callot'
    . . . The composer received the external stimulus to this
    movement from [Callot's] parodistic picture *Des Jägers
    Leichenbegängnis* [The Huntsman's Funeral], well known to
    all children, especially in South Germany, as coming from
    an old book of fairy tales: the animals of the forest accom-
    pany the coffin of the dead hunter to its tomb; rabbits carry
    the flag, preceded by a band of village musicians from
    Bohemia, accompanied by cats, toads, crows etc. playing
    on instruments, and also by stags, does, foxes and other
    quadrupeds and feathered animals of the forest in roguish

attitudes. The movement is intended to express alternately the moods of jesting irony and of eerie brooding. This is immediately followed by

5 'Dall'Inferno al Paradiso' (Allegro furioso), as the sudden cry of a deeply wounded heart.

For a later performance in Berlin in 1896, however, Mahler omitted the title, the description and the second ('Blumine') movement. The published score of 1899 was headed just 'Symphony No. 1 in D major'. Its composer seems to have reassured himself that his music needed no programmatic explanation of its ability to combine the worlds of the two Mahlers – the rhetorical, loudly public stance of the brilliant and ambitious conductor; and the private thoughts of the solitary Romantic artist whose voice, even in the hugest and most epic statements, seems to be speaking personally to each of us.

The symphony begins with two ideas defining the symphony's mood and material, against a still tapestry of strings: a woodwind theme based on the interval of the falling fourth (borrowed, consciously or otherwise, from the finale of Brahms's First Symphony); and a sequence of fanfares on low clarinets and distant trumpets, recalling the sounds of the military barracks next to the house where Mahler grew up. A high clarinet imitates a cuckoo (also calling in fourths). Out of these beginnings emerges a second, jauntier theme on the cellos. A haunting return to the stillness of the introduction follows, its tension eventually broken by a sprightly theme on the horns. Further adventures lead to a rousing restatement of this, and to a riotous conclusion.

Strings and woodwind begin the second movement with a stamping dance in triple time, in the style of a rustic *Ländler* waltz. A pair of trumpets joins in with a five-note rising motif (long, short–short–short–long), which cheekily reappears during the slower, languid Trio section. Then the opening dance is repeated.

The third movement evokes the huntsman's funeral with a bleak, minor-key version of the children's round 'Frère Jacques', first played by a solo double bass above muffled drumbeats. Pairs of oboes and trumpets offer a mock-sentimental commentary. A dreamlike central interlude arrives, with muted violins murmuring a melody from Mahler's *Lieder eines fahrenden Gesellen* (Songs of a Wayfaring Lad, 1896). The march returns, and a sudden spurt of pace speeds the huntsman towards his grave.

An orchestral scream of despair launches the long finale. Furious strings and a shrill triplet motif on wind and brass hurtle towards the grimly determined first theme. When this collapses, exhausted, the violins sing a long, consoling tune in reply. A hint of the first movement's introduction leads to another wild outburst, out of which a new, optimistic version of the finale's first tune appears, tentatively sounded by the trumpets. The struggle continues, until the trumpet theme breaks through in a huge climax with thundering drums and percussion, continued by a heroic chorale on the horns (itself a new version of the first movement's opening idea). More material from the first movement's introduction leads to further doubts and questionings, before the brisk main tune returns, quietly at first on the strings, then rising in intensity. This time the trumpet theme's climax is irresistible. The horns restate their chorale (a note in the score asks them to stand) in a life-affirming peroration whose power Mahler was to equal in later works, but not surpass.

Malcolm Hayes © BBC

∾ Symphony No. 2 in C minor, 'Resurrection' (1888–94)

1   Allegro maestoso: Mit durchaus ernstem und feierlichem Ausdruck [With a serious and solemn expression throughout]

2   Andante moderato: Sehr gemächlich. Nie eilen [Very moderate – Never rushing]

3   In ruhig fliessender Bewegung [Calmly flowing] –
4   'Urlicht': Sehr feierlich, aber schlicht (Choralmässig)
    [Very solemn but simple, like a chorale] –
5   Im Tempo des Scherzo: Wild herausfahrend [In the
    same tempo as the Scherzo; in a wild outburst] –
    Langsam [Slow] – Allegro energico – Langsam

From his very first engagement at a tiny provincial operetta
theatre in 1880 until his death thirty-one years later, the outward course of Mahler's life was almost entirely dictated by
his conducting schedule. Composition was confined to the
summer months when theatres were closed, so most of
Mahler's works were written down during intense bursts of
creativity preceded by months, sometimes years, of gestation.
The Second Symphony took over six years to reach its final
form. It was largely composed in three stages: the first movement in 1888, the three middle movements in 1893, and the
finale in the summer of 1894.

In August 1888, five months after finishing the First
Symphony, Mahler completed an enormous symphonic
movement in C minor. He later called it *Totenfeier* ('funeral
ceremony' or 'funeral rites'). This was eventually to become
the first movement of the Second Symphony. Two themes for
an Andante movement were also sketched at about the same
time. For the next two and a half years, however, further composition was out of the question: Mahler had been appointed
director of the Budapest Opera, where his artistic and admin-
istrative duties left him no time for other work. After three
years in Budapest, Mahler then moved to Hamburg. Once
established there, he was eager to show *Totenfeier* to the great
pianist and conductor Hans von Bülow, who was a staunch
supporter of Mahler's conducting; but despite his champi-
onship of the music of Berlioz, Liszt, Wagner, Brahms and
latterly Richard Strauss, Bülow's reaction to Mahler's score,
when the composer played it through to him in September
1891, was painful: covering his ears with his hands, he simply
groaned. Mahler was bitterly disappointed.

The next stage in the composition of the symphony involved a return to the world of *Des Knaben Wunderhorn*, the early-nineteenth-century collection of folk poetry that influenced so much of Mahler's music. His settings of these poems conjure up a world of lovers – naive, ironical, happy, faithless or wretched; of soldiers leaving for the wars, returning to haunt their lovers, facing execution for desertion; of simple people close to nature; of unquestioning religious faith. The musical devices Mahler uses permeate his early music, and have crucial parts to play in the Second Symphony: drumbeats, fanfares and marches; simple folk melodies, and also ironic distortions of these melodies; popular dance measures; chorales expressing naive religious faith; natural sounds of all sorts, from the inanimate rumbling of rocks and the rushing of wind and water to the cries of animals and birdsong.

Mahler spent the summer of 1893 in complete isolation at Steinbach-am-Attersee in the Salzkammergut. In the previous year he had composed five 'Wunderhorn' songs for voice and piano, and then orchestrated the accompaniments. Two further 'Wunderhorn' songs were now to provide the third and fourth movements of his symphony. The Scherzo, dated 16 July, is an elaborate reworking of the song 'Des Antonius von Padua Fischpredigt' (St Anthony of Padua's Sermon to the Fishes). 'Urlicht' (Primeval Light) was orchestrated by 19 July. The symphony's second movement, based on ideas dating back to 1888, was ready by the end of July.

The stimulus for the composition of the finale came – posthumously – from von Bülow, who had died in Cairo on 12 February 1894. His body was brought back to Hamburg, and on 29 March a funeral service was held in the Michaeliskirche. Mahler was present, and in a moment of illumination vividly experienced the nature of his unwritten finale:

> The frame of mind in which I found myself and the thoughts I devoted to the dead man were very much in the spirit of the work I was then harbouring within me.

All of a sudden the choir, accompanied by the organ, intoned Klopstock's chorale *Aufersteh'n*. It was as if I had been struck by lightning, everything suddenly seemed crystal clear!

In June Mahler went again to Steinbach, where by the end of July the gigantic finale was ready in draft score. The fair copy of the entire symphony was completed by 18 December. Anxious to perform the work as soon as possible, he conducted the first three movements in Berlin the following March; and then on 13 December 1895, also in Berlin, he gave the symphony's first complete performance.

Several versions exist of a programme for the Second Symphony (all written after its first performance), but Mahler's own attitude towards them was cautious, to say the least. Whatever their relevance, they do stress Mahler's almost reckless faith in the power of his music to tackle the deepest questions of human existence. In its urgency to convey spiritual truths, the Second Symphony is very much the work of the man who is reputed to have advised young musicians to 'study less counterpoint and read more Dostoyevsky'. Early in 1896, Mahler was describing the symphony as follows:

The first movement depicts the titanic struggle against life and destiny fought by a superman who is still a prisoner of the world; his endless, constant defeats and finally his death. [In later versions of his note, Mahler placed the first movement after the hero's death: 'We are standing by the grave . . .'] The second and third movements are episodes from the life of the fallen hero. The Andante tells of his love. What I have expressed in the Scherzo can only be described visually. When one watches a dance from a distance, without hearing the music, the revolving motions of the partners seem absurd and pointless. Likewise, to someone who has lost himself and his happiness, the world seems crazy and confused, as if deformed by a concave mirror. The Scherzo ends with the fearful scream of a soul that has experienced this torture.

In 'Urlicht' the questions and struggle of the human soul for God, as well as its own divine nature and existence, come to the forefront. Whereas the first three movements are narrative, the last is altogether dramatic. Here, all is motion and occurrence. The movement starts with the same dreadful death cry which ended the Scherzo. And now, after these frightening questions, comes the answer, redemption. To begin with, as faith and the Church picture it: the Day of Judgement, a huge tremor shakes the earth. The climax of this terrifying event is accompanied by drum rolls. Then the Last Trump sounds. The graves burst open, all the creatures struggle out of the ground, moaning and trembling. Now they march in mighty procession: rich and poor, peasants and kings, the whole church with bishops and popes. All have the same fear, all cry and tremble alike because, in the eyes of God, there are no just men. As though from another world, the Last Trump sounds again. Finally, after they have left their empty graves and the earth lies silent and deserted, there comes only the long-drawn note of the bird of death. Even he finally dies.

What happens now is far from expected: no divine judgement, no blessed and no damned, no Good and no Evil, and no judge. Everything has ceased to exist. Soft and simple, the words gently swell up: 'You will rise again, yes, rise again, my mortal dust, after a short repose.' Here the words suffice as commentary and I will not add a single syllable.

Mahler came to see the first movement as the 'exposition' of the whole work, presenting, as it were, the terms on which the rest of the symphony would evolve. Its vehement opening shows at once one of his devices for large-scale construction: the musical material in itself is 'self-developing'; that is to say, by extending his themes melodically, by basing them on simple rhythmic elements, Mahler is able to transform them at the same time as presenting them. Musical 'characters' (such as marches, fanfares, birdsongs, chorales – Mahler's 'Wunderhorn' vocabulary) also stand out on their own terms, independent of more exact thematic characterisation. This becomes an important factor in Mahler's prodigality of invention, and his ability to work in a colossal dimension.

The central movements, as Mahler wrote, are 'conceived as intermezzi', throwing into relief a dramatic antithesis between the 'death' movements and the central 'life-in-retrospect' movements. The Andante has neither the tempo nor the weight of a real slow movement, and its remoteness from the first movement is emphasised by its keys – A flat major alternating with G sharp minor – which have hardly been touched upon previously.

The song on which the third movement is based is a wry comment on Mahler's own battles with cloth-eared audiences and critics. The text tells of St Anthony finding his church empty and resolving to preach instead to the fishes. His exhortations attract a large congregation of carp, pike, cod, eels, crabs, sturgeons and so on. They listen devoutly, but the sermon is in vain; as soon as the saint leaves the river bank, the fishes return to their habitual vices as though he had never spoken. The orchestral movement is much weightier. Mahler explained that, in composing it, he had 'been driven further and further from my original form'. And later, 'It's a big and remarkable piece . . . I had not realised this while I was composing it.' The music is inevitably darkened by its return to the first movement's C minor after the A flat of the Andante; and the orchestral colouring, the symphonic development and the great outburst near the end – the 'cry of despair' that returns to open the finale – further contribute to its more sinister character.

The magical entry of the solo alto, the voice of naive faith, acts as both a comment on the two preceding movements and a musico-dramatic preparation for the revelations of the finale. This last movement, as we have seen, was directly inspired by the choir at Hans von Bülow's funeral singing the chorale *Aufersteh'n* by the devotional poet Friedrich

Klopstock (1724–1803). Only the first section of the text is by Klopstock, however; from the alto soloist's '*O glaube, mein Herz, o glaube . . .*' the words are Mahler's own.

The turning point of the symphony is a moment of solemn drama: the orchestra falls silent, and time is suspended. Remote brass fanfares ('the Last Trump sounds again') are answered by solo flute and piccolo ('the long-drawn note of the bird of death'); the almost imperceptible entry of the chorus initiates a progress which culminates in a blaze of sound deploying all the resources of soloists, chorus, orchestra and organ. As Mahler quite rightly said, 'Here the words suffice as commentary and I will not add a single syllable.'

© Andrew Huth

✑ Symphony No. 3 in D minor (1893–6)

Part One
1   Kräftig. Entschieden [Powerful. Resolute]
Part Two
2   Tempo di Menuetto. Sehr mässig [At a very moderate pace]
3   Comodo. Scherzando. Ohne Hast [Unhurried]
4   Sehr langsam. Misterioso. Durchaus *ppp* [Very slow. Mysteriously. As quiet as possible] –
5   Lustig im Tempo und keck im Ausdruck [At a jaunty tempo with bold expression] –
6   Langsam. Ruhevoll. Empfunden [Slow. Peaceful. With feeling]

'Everyone knows by now that some triviality always has to occur in my work, but this time it goes beyond all bounds.' Thus wrote Gustav Mahler, in the summer of 1896, gleefully looking forward to the consternation his new Third Symphony was going to cause the critics. No doubt he was remembering some of the barbed comments in the press after the first performance of his Second Symphony the previous year – 'cynical impudence' was one choice verdict. And now, far from being chastened, Mahler had created a successor to the Second that was even longer and more bizarrely structured. This time there would be six movements, one almost as long as the other five put together, mixing elements of symphony, tone poem, Lieder, oratorio, folk music, and, most bewilderingly, juxtaposing the sublime and the deliberately 'trivial' – the sweetly naive post-horn tune in the third movement, the children's playground songs of the fifth. Despite his heroic cheerfulness, internally Mahler must have braced himself for another massed rejection.

If so, he was in for a surprise. The world premiere of the Third Symphony – in the small German town of Krefeld, in 1902 – was a huge success, despite the sweltering summer heat and the fact that Mahler, conducting, was forced to work with an ad hoc orchestra, thrown together at the last minute. Mahler was given a standing ovation, and the press enthused. But this turned out to be a false dawn. The symphony's 1904 Viennese premiere incensed the critics. One of them, unable to last the whole ninety minutes, left the hall muttering that Mahler deserved a spell in jail for perpetrating such nonsense. Half a century later, the English composer William Walton summed up the feelings of many when he remarked, 'It's all very well, but you can't call that a symphony.' And yet amid the scandalised, outraged comments one can find equally impassioned praise. After hearing that same 1904 Viennese performance, the young Arnold Schoenberg (originally hostile to Mahler) told Mahler ecstatically that the symphony had revealed to him 'a human being, a drama, truth, the most ruthless truth!'

It is easy to see why the Third Symphony should provoke such extreme reactions. In both form and content it is Mahler's most outrageous work. The orchestral forces may be slightly smaller than those used in the 'Resurrection' Symphony or the so-called 'Symphony of a Thousand' (No. 8), but in other respects it is breathtakingly ambitious. Mahler once remarked that 'the symphony must be like the world. It must embrace everything.' If that all-inclusiveness is the key to his philosophy of the symphony, then the Third is his most 'symphonic' work. Mahler revealed a great deal about the Third Symphony in his letters to the soprano Anna von Mildenburg, who at the time was his lover. 'Just imagine a work of such magnitude that it actually mirrors the whole world – one is, so to speak, an instrument played upon by the universe . . . My [third] symphony will be something the like of which the world has never heard! . . . In my symphony the whole of nature finds a voice . . . Some passages in it seem so uncanny that I can hardly recognise them as my own work.'

Mahler thought about giving the Third Symphony a title. Perhaps it could be called *Pan*, after the Greek god of nature, or *The Joyful Science*, after of one of Friedrich Nietzsche's philosophical works, *Die fröhliche Wissenschaft*. The young Mahler soaked himself in Nietzsche's writings. And in the fourth movement of the Third Symphony he sets the most famous lines from Nietzsche's *Also sprach Zarathustra* (Thus spake Zarathustra). This was the work in which Nietzsche first put forward the ideal of the 'Superman', the man who can embrace life – nature – in all its fullness, who can confront both the beauty and the horror of existence without faltering. Nietzsche's ideas found sympathetic echo in Mahler. After writing the Third Symphony's second movement Mahler made this very Nietzschean observation: 'It always strikes me as strange that most people, when they speak of "nature", think only of flowers, little birds, and woodsy smells. No one knows the god Dionysus, the great Pan. There now! You have a sort of programme – that is, an example of how I make music. Everywhere and always it is only the voice of nature!'

Initially, Mahler was prepared to be specific about that 'sort of programme'. He gave the symphony's six movements subtitles: 1. 'Summer marches in'. 2. 'What the flowers of the meadow tell me'. 3. 'What the animals of the forest tell me'. 4. 'What night tells me (mankind)'. 5. 'What the morning bells tell me (the angels)'. 6. 'What love tells me'. As Mahler noted, a kind of philosophical plan emerges, in which each movement aspires higher than the one before. The awakening of elemental nature leads ultimately to transcendent love, and perhaps to faith in God. But Mahler's faith in titles and literary programmes had already been sorely tried. Soon afterwards he was to declare 'Perish all programmes!' and in later performances the Third Symphony appeared without such detailed explanatory notes.

All the same, this should not be taken as meaning that Mahler wants us to hear the Third Symphony as 'absolute music'. There are elements in the Third Symphony that cry out for non-musical explanation – how else can we make sense of his choice of texts in the fourth and fifth movements? Clearly there is a message to be read here, and it is more than helpful to know what Mahler's thoughts were – after all, he does seem to have taken care to ensure that they were preserved for posterity.

The listener also needs to be prepared for the Third Symphony's extraordinary proportions. The first movement is huge: around thirty-five to forty minutes in most performances. Attempts to make sense of its structure along traditional formal lines usually end in confusion. At times it feels more like a fantastic kaleidoscope of wildly contrasting sounds than a coherent symphonic argument. Broadly speaking, this movement alternates three kinds of music: the dark, primordial sounds of the opening (described by Mahler as 'Pan awakes'), pastoral sounds (murmurous wind and string trills, woodwind bird calls), and raucous, garish military march music (brass fanfares, dotted rhythms and plenty of percussion). Eventually it is the martial music which triumphs – 'Summer marches in'.

The 'flowers of the meadow' minuet that follows is on a much more intimate scale. It is delicately scored, and full of folksy tunefulness. Mahler was persuaded to let this movement be heard performed on its own before the whole symphony was performed. It was an instant hit, causing Mahler mixed feelings:

If I ever want to be heard I can't be too fussy, so this modest little piece will no doubt present me to the public as the sensuously perfumed singer of nature. That this nature hides within itself everything that is frightful, great and also lovely (which is exactly what I wanted to express in the entire work in a sort of evolutionary development) of course, no one ever understands that.

The third movement is more complex. The naive vitality of the 'animals of the forest' is twice interrupted by a distant post-horn, sounding through a halo of hushed high strings – a nostalgic memory, perhaps, or an evocation of primal innocence. Then, near the end of this movement, comes a ferocious fortissimo outburst: Pan is revealed again in all his 'frightful' majesty.

Quiet echoes of the deep bass stirrings from near the beginning of the symphony introduce the fourth movement, almost all of which is delivered in an awestruck pianissimo. Here the subject is mankind's struggle to make sense of the world, its joy and its grief, as expressed enigmatically in Nietzsche's verses. Then the sound of bells (literally and mimicked by the boys' choir) introduces the fifth movement. With childlike delight, angels tell of God's forgiveness of Peter, the 'all too human' disciple of Christ who became the rock on which the Christian Church was built.

The sixth movement combines the functions of slow movement and finale, moving from rapt meditation to grand summing up. An ardent, hymn-like theme for strings alternates with troubled, searching music – there is room for doubt here too. Ideas from earlier in the symphony return, then the hymn builds to a grand apotheosis, using the force of the full orchestra (minus the harps) for the first time since the end of the first movement. Mahler confided to Anna von Mildenburg that he had a literary motto in mind when he wrote this movement:

'Father, see these wounds of mine! Let no creature of yours be lost!' I could almost call this [the finale] 'What

God tells me'. And truly, in the sense that God can only be understood as love. And so my work begins as a musical poem embracing all stages of development in a step-wise ascent. It begins with inanimate nature and ascends to the love of God.

© Stephen Johnson

∾ Symphony No. 4 in G major (1892, 1899–1900; rev. 1901–10)

1 Bedächtig. Nicht eilen [Deliberately. Unhurried]
2 In gemächlicher Bewegung. Ohne Hast [Moving comfortably. Without haste]
3 Ruhevoll [Peacefully]
4 Sehr behaglich [Easefully]

Composed mainly between 1899 and 1900, Mahler's Fourth Symphony brings to a close his period of exploration of the spooky, grotesque world of *Des Knaben Wunderhorn*, and, appropriately, it ends with a beatific setting for soprano of one of the *Wunderhorn* poems, 'Das himmlische Leben' (Heavenly Life).

Mahler was forty when he finished drafting the symphony at Maiernigg on the Wörthersee in Carinthia. Building work was already under way there on the holiday home where he would later spend the summers with his future wife Alma (their first encounter was still a year away) and their two daughters. Here most of the later symphonies were also to be composed, until the catastrophic year of 1907, when within a few days the couple's elder daughter died in the house, and Mahler's own (ultimately fatal) heart condition was diagnosed.

With the Fourth Symphony essentially completed, and only finishing touches to add – which, he wrote, would give his life a focus over the winter months – Mahler returned to Vienna to start his fourth season as Musical Director of the

Court Opera. He was busy expanding the repertory with a variety of works new to Vienna, by Leoncavallo, Giordano, Tchaikovsky and Bizet, as well as a Haydn opera, but the programming was dominated by Wagner (the most performed composer in the previous season) and Mozart. Contemporary reports had already remarked on how Mahler had 'regenerated' Mozart's *Marriage of Figaro* at the opera house, and the worldly-wise comedy of *Così fan tutte*, a neglected and misunderstood opera by comparison, was to follow in October 1900. This is the experience which the Fourth Symphony seems to reflect in its opening movement, as it casts a glance backwards, past German Romanticism, to the era of Mozart and Haydn: a movement of untroubled themes, at a trotting pace and with pointedly classical gestures and rhythms.

As well as being of less massive proportions than the Second and Third Symphonies (around sixty minutes compared with their eighty and hundred minutes respectively), structurally, too, the Fourth is a more conventional work. Mahler had been uncertain about embracing the term 'symphony' for his First (originally designating it a 'symphonic poem'), and he initially conceived the Fourth as a 'symphonic humoresque'. But it has the customary four movements: an allegro, conceived on a large scale, and packed with ideas; a scherzo; a slow movement; and a rondo finale. It also employs a smaller orchestra than the Second and Third Symphonies, although the Fourth's characteristically transparent scoring and instrumental combinations were to survive in the later symphonies, even after the larger orchestra had been restored.

Mahler famously declared, in the course of a conversation with Sibelius (whose music, and personality for that matter, did not impress him), that the symphony 'must be like the world – it must embrace everything'. Here the world is the one of the final movement, which casts its shadow back over the preceding three. Unlike the technique of thematic reminiscences, widely used in opera of the period, the themes and ideas that reappear in the final movement are at last being heard in their true home, rather than referring back nostalgically to the point at which they were first heard.

Mahler gave a memorable depiction of the mood of the Fourth Symphony to his close friend, the violinist Natalie Bauer-Lechner, as 'the uniform blue of the sky, which is more difficult to render than all its changing and contrasting hues'. This clear blue is disturbed by frequent threatening clouds, however: the terrors of the scherzo, led by a solo violin tuned up a tone (and originally intended to portray Freund Hein, the dark fiddler of German folk tradition who leads the dead into the next world), and the moments of anxiety into which the otherwise peaceful, Beethovenian slow movement is prone to descend. But this tension is always successfully resolved, and the third movement finally erupts into an elaborately scored vision of glory, and ends in a mood of grace, the perfect preparation for the wide-eyed innocence of the finale.

This last movement is a child's vision of the 'heavenly life' ('*Das himmlische Leben*') – a counterpart to the grim tale of starvation and death contained in the 'earthly life' ('*Das irdische Leben*', one of Mahler's ten orchestral settings of *Wunderhorn* poems). Here in Heaven there is food in abundance and the bread, whose lack caused the child on earth to die, is baked by angels; while for the final stanza about the music that can be heard in Paradise, Mahler modulates from the symphony's home key of G major into a bright E major, the Baroque key of Heaven.

© Kenneth Chalmers

∾ Symphony No. 5 in C sharp minor
(1901–2)

Part One

1 Trauermarsch: In gemessenem Schritt. Streng. Wie ein Kondukt [Funeral March: At a measured pace. Strict. Like a cortège]

2 Stürmisch bewegt. Mit grösster Vehemenz [Tempestuously. With utmost vehemence]

Part Two

3 Scherzo: Kräftig, nicht zu schnell [Sturdy, not too fast]

Part Three

4 Adagietto: Sehr langsam [Very slow]

5 Rondo-Finale: Allegro – Allegro giocoso

Mahler started work on his Fifth Symphony in the summer of 1901, in the composing studio built for him up the hill from his lakeside house at Maiernigg, on the wooded south shore of the Wörthersee.

The following winter in Vienna changed Mahler's life. At a dinner party he met the much younger Alma Schindler, whose beauty, strong personality and musical talent soon had him falling feverishly in love with her. She became pregnant, and they married in March 1902. Mahler completed the draft of the Fifth Symphony at Maiernigg that summer. It had grown to a highly unusual five-movement structure, whose orchestral requirements are not large compared to those of some of Mahler's earlier symphonies, but still large enough: woodwind in threes (plus a fourth flute), six horns, four trumpets, three trombones, tuba, harp, percussion and strings.

Each of Mahler's symphonies is to some extent a self-portrait. So it is natural that this one, written at one of the happiest periods of his life, should contain some of his sunniest music. But he remained haunted by memories of his childhood, during which several of his younger siblings had died in infancy: the fanfares sounding from the nearby army barracks became connected in his mind with this death-shrouded world. And in February 1901 a haemorrhage, caused by years of relentless overwork as a conductor, had very nearly killed him too. Perhaps both that experience and the exhilaration of his recovery are reflected in the Fifth Symphony's extremes of convulsed terror and bounding energy.

But a work of this magnitude also amounts to something more than a chapter of autobiography. The Austro-German musical tradition of the nineteenth century was rooted in artistic certainties which, much as Mahler admired and understood them, it was in his nature to challenge. There are no certainties, his music seems to be saying: the kind of optimistic and absolute resolution of dark conflicts that propels Beethoven's symphonies, for instance, is no longer possible in the modern age. Perhaps it is this sense of tumultuous ambivalence that now communicates so urgently to our post-Holocaust, nuclear era, in which certainties of any kind – social, political, spiritual – seem ever harder to find.

The symphony begins with a solo trumpet ('like a military fanfare'). After the thunderous entry of the full orchestra, a quieter second theme, also in C sharp minor, is introduced by the violins. An outburst of despair ('Suddenly faster – passionate – wild') is led by the trumpet and violins in agonised duet with each other, eventually subsiding into a return of the march. A restatement of the fanfare idea – very quietly, on unaccompanied timpani – introduces another episode. This is in the new key of A minor, and the violins' melody is accompanied by the other strings in an insistent short–short–short–long rhythm. But the march returns with pitiless bleakness, and a muted trumpet and flute lead it away into the distance.

Taking up the key of A minor, cellos and basses furiously launch the second movement, which explores further the ideas heard in the first. The frenetic, driving pace is punctuated by slower episodes, where the first movement's accompanying short–short–short–long figure now appears in the woodwind (like a cackling bird call) and brass, as well as in the strings. Eventually a triumphant chorale in D major manages to fight its way to the surface, before the movement peters out on the cellos, double basses, and a single drum stroke.

Perhaps the greatest of all Mahler's musical 'forest walks', the self-contained central Scherzo in D major is a tumultuous dance of life and nature, blending elements of the whirling Viennese waltz with its leisurely and genial country counterpart, the *Ländler*. The vigorous main opening section is spurred on by an elaborate part for the principal horn, and contrasted by a gentle, lilting idea introduced by the violins. A thrilling climax, where the horns seem to call to each other down dark ravines, leads to an enchanting, delicately scored central Trio section, begun by solo pizzicato strings. Then the rousing dance is taken up again. More horns lead to a hinted-at reprise of the Trio, then to a storming conclusion.

The Adagietto in F major is scored only for strings and harp. Mahler wrote it as a love song to Alma, and its tempo marking of 'Very slow' surely implies sustained warmth and soulfulness, rather than the funereal dirge to which some performances reduce it. The beautifully judged scoring allows moments of darkness to contrast with the music's radiance. After the more urgent central section, the return of the main theme is a quiet masterstroke: Mahler gives it to the second violins, allowing them a rare moment in the limelight while the first violins, for once, accompany.

The principal horn enters and, along with the woodwind, introduces the main ideas of the D major Rondo-Finale. Critics have always had a field day debating the complex design of this movement, which fuses elements of sonata and rondo form with such mastery that the result conforms arguably to both, or to neither. But there is the unmistakable feel of a classical rondo in the music's free-wheeling, tension-releasing effervescence. Among the several themes explored and developed is one from the preceding Adagietto. The eventual arrival of the second movement's chorale – blazing out on full brass as before – crowns the entire symphony, balancing out its incandescent interplay of the forces of darkness and light.

Malcolm Hayes © BBC

∾ Symphony No. 6 in A minor (1903–4)

1 Allegro energico, ma non troppo: Heftig, aber markig [Vehement, but concentrated]
2 Scherzo: Wuchtig [Heavy] – Altväterisch [In an old-fashioned style], Grazioso
3 Andante moderato
4 Finale: Sostenuto – Allegro energico

Ever since Mahler conducted the first performance of his Sixth Symphony in May 1906, commentators have tried to pin down what it is 'about'. Mahler's widow, Alma, maintained that the Finale portrayed an individual's heroic struggle against implacable fate, symbolised by the three huge hammer blows that occur at strategic points throughout the movement. Yet the Sixth Symphony was written at the most fulfilled period of Mahler's life. He had married the young and beautiful Alma in 1902; they now had two children; and, as director of the Vienna Court Opera, Mahler's career as a conductor was at its apogee. His idyllic summer home at Maiernigg had been built on the lucrative proceeds of these years of success, complete with an isolated forest hut, to which Mahler would retreat every day to compose.

Other commentators have looked for a different interpretation – for instance, that the symphony was an artist's premonition of the First World War and the subsequent horrors of Nazi Germany. Alma maintained that the element of premonition was personal. In 1907 Mahler's daughter Maria died of a combination of scarlet fever and diptheria in the house at Maiernigg; his career at the Vienna Court Opera came to an embittered end; and he was diagnosed with the heart condition that was to cause his death four years later. Three hammer blows – the scenario fits. Too neatly, perhaps? The Sixth Symphony simply exists: disturbing in its nihilistic despair, yet ultimately attaining a true and monumental grandeur.

The orchestral forces used are formidable. Including extra instruments added in the Finale, there are woodwind in groups of five, eight horns, six trumpets, four trombones, tuba, a fairly extensive percussion section, two harps and a celesta (Mahler asks for these to be augmented 'if possible'), and strings to match. In his earlier symphonies Mahler had experimented with unusual numbers of movements, but in the Sixth he reverted to a classical four-movement design. The Scherzo originally came second and the Andante third, but after the first performance Mahler had doubts about this and switched their order round. He also omitted the Finale's third and final hammer blow from the score. Later, he seems to have moved towards reinstating both this and the original order of the middle movements, but he died apparently before reaching a final decision.

The first movement's opening bars introduce the march rhythms in A minor that haunt the symphony. Violins introduce the grimly determined main theme, continued by all four oboes wailing in unison. A new march rhythm, thundered out on the timpani, introduces the symphony's motto idea: a loud major triad on the trumpets, changing at once to a minor one. A quiet chorale on the woodwind leads to the second theme, impulsive and passionate (Mahler told Alma it was a musical portrait of her). True to classical procedure, Mahler indicates that this opening section should be repeated, before the music strides into its development. A sudden quieter interlude introduces a return of the chorale and the distant clattering of cowbells, symbolising the remoteness of serene (and very Austrian) mountain heights. Then the hectic marching resumes, eventually spurring the movement to a noisy conclusion in an embattled A major.

This temporary triumph is at once negated by the Scherzo: a kind of strange, triple-time march, also in A minor, launched by timpani thudding across the main beat. The music seems to move in aimless circles; the metre changes erratically between three and four beats; the scoring is wilfully harsh (*wie gepeitscht* – 'whipped' – is written above a violin figure). A quieter second idea, coyly introduced by the oboe, dispels some of the tension, but not the weirdly fluctuating metre. The two moods alternate until the movement ebbs to its close, with some final muttering from the contrabassoon and timpani.

The key of the Andante moderato, E flat major, is at an opposite pole to the symphony's main A minor tonality. There is a beautiful opening theme on the first violins and, soon after, a little oscillating figure introduced by the flutes, beneath which the cor anglais adds a second tune. These two main ideas are extended in turn, the first largely keeping its repose, while the second becomes each time more intense and passionate. Both eventually combine, to lead the movement to a close whose loveliness belongs to a world too remote from the rest of the symphony to be disturbed by it.

A soaring violin theme, and an ominous return of the major-to-minor motto idea, together launch the massive Finale – a much-expanded sonata-form structure, with a double development section. The brooding introduction helpfully lays out the other main ideas in turn: an insistent little three-note march-figure on the solo tuba; a recall of the first movement's mountain interlude, again with distant bells, and now with a more confident theme on the solo horn; a sombre chorale on low woodwind and brass; and a new, leaping march theme on low horns and woodwind, leading towards the main Allegro energico.

The first development begins quietly (cowbells again) before building to a huge climax and the first hammer blow ('like an axe stroke', says a note in the score). A march-rhythm viciously beaten out by the *Rute* (birch-twig switch) marks the start of the second development. The cataclysm unleashed by the second hammer blow – roaring brass, berserk strings – hurtles towards a return of the slow introduction. What follows is a final, fearless and magnificent assault, as the march rhythms charge on, to be cut down at last by the third hammer blow. All that remains is a coda, quietly and mournfully sounded by trombones and horns, and some last traces of life in the basses and cellos. The ending itself is perhaps the bleakest in all music.

Malcolm Hayes © BBC

∾ Symphony No. 7 in B minor (1904–5)

1   Langsam (Adagio) – Allegro con fuoco
2   Nachtmusik [Night music] 1: Allegro moderato
3   Scherzo: Schattenhaft [Shadowy]
4   Nachtmusik 2: Andante amoroso
5   Rondo-Finale: Allegro ordinario

Mahler was once asked an impossible question: how did he compose? 'Do you know how to make a trumpet?' he replied. 'You take a hole and wrap brass around it; that's about what happens in composing.' It is an appropriate image for the Seventh Symphony, which was composed, as it were, inside out. Mahler usually concentrated on one work at a time, but in the summer of 1904, while finishing his Sixth Symphony, he composed two *Nachtmusik* movements, evocative pieces in complete contrast to the tragic world of the symphony he was completing. He realised that they would form part of his next symphony, but it took him some time to find the way ahead.

Because of his heavy conducting schedule, composing was impossible during the following winter. It was only in the summer of 1905 that Mahler returned to the new symphony, and still the ideas refused to come. Suddenly, however, there came one of those flashes of illumination that had such importance for Mahler. He was on the shore of an Alpine lake, waiting to be ferried across. 'I stepped into the boat to be rowed over. At the first stroke of the oars, I hit upon the theme (or rather, the rhythm and the style) of the introduction to the first movement, and within four weeks the first, third and fifth movements were completely finished.'

Mahler conducted the first performance three years later in Prague, on 19 September 1908. By then his life had changed drastically. After the grand affirmation of the Eighth Symphony (1906) came a year of disasters: his forced resignation from the Vienna Court Opera, the death of his eldest daughter and the diagnosis of the heart disease that would kill him two and a half years later. When the Seventh was performed, he was already working on those death-haunted works, *Das Lied von der Erde* and the Ninth Symphony.

Mahler's contemporaries, most of whom reacted to the Seventh Symphony with sarcasm and even anger, suffered from two disadvantages that time has removed. The first was that they could not have an overall view of the connections that exist between all of Mahler's works and allow us to appreciate his whole achievement as a unity. The Seventh shares many features with the Fifth and Sixth Symphonies. The vigorous march theme which launches the first movement's Allegro and returns in the finale is a variant of the march theme that opened the Sixth; two other features carried over from the Sixth are the sound of distant cowbells (a symbol of remoteness and solitude) and the feature of a major chord dissolving into a minor one, the basic 'fate' motif of the Sixth. The Rondo-Finale of the Seventh Symphony looks forward to the first movement of the Eighth.

The other obstacle Mahler's contemporaries found was the reckless mixture of styles that was Mahler's way of expressing his complex vision of the world. The combination of elements that he throws together, his outrageous veering between sophistication and naivety, offended against all established ideas of good taste. The Seventh Symphony is also full of reminiscences of other music, something that went completely against the prevailing idea that thematic originality was essential to any musical work.

There are the sounds of nature found in all Mahler's music: the sounds of wind and water, bird and animal calls. There are popular dances, marches and songs, sometimes played straightforwardly, sometimes distorted. Passing references, perhaps not intentional, can be heard to music by Schubert, Schumann and Wagner, to Bizet's *Carmen* and even Lehár's *The Merry Widow*. This range of sound was Mahler's world, and it is all moulded into a vast five-movement structure lasting nearly eighty minutes.

The symphony as a whole describes a 'darkness to light' process, a common Romantic scheme; but in Mahler's case nothing is quite straightforward, and the progress is often ambiguous. Rather than the subjective emotional progress of such works as the Second and Fifth Symphonies, the Seventh seems to stand at a distance from personal emotion and to develop as a series of tableaux of the natural world. The opening 'darkness on the lake' image, marked by the penetrating sound of the tenor horn, has something of a veiled funeral march; but the big Allegro movement that follows shakes off this sense of foreboding and moves into a world which offers a strange mixture of mystery and energy.

The three central movements provide Mahlerian images of march, dance and song. The first *Nachtmusik* begins with answering horn calls – a fundamental Romantic forest evocation – which introduce a kind of nocturnal procession moving against a background of nature sounds. The dance of the third movement is a waltz, but not a social or friendly one. Marked *Schattenhaft* ('shadowy'), it is a nightmare vision of disintegration. The song of the fourth movement (the second 'night music' movement) recalls something of the enchanted worlds Mahler invented in his Third and Fourth Symphonies, and the orchestra includes a guitar and a mandolin, the archetypal serenade instruments.

Brass fanfares and drum tattoos launch a Finale that seems to be driven by a determination to be joyful at any cost, as though Mahler were recalling Schubert's reported words: 'Do you know any music that is really happy? I don't.' Many people have found the Seventh to be the most problematic of Mahler's symphonies, generally on account of this Finale. Not the young Arnold Schoenberg, however. For him, this was the gateway into Mahler's world, and his experience of the Seventh Symphony had a profound effect on his own music and, through him, twentieth-century music as a whole.

© Andrew Huth

❧ Symphony No. 8 in E flat major, 'Symphony of a Thousand' (1906–7)

Part 1   Hymn: *Veni, creator spiritus*
Part 2   Final Scene from Goethe's *Faust*

> Imagine that the universe begins to ring and resound.
> No longer with human voices but with revolving planets
> and suns.
>
> Mahler to Willem Mengelberg, August 1906

In the scope of its ambition as well as its sheer physical dimensions, Mahler's Eighth Symphony is one of the largest musical works ever created. The forces required to perform this vast symphony are almost without parallel in musical history: two very large mixed choirs, children's choir, eight vocal soloists, organ, a huge orchestra, plus an additional brass choir placed at a distance from the other performers. At its first performances, in Munich on 12 and 13 September 1910, 1,029 performers took part and the concert promoter, quite reasonably, dubbed it 'Symphony of a Thousand'.

Those performances, the last time Mahler ever conducted a work of his own, represented the greatest triumph of his career and their success meant much to him. Consciously intended as his magnum opus, the Eighth was described by its composer as 'my gift to the nation'. Emerging triumphantly from the dark night of the Sixth and Seventh Symphonies, the new work was an act of both public and private affirmation. For once, popular appeal was, for its composer, a legitimate index of artistic success.

Mahler sorely needed affirmation at this stage in his career. Four turbulent years had passed since the Eighth's composition. During this time, Mahler had been forced to resign from the Vienna Court Opera, his four-year-old daughter had died of diphtheria and scarlet fever, his marriage had virtually disintegrated and he had been diagnosed with a potentially fatal heart condition. The work's triumphant reception undoubtedly offered a brief, precious glimpse of pure happiness during the agonising final months of Mahler's life.

The story of the symphony's composition is well known. Writing in May 1910, Mahler recalled that 'Four years ago, on the first day of the holidays, I went up to the hut at Maiernigg with the firm intention of idling the holiday away . . . On the threshold of my old workshop, the Spiritus Creator took hold of me and shook me and drove me on for the next eight weeks until my greatest work was done.'

Although the absolute accuracy of Mahler's recollection has been questioned (a lack of surviving manuscript sketches makes it impossible to determine exactly how much was completed during the summer of 1906), there is no doubt that most of the symphony was composed in a fever of inspiration. This is important, because the union between man and the 'creator spirit' forms the symphony's main philosophical theme – a concept embodied in the very act of its conception.

The German language has a word for the kind of inspiration Mahler experienced: *Einfall*. Essentially untranslatable, it implies the sudden manifestation of unlooked-for enlightenment – an epiphany. This notion was a staple of nineteenth-century German aesthetics, which often made a distinction between the artist as 'vessel', through which inspiration passes (think of the popular – if somewhat inaccurate – image of Mozart as the uncomprehending lout through whom the voice of God happened to speak), and the artist who consciously strives to achieve enlightenment through a sustained effort of will (the figure of Beethoven perhaps provides the most striking example, or even that of Mahler himself).

The dichotomy is attractive because it also encompasses some fundamental polarities that lie at the heart of the Eighth: passive/active; feminine/masculine; traditional/progressive. These in turn offer a key to understanding Mahler's curious, and apparently contradictory, choice of texts for this, the world's first truly choral symphony.

The symphony has just two movements. First comes a setting of the great Latin hymn *Veni, creator spiritus*, attributed (wrongly, it now seems) to the ninth-century Archbishop of Mainz, Hrabanus Maurus. The second movement sets a slightly shortened version of the closing scene of Part Two of Goethe's *Faust*. Separated by a millennium, these texts stand respectively among the supreme summits of the sacred and the humanistic traditions and their juxtaposition in Mahler's work is both audacious and provocative.

In fact, the texts are fundamentally complementary. Each is concerned with achieving, or receiving, 'grace', and Mahler's music reflects this in profound and subtle ways. For example, the Latin hymn passively invites the creator spirit to dwell within us, while the *Faust* scene would appear actively to draw us onwards to that creator spirit. Yet Mahler's musical treatment of the texts confounds expectation by inverting these passive/active characteristics, reflecting the fact that the creator spirit entering Part 1 is undoubtedly masculine, while the spirit drawing us through Part 2 is surely feminine – Goethe's *Ewig-Weibliche* (eternal feminine).

This is nicely encapsulated in two contrasting settings of the crucial word 'come' (Latin: *Veni*; German: *Komm*). Part 1 opens with a resounding cry of 'Come, come, creator spirit!' The exclamation mark is Mahler's own – this is a demand, not an entreaty! – and an urgent sense of assertion is rarely absent from this Allegro impetuoso movement. Conversely, towards the end of Part 2, Mater Gloriosa gently beckons the souls of Gretchen and Faust with the words 'Come! Come! Soar to higher spheres.' Here the ethereal sound-world enfolding the distant voice of the 'Glorious Mother' sums up the prevailingly lyrical and contemplative mood of Part 2.

As well as reconciling sacred Latin and secular German texts, the symphony also attempts a remarkable musical-historical synthesis. Part 1 employs a kind of *stile antico* ('old style'), full of traditional, 'learnèd' procedures. Part 2 is very much in a *stile moderno* ('new style'), less formal and more overtly dramatic.

The 'old-style' Part 1 is packed with Baroque contrapuntal devices and also conforms to a clearly recognisable classical sonata-form plan. The Latin hymn has just 110 words and the music devours them with such voracity that words and phrases are repeated, juxtaposed and re-ordered by Mahler, seemingly at random. Textual clarity here becomes the servant of the musical process.

Part 2 reverses this. Clarity is now all-important in Mahler's setting of 220 lines from Goethe's drama. Old-style polyphony yields to predominantly solo lines and a respect for textual meaning that has its roots in the music dramas of Wagner.

So what binds together this extraordinary and ambitious conflation of literary, philosophical and musical traditions? What, if anything, rescues it from incoherence and impossible pretentiousness? There are two main reasons why it succeeds. Firstly, the symphony displays absolute unity of purpose throughout both its parts: that purpose is to celebrate and to affirm. In this respect one might argue that the symphony is over almost as soon as it has begun, the joyous opening chorus never being seriously called into question at any subsequent point. For the writer Theodor Adorno, who thought Mahler 'a poor yea-sayer', this represented a fatal flaw. For him the Eighth's unalloyed optimism represented a climb-down in artistic aspiration. Secondly, and more importantly, for all its apparent extravagance, the Eighth is thematically the most tightly integrated of all Mahler's works. The better one knows it, the more astonishingly apparent it is that almost every aspect of this mighty edifice grows from the intervals and rhythms of the opening bars.

A thunderous organ chord is the sole preparation for the chorus's opening invocation of the creator spirit. The words are set to an energetic leaping theme that provides so much of the subsequent musical material.

As the cries of '*Veni*' subside, the more lyrical second subject introduces seven of the vocal soloists ('*Imple superna gratia*'). Complex but radiant polyphony between chorus and soloists is allowed to expand lyrically throughout this extended passage ('*Qui tu Paraclitus diceris*').

The central development falls into two large spans. The first, beginning '*Infirma nostri corporis*', introduces a rare note of anxiety into the work, extending through an edgy orchestral interlude dominated by the tolling of bells.

All doubt is abruptly swept aside with the development's second phase, launched by a cry of '*Accende lumen sensibus*'. These words set a new variant of the opening theme and have far-reaching implications for the rest of the symphony. The following energetic march ('*Ductore sic te praevio*') incorporates a double fugue of great contrapuntal complexity preparing the way for an ecstatic recapitulation of the opening '*Veni, creator spiritus*' and a varied reprise of the earlier sections.

Children's voices announce the concluding '*Gloria sit Patri Domino*' and the movement ends in a mood of jubilation, the final bars crowned with fanfares from an additional brass choir.

An extended orchestral prelude to Part 2 evokes the rocky chasms and forests of the closing scene of Goethe's drama. Its spare orchestration, the blueprint for Mahler's late orchestral style, could hardly offer greater contrast from what preceded it. Nevertheless, the music is actually a development of previously heard material: the theme in the pizzicato double basses comes from the '*Accende*' theme of Part 1, symbolising the physical and spiritual ascent that is the subject of the rest of the symphony.

The prelude has an almost operatic function. Not only does it set the scene but it also provides a glimpse of many of the musical ideas that follow and emphasises the shift between the two parts from motet to music drama.

It is well known that Goethe had musical setting in mind for much of *Faust* and this scene's opening 'Chorus and Echo' obviously cries out for music. Mahler responds with choral writing of startling originality and evocative power.

In contrast with Part 1, the vocal soloists now become named characters, each with at least one solo passage. In Goethe's drama, four devotional father figures, presumably saints, are identified: Pater Ecstaticus, Pater Profundus and Pater Seraphicus (the last of them omitted by Mahler), along with Doctor Marianus. They reveal progressively higher, purer forms of love, from the sensuality of Pater Ecstaticus to the selfless devotion to the Virgin shown by the 'Marian Doctor'.

Following extended arias from Pater Ecstaticus and Pater Profundus, the music takes on an airy, scherzo-like character, with the appearance of the choirs of Angels and Blessed Boys. They bear Faust's soul, victoriously rescued from combat with Satan. To a further variant of the '*Accende*' theme from Part 1, they intone words described by Goethe as 'the key to Faust's salvation': 'He who endeavours, ever striving, / Him we have the power to redeem.'

Almost imperceptibly, the choruses are joined by Doctor Marianus for the first of his ecstatic hymns of adoration. In response, the Mater Gloriosa (Glorious Mother) herself soars into view. At this crucial juncture, Mahler introduces both a completely new theme and a new orchestral sonority of harps, piano and harmonium – none of these instruments having been used up to this point.

The new theme dominates much of the following music, especially that of the Penitent Women accompanying the Glorious Mother. Two are biblical figures: Magna Peccatrix (the repentant sinner from St Luke's Gospel who washed Christ's feet with her tears) and Mulier Samaritana, the woman of Samaria from St John's Gospel. The third, Maria Aegyptiaca (Mary of Egypt), is a character taken by Goethe from the seventeenth-century Acts of the Saints. Their state of grace is reflected by the innocent little canon they sing (like a children's round – how different from the driving counterpoint of Part 1!) as they intercede on behalf of a fourth penitent (Una Poenitentium).

This is the soul of Gretchen, the woman Faust seduced and who was executed for the infanticide of the child she conceived by him. She in turn pleads for Faust's soul and is rewarded by a response from the Glorious Mother herself (the eighth vocal soloist, so far unheard and now, magically, calling from on high). She invites Gretchen's soul to 'soar to higher spheres', assuring her that Faust's will follow.

The symphony's closing minutes incorporate Doctor Marianus's apotheosis of the Glorious Mother and the 'Chorus Mysticus', a solemn chorale setting the final lines of Goethe's drama: 'The eternal feminine / Draws us heavenward.' Gradually the music grows in power and intensity to a climax of overwhelming splendour, crowned by the extra brass choir intoning the '*Veni, creator*' hymn from the work's opening.

© John Pickard

✎ Symphony No. 9 in D major (1909–10)

1 Andante comodo – Allegro
2 Im Tempo eines gemächliches Ländlers. Etwas täppisch und sehr derb [In the tempo of an easy-going country waltz. Somewhat clumsy and very rough]
3 Rondo-Burleske. Allegro assai. Sehr trotzig [Very defiant]
4 Adagio. Sehr langsam und noch zurückhaltend [Very slow and even held back]

In April 1909, after a successful winter spent conducting in New York, Mahler returned to Austria for his usual summer holiday of hard work on a new composition. Two years earlier his life had been devastated by the death of his oldest daughter from scarlet fever and diptheria, the intrigue-ridden end of his reign as artistic director of the Vienna Court Opera, and the diagnosis of a heart condition which, in theory at least, was supposed to restrict his hyperactive lifestyle. His marriage to his much younger wife, too, had become unhappy. Given their two impossibly intense natures, the age gap between them, and the tragedy of their daughter's death, the emotional impasse that had resulted was really the fault of neither. But it was causing both Gustav and Alma much pain.

They took up residence on the upper floor of a farmhouse near Toblach (now Dobbiaco), among the Dolomite mountain peaks of South Tyrol. Here they had spent the previous summer, with Mahler retreating to his hut to compose. Alma now left her husband to his own devices, however, and took herself and their surviving daughter to stay with her mother elsewhere. The Ninth Symphony duly took shape against this background of distraught memories, frustrated love, and a life about to be cut short.

Musical history has since given Mahler's last completed work a special place among the symphonic masterworks of the Austro-German tradition. Great symphonies were to be written in the future, of course, but not in the direct line of descent from Haydn, Mozart and Beethoven, as Mahler's were. In that sense his Ninth is truly the end of something. But if despair and anguish are all harrowingly present in the music, they co-exist with other Mahlerian qualities also – a passionate love of life and nature; an idealistic instinct to confront despair with heroic endeavour; and a magnificent pride in creative powers which, despite his illness, remained undiminished.

The Ninth Symphony's orchestra is modest by Mahlerian standards: woodwind in groups of four or five, but a standard-size brass section, with percussion (including deep bells), harp and strings. The design is much more unusual. The layout of two large, slow movements enclosing two shorter, quicker ones has an obvious symmetry, and the symphony does indeed end as quietly as it begins. Yet, on another level, the work proceeds in a different way from that of symphonic tradition, where the finale represents the goal and summing up of the entire musical journey. Here, the response to the first movement's yearning questioning is the nihilistic negation of the second-movement Scherzo, followed by the manic hyperactivity of the Rondo-Burleske. Far from drawing these contradictory musical strands together, the closing Adagio widens the gulf between them, answering the first movement's key of D major with its own resigned, lower D flat major.

The symphony's understated opening, lasting only a few seconds, presents a complex of ideas out of which the entire first movement is built: a rhythmic figure articulated across the main beat by cellos and a low horn; a four-note theme in the harp's bass register; a fanfare on a muted horn; and a quivering two-note figure on violas. With the tempo now set in motion, the second violins sing the beautiful main theme, supported by a solo horn. They are soon joined by the first violins in a mood of ecstatic serenity, which is promptly darkened by a second theme in a restless D minor. A quickening of pace and a flurry of fanfares lead to the hushed start of the development (the cross-beat rhythm on horns, repeated on trombones) and an epic journey through extremes of emotionalism and wild unease. A huge climax, with the trombones hurling out the cross-beat rhythm, gives way to a bleak funeral march, followed by a passionate reprise of the movement's main themes. This leads eventually to a coda, signalled by the last and loveliest of all Mahler's horn calls. A solo flute, hovering alone in mid-air, and a solo violin lead the movement to its serene close.

The Scherzo's response is wilfully grotesque: a crude country *Ländler* (slow waltz), dry and expressionless, with pattering bassoons and violas answered by clarinets and horns. The music's directionless course gives no sense of why one particular idea should follow another, nor why the entire movement might not continue like this indefinitely. A quick, frenetic waltz suddenly bursts in on the strings; a third idea, wistful and lilting, introduced by the violins and oboe, alternates with the other two. Eventually, having made a point of going on too long, the movement peters out.

The Rondo-Burleske is launched by solo trumpet, strings and horns. Groups of ideas fly past the ear in a virtuoso tour de force that does not conceal a sense of hollowness behind all the feverish activity. A sudden slowing of the pace transforms the music's cackling demons into angels, but their serene song is shrilly mocked by the clarinets, and the movement's course resumes even more frantically than before, chasing its tail in ever-decreasing circles.

Strings begin the Adagio with an intense, richly harmonised theme, out of which Mahler builds an immense set of slow variations. The tune's first statement is momentarily interrupted by a quiet solo on low bassoon, but already the passionate string harmonies seem to be pushing further out into the vast spaces around them. An interlude of calm arrives, with high violins and a subterranean contrabassoon exploring new and haunting regions, before the strings and a solo horn renew the variation sequence. A quiet, rocking figure on clarinets and harp introduces a second interlude. The third and final phase of variations then leads the symphony to its climax, after which the music seems not so much to end as to dissolve into an overhead sky which, while vast and empty, is at least calm and cloudless.

Malcolm Hayes © BBC

∾ **Symphony No. 10** (sketched 1910)
Performing version of the draft, prepared by Deryck Cooke in collaboration with Berthold Goldschmidt, Colin Matthews and David Matthews (1964–76)

1 Adagio
2 Scherzo
3 Purgatorio: Allegretto moderato
4 [Scherzo]: Allegro pesante. Nicht zu schnell [Not too fast]
5 Finale: Introduction: Langsam, schwer [Slow, serious] – Allegro moderato

When Mahler died in May 1911, *Das Lied von der Erde* and the Ninth Symphony had not yet been performed, and his Tenth Symphony was left unfinished. The last of his works to reach the public during his lifetime was the Eighth Symphony, which Mahler conducted in Munich in September 1910 – his greatest personal triumph as a composer. Few of those in the audience who heard the heaven-storming sounds of the 'Symphony of a Thousand' could have guessed the new paths that Mahler's music had taken since that work. In 1907, the year he completed the Eighth, Mahler discovered that he had a serious heart disease, and that he probably had only a few more years to live. He wrote to his friend Bruno Walter: 'at one fell stroke, I have lost everything of clearness and reassurance that I had ever won for myself . . . now, at the end of my life, I must learn anew how to walk and stand.'

Mahler was, above all, a Romantic composer whose music expresses in an extraordinarily direct way his most intimate feelings about his own life. So it is not surprising that *Das Lied* and the Ninth Symphony reflect his new attitude. In both works the conflict between affirmation and negation, life and death – a familiar feature in earlier Mahler symphonies – is intensified to an unprecedented degree. In both works the conflict ends with a serene but resigned acceptance of death as an end. Faith in the Christian God, which Mahler had proclaimed in his early symphonies, or the humanist optimism of the Fifth, Seventh and Eighth symphonies, were now inconceivable. Against their loss Mahler could now only set his continuing joy in the beauty of the natural world, and the tenuous peace of a quasi-Buddhist nirvana.

Yet the infinitely lingering coda of the Ninth Symphony's Adagio finale was not Mahler's last word. In the summer of 1910 he sketched a Tenth Symphony, in which the conflict with death was to take a different and more vital form. One crucial reason for this change is again bound up with his personal life, for it was while he was composing the symphony that Mahler discovered his wife Alma was having an affair with the architect Walter Gropius (whom she was to marry some years after Mahler's death). Gropius asked Alma to leave her husband in a letter he inadvertently addressed to Mahler. Mahler was devastated: he had perhaps never had a realistic understanding of his young wife, whom he all too easily turned into a Romantic symbol (as, for instance, Goethe's *Ewig-Weibliche* in the Eighth Symphony). His helplessness convinced Alma that she should stay with him. Meanwhile, all his turbulent emotions went into the symphony he was writing, and out of them he drew the strength to reach, once again, a positive resolution: the Finale ends with a passionate reaffirmation of his love for Alma. It should be noted, however, that a feeling of renewed vitality is already strongly present in the second movement, which was almost certainly drafted before the marital crisis occurred. Like Berlioz's *Lélio* (though with added Mahlerian irony), the Tenth Symphony might be subtitled 'The Return to Life'.

It was Mahler's practice to sketch a symphony in his summer holidays and to revise and score it during the following winter. But he had no opportunity to complete the Tenth Symphony, as during the winter of 1910–11 he was preoccupied with extensive revisions to the Ninth Symphony, and then came his final illness. He left behind the draft of a five-movement work in a complex state of incompleteness, which may be summarised under four headings:

(a) For the first movement, Adagio, there is a draft full score, from which, had he lived, Mahler would have made a fair copy. The existing score can be played more or less as it stands, though no doubt Mahler would have refined it.

(b) The second movement, Scherzo, exists in a full-score sketch. For about half its length this is fairly complete, but in the latter part the texture is often extremely sparse. This is the most problematic movement, chiefly because it is not entirely convincing in its shape. It is likely that Mahler would have made revisions – perhaps quite drastic ones – to the structure, just as he did with the Scherzo of the Ninth Symphony when it had reached its draft full-score stage (this was one of the things he did in the winter of 1910–11).

(c) The brief third movement: the first twenty-eight bars are written out in full score, and from then onwards there is a short score with enough details of instrumentation to make realisation fairly simple, though for the repeat of the first section, Mahler simply wrote 'da capo'.

(d) For the fourth and fifth movements there is only a short score with a few hints of instrumentation. Both movements, however, are convincing as structures, particularly the Finale.

For many years it was assumed that it was impossible to play the whole symphony. At first the sketches were shrouded in mystery, amidst rumours that Mahler had asked his wife to destroy them. But in 1924 Alma arranged for a handsome facsimile of the manuscript to be published, and at the same time she asked Ernst Krenek, then her son-in-law, to prepare the first and third movements for performance. There was some hostile criticism of these moves at the time, but the first movement thereafter quite often found its way into concerts. After the Second World War, several musicologists began working independently on realisations of the other movements, including, from 1959, Deryck Cooke.

Cooke first became interested in the symphony while he was writing a booklet for the BBC's celebrations of the Mahler centenary. Having examined the sketches, Cooke decided to prepare for performance as much of the symphony as he could, for an illustrated broadcast talk. He soon found he could realise much more of the score than he had initially thought possible. The Tenth differs from the majority of unfinished works in that, although the texture is very thin in places, sometimes only a single line, there are no gaps, so no free composition is necessary. What Cooke did was to fill out the texture where this was required, particularly in the latter half of the second movement where extra counterpoint derived from Mahler's thematic material had often to be added; to orchestrate the third movement partially (Cooke saw no alternative to following Mahler's 'da capo' literally, using the same orchestration, though he was well aware that there is no precedent for such a literal repeat in other Mahler symphonies) and the fourth and fifth movements entirely; and to tidy up Mahler's full score of the first movement. In the eventual programme, then, broadcast in December 1960, he was able to present virtually the whole symphony, except for some gaps in the second and fourth movements. Berthold Goldschmidt, who conducted this preliminary performance, had given Cooke much expert assistance with the orchestration (though a composer himself, Cooke had little experience of writing orchestral music) and he helped Cooke to revise the whole work after Cooke had decided he could without too much difficulty fill in the gaps in the score. This full-length version was first performed at a Prom in August 1964, with Goldschmidt again conducting. The first American performance followed in 1965, conducted by Eugene Ormandy, who went on to make the first recording.

It was only when the symphony was heard in its entirety that it became possible to judge just how far Mahler had progressed since the Ninth. And the quality of what was revealed was such as effectively to silence those purist critics who argued that an unfinished, imperfect work should not be played at all. For, as Deryck Cooke wrote:

Mahler's actual music, even in its unperfected and unelaborated state, has such significance, strength and beauty, that it dwarfs into insignificance the momentary uncertainties about notation and the occasional subsidiary pastiche-composing, and even survives being largely presented in conjectural orchestration, so long as Mahler's characteristic widely spaced texture is faithfully preserved. After all, the thematic line throughout, and something like ninety per cent of the counterpoint and harmony, are pure Mahler, and vintage Mahler at that.

Nevertheless, it is important for the listener to bear in mind exactly what it is he or she is listening to. Cooke called his realisation 'a performing version of the draft for the Tenth Symphony', and he was always concerned to stress that it was in no sense a completion, since only Mahler himself could have completed the work. We were aware, while we were revising the score, of the paradox that what we were trying to make as perfect as we could was something that was intrinsically imperfect. And we were also aware that the closer we got to what we believed was a Mahlerian sound, the more likely it was that the audiences would forget that what they were listening to was only the realisation of a draft and accept it simply as Mahler's Tenth Symphony, which it could never quite be. Yet we all believed the risk was worth taking.

The symphony is cast in two parts. The first two movements are both in the key of F sharp, and could almost stand independently as a two-movement work. The first movement is a twenty-five-minute slow movement, an unprecedented way to begin a symphony; but it follows on directly from the last movement of the Ninth. The dark, searching opening theme for violas alone alternates with a consoling Adagio for strings and trombones, related not only to Mahler's Ninth but also to Bruckner's, and to a common background in the prelude to Act 3 of *Parsifal*. The whole movement, indeed, is a *Parsifal*-like quest, whose ending is a precarious and temporary haven. For midway through the movement there occurs a great outburst in A flat minor, leading to a terrifying nine-note dissonant chord, which casts its shadow over the rest of the movement, and is not exorcised until the Finale.

The F sharp major Scherzo, however, is full of confidence: a busy neo-classical movement with constantly changing time-signatures. It has a relaxed *Ländler* trio. Mahler had not written a scherzo so free from malice since the Fifth Symphony; and its coda, with its exultantly whooping horns, directly recalls the scherzo of the Fifth. So ends Part 1 of the symphony.

If, as seems likely, the first two movements were drafted before the crisis in Mahler's marriage, which occurred at the end of July, then the little B flat minor third movement, which Mahler entitled 'Purgatorio oder Inferno' (the last word has been crossed out, probably by Alma) was his immediate reaction to the shock of the discovery. In several places in the manuscript Mahler wrote anguished exclamations over the music, including at one point '*Erbarmen!*' ('Have mercy!' – the wounded Amfortas's cry in *Parsifal*) and, at another, '*Tod! Verk!*' At the latter point the music alludes to Wagner's fate motif in the *Ring*, whose first occurrence is in the scene from Act 2 of *Die Walküre* where Brünnhilde appears before Siegmund to tell him he must die, known as the *Todesverkündigung* ('Annunciation of Death'). In the

Todesverkündigung the fate motif is followed by another motif for the brass, at first in F sharp minor, then in A flat minor. This motif is strikingly similar to the A flat minor brass chorale in the first movement's central outburst, which is clearly also an Annunciation of Death, and the tonal parallels are surely too close to be coincidental. Possibly this passage was inserted into the first movement after the July crisis: the existing sketches suggest that it was an afterthought (though the crucial page is missing).

The structural function of the third movement is to act as a prelude to the last two movements, and to supply them with most of their thematic material. The fourth movement, a lamenting fast waltz in E minor, is closely related to the 'Trinklied' from *Das Lied von der Erde*. A wild inscription on the title page begins *'Der Teufel tanzt es mit mir'* (The Devil dances it with me). At its start the music is forceful and energetic, but it gradually exhausts itself under the weight of its climaxes, and at the end the dance runs down to a standstill, finishing with the dead sounds of percussion (Mahler's instrumental indications here) and, last of all, a loud stroke on a muffled bass drum. Alma Mahler has described how Mahler heard this sound at a fireman's funeral in New York, and how he watched from his hotel window, his face streaming with tears. The experience deeply affected his death-obsessed mind. *'Du allein weisst was es bedeutet'* (You alone know what it means), he wrote for Alma on the last page of the score.

The Finale brings redemption. It opens in D minor, in utter darkness. Fragments of themes grope upwards from the depths of the orchestra, to be beaten down relentlessly by repeated strokes of the muffled drum. Then in sudden calm a solo flute (another of Mahler's own indications of instrumentation) plays a long, arching melody of serene and strange beauty, a metamorphosis of elements from the third and fourth movements. Violins take it up with a glorious modulation to B major and move slowly to a climax, whose apex is violently cut off by the drum stroke. The darkness of the introduction returns, heralding a central Allegro moderato –

nervously agitated music derived from the third movement. Its middle section develops the flute theme, with a noble continuation for high trumpet (here too Mahler has indicated the specific instrument), after which the crisis comes quickly with the return of the dissonant chord from the first movement. It is followed by the opening theme of the symphony, played by the horns. A gentle modulation to B flat brings back the flute theme; all tension subsides, and the climax of a long, tranquil ascent is a radiant restatement of the flute theme in F sharp major on all the violins (Mahler's marking). The last pages are full of tenderness, and over the final passage Mahler wrote Alma's name, as a last gesture of love. It is no coincidence that these final pages are reminiscent of the Adagietto from the Fifth Symphony, Mahler's first music inspired by Alma, written after he fell in love with her. It was by recreating her image in its original purity that Mahler was able to come to terms with the trauma of her infidelity, and to end his life's work with a victory of love over death.

© David Matthews

Felix Mendelssohn (1809–47)

The grandson of a philosopher, Mendelssohn combined musical precociousness of a Mozartian order with a lifetime of learning and travelling. He gave his first performance as a pianist aged nine, and composed thirteen early string symphonies between 1821 and 1823. By the time of his first visit to London, aged twenty, he had already spent time in Paris. After returning to Berlin, where he had studied philosophy with Hegel, he undertook a major tour of Europe, which inspired the 'Scottish' and 'Italian' Symphonies as well as the *Hebrides* overture. He became conductor of the Lower Rhine Music Festival, Music Director of the Leipzig Gewandhaus Orchestra (1835), and founded the Leipzig Conservatory (1843). He showed vivid scene-painting ability in his overtures (especially *A Midsummer Night's Dream* and *Calm Sea and Prosperous Voyage*), but he produced some of his best work in the standard classical forms: an enduringly popular Violin Concerto, six string quartets and two piano concertos. Of his three oratorios, *Elijah* was especially favoured by the English choral societies of the Victorian era.

∾ Symphony No. 3 in A minor, Op. 56, 'Scottish' (1829–42)

1 Andante con moto – Allegro un poco agitato
2 Vivace non troppo
3 Adagio
4 Allegro vivacissimo – Allegro maestoso assai

In July 1829 the twenty-year-old Mendelssohn and his friend Karl Klingemann went on a three-week walking tour of Scotland. Klingemann's detailed diary of the trip records that they visited Arthur's Seat and the Palace of Holyrood in Edinburgh, then went up the river Forth by steamer to

Stirling, by pony and cart north to Dunkeld, west to Loch Tay, Glencoe (shrouded – as usual – in mists) and Fort William, and once more by paddle steamer down Loch Linnhe to Oban on the west coast. From there they took a boat trip to Mull, Iona and Staffa – then an up-and-coming tourist attraction – and finally returned to England via Glasgow.

Scotland made a deep impression on the young composer's Romantic susceptibilities: he drew inspiration from its 'comfortless, inhospitable solitude' to produce two of his best known works: the *Hebrides* overture and the Third Symphony (known as the 'Scottish'). Mendelssohn had evidently had it in mind to write such a symphony before leaving Germany, since he wrote to his family from Edinburgh, after visiting Holyrood Palace: 'The chapel is now roofless; grass and ivy grow there, and at that broken altar Mary was crowned Queen of Scotland. Everything around is broken and mouldering, and the bright sky shines in. I believe I found there today the beginning of my Scottish Symphony.'

Thirteen years were to elapse before Mendelssohn completed the symphony, and by that time his memories of the trip must have dimmed. Once back in Germany, he found himself occupied with other projects, including a trip to Italy less than two years later. Under the bright Italian sunshine another symphony took shape (No. 4), and he wrote that he found it 'impossible to return to my misty Scottish mood. I have therefore laid aside the Scottish Symphony for the present.' Finally completed at the beginning of 1842, the 'Scottish' Symphony was given its premiere on 3 March in Leipzig, by the Leipzig Gewandhaus Orchestra under the composer's direction. A few months later he conducted it in London, where it was very well received. The score was published the following year with a dedication to Queen Victoria, and a note by Mendelssohn to the effect that all four movements should be played without a break.

By the late eighteenth century, the influence of the classical revival on contemporary culture had almost run its course, and the new Romanticism was eager for an alternative view of history. One such was provided by James Macpherson's timely 'discovery' of supposedly ancient Celtic poetry lauding the exploits of heathen heroes such as Fingal and Ossian. These poems were particularly popular in Germany, where nascent nationalism seized on the Enlightenment theme of the 'noble savage'. The young Mendelssohn had been reared on the writings of Sir Walter Scott – the 'wizard of the North' – and would doubtless have been familiar with Macpherson's 'Ossianic' transcriptions. Seen within the context of Mendelssohn's output, the 'Scottish' Symphony clearly falls into a category which could be labelled 'Ossianic' compositions. These date from the years between 1829 and 1846, and include: the *Hebrides* overture; the *Sonate écossaise*, Op. 28; a set of six Scottish folk songs; a hunting song setting a text by Sir Walter Scott; a vocal duet on a Burns poem, and finally a setting of a poem by 'Ossian' himself, *On Lena's Gloomy Heath* (1846).

Scholars have drawn attention to the close connections, both thematic and structural, between the 'Scottish' Symphony and the overture *Echoes of Ossian* (1840) by Mendelssohn's younger Danish contemporary Niels Gade, who in turn had been influenced by the *Hebrides* overture. It has been supposed that one of the reasons for the symphony's unusually long gestation was that Mendelssohn was held up by structural problems, which he eventually solved by the use of cyclic principles perhaps suggested to him by Gade's work. The material of the slow introduction to the first movement – the 'Holyrood' theme – returns at the end of the movement (as in the Gade overture), and not only fuels the main theme of the ensuing Allegro, but reappears in pentatonic guise in the scherzo and, in a different order, in the finale – both movements influenced by Scottish folk song. This thematic unity was noted in an early review in the *Allgemeine musikalische Zeitung*, which stated that 'all four movements are very closely related to one another and are bound by an inner connection'. Echoes of Ossian's horn resound in hunting calls throughout the symphony, while the other instrument most closely associated with the Celtic bard – the harp – is imitated in the pizzicato string accompaniment to the Adagio, a scene which may have been inspired by an episode from Scott's *The Lady of the Lake*.

© Wendy Thompson

❧ Symphony No. 4 in A major, Op. 90, 'Italian' (1833)

1 Allegro vivace
2 Andante con moto
3 Con moto moderato
4 Saltarello: Presto

In the autumn of 1830 Mendelssohn, then twenty-one years old, crossed the Alps into Italy, where he spent the next ten months. He visited Florence and Naples but his base was Rome, and it was there, in a sunny room on the Piazza di Spagna, that he wrote most of the Symphony in A known as the 'Italian'. The work is a paean of praise to the warm south; it celebrates the Northerner's response to Goethe's 'land where the lemon-trees bloom'. Mendelssohn, no less than Berlioz (the two composers were in Rome at the same time), was disgusted with what he considered the degraded condition of contemporary Italian musical culture, but his pleasure in the light and colour and animation of the Italian landscape was intense. 'Why should Italy still insist on being the land of Art', he wrote to his family, 'when in reality it is the land of Nature, delighting every heart? No lack of music *there*; it echoes and vibrates on every side – not in the vapid and vulgar theatres.'

The famous opening chord of the work – pizzicato strings, woodwind and horns *fortepiano* – signals the release of a flow of high spirits unsurpassed in music. The long violin theme which unfolds beneath luminous, pulsating wind chords has that combination of pace and leisurely stride – like a perfectly ridden thoroughbred – that was Mendelssohn's secret. The mixture of graceful, broadly arched melody and busy accompanying figuration continues throughout the movement. A new, rhythmical theme in the minor dominates the development, leading to an impassioned climax from which, after a diminuendo, the solo oboe in a long crescendo leads the way back to the reprise – one of the most magical passages in nineteenth-century music.

As with the slow movement of Berlioz's Italian symphony (*Harold in Italy*), a religious procession inspired Mendelssohn's Andante. The elements of this beautifully poised and evocative movement are an introductory chant-like figure, which recurs halfway through and again at the end, a continuous patter of marching quavers in the bass, a melancholy tune intoned in unison by woodwind and violas (joined at its repetition by the soft counterpoint of two flutes), and a second theme in the major which, as Donald Tovey remarks, introduces a note of human wistfulness into the austerity of the litany. At the end, as the procession passes into the distance, the chant fades, and only the marching quavers are still audible. Then they too are heard no more.

The minuet-like third movement is a fine example of Mendelssohn taking the classical tradition and making it more Romantic and personal. The poetic trio, in E major (like the *Midsummer Night's Dream* overture), begins with the horns of elfland blowing a far-off fanfare, but works up to a vigorously rhythmic forte in A minor which foreshadows the finale.

The last movement is a saltarello – an Italian popular dance, quick, flowing but interrupted by sudden hops. Haydn sometimes concluded major-key sonata works with finales in the minor, but he liked to end them in the major. Mendelssohn, unprecedentedly, remains in the minor to the very last bar. He also sustains to the end the music's sense of furious, whirling movement. This whole finale is a rhythmic tour de force whose excitement is intensified by the contrasts of scoring, articulation and dynamics. Near the end the music, still drumming out the rhythm of the saltarello, sinks to a far-off pianissimo, before the final irresistible crescendo.

© David Cairns

Olivier Messiaen (1908–92)

Born to literary parents in Avignon, Messiaen devised a highly personal musical language based on a diverse range of elements, including plainsong, and Indian and Greek rhythms. He studied at the Paris Conservatoire, and in 1931 was appointed organist at the Church of La Sainte Trinité, where he continued his duties until his death. During the Second World War he was interned in Silesia, where his *Quartet for the End of Time* (1941) was written and first performed. Returning as professor to the Conservatoire, he produced the massive, meditative *Vingt regards sur l'Enfant-Jésus* – one of a number of piano works from the 1940s inspired by Yvonne Loriod, one of Messiaen's students, who became his second wife in 1962. Abundant, meticulously transcribed birdsong featured in many of his compositions after *Réveil des oiseaux* (1953). He pioneered the use of the ondes martenot (the electronic instrument whose ethereal swooping sounds would later become associated with science-fiction films), but throughout his life the theme closest to his heart was the celebration of love and of his Catholic faith.

✍ *Turangalîla Symphony* (1946–8)

1 Introduction
2 Chant d'amour 1
3 Turangalîla 1
4 Chant d'amour 2
5 Joie du sang des étoiles
6 Jardin du sommeil d'amour
7 Turangalîla 2
8 Développement de l'amour
9 Turangalîla 3
10 Final

When Germany invaded France in the Second World War, Messiaen was called up as a medical orderly in the French army. Captured in May 1940, he was imprisoned in a camp in Silesia. While there, he composed his *Quartet for the End of Time* and, with three colleagues, gave its world premiere before an audience of five thousand fellow prisoners. Messiaen later recalled: 'Never have I been heard with as much attention and understanding.' The experience seems to have decisively changed his view of the kind of artist he felt he needed to be.

Repatriated to France in 1941, he set about composing a series of masterworks whose rhetorical, public stance is very different from that of their more contemplative predecessors. Among Messiaen's new intake of pupils at the Paris Conservatoire was the young pianist Yvonne Loriod, his future second wife, whose brilliant playing inspired several new works. The exultant, life-affirming tone of these reflected Messiaen's gratitude and exhilaration at having survived his captivity. And all these elements came together spectacularly in the *Turangalîla Symphony* – the central panel of a trilogy of works based on the Tristan legend and its theme of transcendent love.

Commissioned by Serge Koussevitzky for the Boston Symphony Orchestra but actually premiered by them under Leonard Bernstein in 1949, the new symphony astounded its first audiences with its hectic invention, fearless decibel level, total lack of inhibition and its sense of joyful excess at every level. The orchestral forces required, however, are not extreme: woodwind in normal threes, a cornet and high trumpet augmenting a standard brass section, a modestly expanded percussion department with prominent parts for glockenspiel and vibraphone, and strings. There are also two solo parts: one for piano (written for Loriod), and one for ondes martenot, the electronic keyboard instrument whose sweet expressiveness had already featured in Messiaen's recent music.

The symphony is laid out in two parts of five movements each. Messiaen sustains this huge structure by intercutting movements of passionate love music with others involving intricate rhythmic number games. In the composer's own words:

> *Turangalîla* is a word in Sanskrit . . . *Lîla* literally means play – but play in the sense of the divine action upon the cosmos, the play of creation, of destruction, of reconstruction, the play of life and death. *Lîla* is also Love. *Turanga*: this is time that runs, like a galloping horse; this is time that flows, like sand in an hourglass. *Turanga* is movement and rhythm. *Turangalîla* therefore means all at once love song, hymn to joy, time, movement, rhythm, life and death.

1 *Introduction* (Modéré, un peu vif)

Agitated strings and brass launch the work. Then two themes that occur throughout the symphony are presented: a loud, strident one for trombones and tuba, and a gentle, curling one introduced by two clarinets. Messiaen called these the 'statue' theme and the 'flower' theme, but he was being circumspect: the musical imagery is straightforwardly sexual. A solo piano cadenza is followed by a passage superimposing several different ideas at once: chord sequences on wind and strings, a stamping theme on high and low strings, and snapping, cascading chords on the brass and piano. The movement ends with an ondes martenot swoop and a percussion thump.

2 *Chant d'amour 1* (Modéré, lourd)

After a brief introduction comes the symphony's 'theme of joy', with two contrasting elements: an exultant shout from trumpets and strings, and a slow, sweet response from the violins and ondes. This double idea functions as a refrain between two orchestral 'verses' – the first with low oboes, cor anglais and swirling ondes martenot, the second with wailing oboes and hectoring brass interruptions. All this is developed to a climax.

3 *Turangalîla 1* (Presque lent, rêveur)

The symphony's three *Turangalîla* movements are all shorter than the others, and their tone is different: depersonalised, remorseless, inscrutable. Here there are three main ideas: a quiet theme exchanged between clarinet and ondes; a loud, menacing one for low trombones; and an oriental-sounding oboe melody. Meanwhile drums and woodblocks beat out their own rhythmic cycles.

4 *Chant d'amour 2* (Bien modéré)

A movement of fantastic multi-layered complexity, built out of two groups of ideas. The first is a hopping, scherzo-like theme introduced by piccolo and bassoon, plus a quicker, perky melody on the upper woodwind; the second is an out-burst of rapture on strings and ondes, answered by a wood-wind chorale. All this is intricately developed, with the 'statue' theme joining in. After a piano cadenza, the final bars are quiet and serene.

5 *Joie du sang des étoiles* (Vif, passionné, avec joie)

A cosmic romp for full orchestra, launched by a dancing ver-sion of the 'statue' theme. The central section develops the 'statue' theme itself several times at once on trombones, horns and trumpets. After the dancing theme's reprise comes an explosive piano cadenza, and a final blaze of light from the full orchestra.

6 *Jardin du sommeil d'amour* (Très modéré, très tendre)

Complete contrast. Muted strings and ondes martenot sing a hushed variant of the 'love' theme, while piano, solo woodwind, vibraphone and glockenspiel add birdsongs and shimmering decoration. Meanwhile the temple blocks gen-tly tap out slow-motion rhythms. In Messiaen's words: 'Time flows forgotten. The lovers are outside time: let us not wake them.'

7 *Turangalîla 2* (Un peu vif – Bien modéré)

Four main groups of ideas: an opening piano cadenza; a remarkable passage for high, descending ondes and low, dark trombone chords; interlocking rhythms on a battery of per-cussion; and a passage for woodwind and solo cello. All are combined and extended. (Messiaen once compared the climax of this movement to the tortures related in Edgar Allan Poe's story 'The Pit and the Pendulum'.)

8 *Développement de l'amour* (Bien modéré)

One of the longest movements, where the symphony's themes are thrown together into a furnace of development. This culminates in a soaring peroration based on the 'love' theme: '*avec passion – charnel* [carnal] *et terrible*' writes Messiaen in the score. In the final bars, in his own words, 'the "statue" theme bends over the abyss'.

9 *Turangalîla 3* (Bien modéré)

The main theme is at first shared between solo woodwind, tubular bells and ondes. Next comes a complex layering of rhythmic cycles on the percussion; the piano then takes up the main theme, while the percussion rhythms are underpinned by chords on thirteen solo strings. Both ideas are simultaneously extended.

10 *Final* (Modéré, presque vif, avec une grande joie)

A dance of transcendent joy, with two main themes: an opening fanfare on brass and strings, and a speeded-up version of the 'love' theme on strings and woodwind. A development section and reprise lead to a final radiant statement of the 'love' theme, and a tumultuous conclusion.

Malcolm Hayes © BBC

Wolfgang Amadeus Mozart (1756–91)

More than two hundred years after his death, Mozart stands as a focal figure of Western classical music, not only for his astonishing precocity and inventiveness, but for the staggering range and quality of his music. His father Leopold, a violinist, paraded his son's talents around the European capital cities when he was as young as six. By sixteen, Mozart had absorbed a variety of musical fashions, having travelled to England, Germany, France, Holland and Italy. He worked for the Prince-Archbishop in Salzburg during his teens, producing symphonies, concertos and masses as well as operas. In 1780 he went to Munich to compose *Idomeneo*, his first great opera, and the following year he moved to Vienna, where in the four years beginning in 1782 he wrote fifteen of his twenty-seven piano concertos. *The Marriage of Figaro*, the first of his three operatic collaborations with the court poet Da Ponte, appeared in 1786, followed swiftly by *Don Giovanni*. In his last three years he produced his last Da Ponte opera, *Così fan tutte*, the three final symphonies (Nos 39–41) and the gem-like Clarinet Concerto, leaving his Requiem incomplete at his death.

∾ Symphony No. 29 in A major, K201 (1774)

1 Allegro moderato
2 Andante
3 Minuet and Trio
4 Allegro con spirito

In 1772 the English musician Dr Charles Burney travelled through Germany, the Netherlands and Austria gathering material for a history of music. *A General History of Music from the Earliest Ages to the Present Period* appeared in four volumes between 1776 and 1789 but, like so many other gentlemen on the Grand Tour in the eighteenth century, Burney published his immediate impressions soon after returning to London. *The Present State of Music in Germany, the Netherlands and United Provinces* contains a section on Salzburg, even though he had not visited the city. To remedy this omission Burney had contacted an English diplomat in Salzburg who provided the following views, which Burney reproduced without acknowledgement:

> The archbishop and sovereign of Saltzburg [*sic*] is very magnificent in his support of music, having usually near a hundred performers, vocal and instrumental, in his service. The prince is himself a dilettante, and a good performer on the violin; he has lately been at great pains to reform his band, which has been accused of being more remarkable for coarseness and noise, than delicacy and high finishing.

It was for this orchestra that Mozart composed most of his symphonies in the 1770s. His father, Leopold, was Vice Kapellmeister at the court and from an early age Mozart had ample opportunity to take part in performances there. In 1769 Wolfgang had stepped on to the lowest rung of the musical ladder at the court when he was appointed to the salaried position of a Konzertmeister, fourth in seniority after Domenico Fischietti, his father Leopold, and Michael Haydn (Joseph's younger brother). He composed several items of church music and, between October 1773 and the end of 1774, five symphonies for the court orchestra. They are remarkably individual works for an eighteen-year-old, projecting a meaningful personality as well as the usual effortless technique; this is especially true of the A major symphony, dated 6 April 1774.

Much of the individuality of the symphony's opening is due to the presentation of the theme over a slow-moving background, rather than the more conventional pulsating movement. The resultant pensive quality is transformed at the first tutti into taut aggression, as the theme is played in close imitation between treble and bass. Eloquent and persuasive argument is a feature of the whole movement, complemented by a wealth of cantabile themes.

For the slow movement, Mozart indicates that the violins should be muted, a favourite technique for him in the 1770s. The movement is in a full sonata form, again with a profusion of melodic material. Near the end of the movement, the composer writes '*si levano i sordini*' (remove the mutes), so that the final phrase has a bold sonority that puts the slow movement into perspective and anticipates that of the Minuet.

Like the Andante, the Minuet makes characterful use of dotted rhythms, especially noticeable in the figure that punctuates the end of each section. The Trio, in turn, is more evenly flowing, requiring those very qualities of 'delicacy and high finishing' that were apparently lacking in the court orchestra.

The finale is a brilliant movement in 6/8, full of pulsating energy and, as throughout the symphony, making pointed use of the wind instruments (two oboes and two horns), so that the texture has as much light and shade as if the orchestra were three times the size.

© David Wyn Jones

∾ Symphony No. 31 in D major, K297, 'Paris' (1778)

1 Allegro assai
2 Andante
3 Allegro

In the couple of decades that preceded the French Revolution, Paris was the musical capital of Europe. It had an active and varied concert and operatic life with, according to a music almanac of 1783, 194 composers, 63 singing teachers, 93 violin teachers, 87 piano teachers, 97 music publishers and 120 instrument makers; in addition it had a lively musical press, both disputatious and gossipy. Thus when Mozart, accompanied by his mother, arrived in the city on 23 March

1778, it was with considerable hope and expectation; certainly Mozart's father expected great things of the visit: 'You are in the one place which, if you are industrious, as you are by nature, can give you a great reputation throughout the world . . . you must turn the coming years to account both for your own sake and for that of us all.'

In the event the visit was a near disaster, and Paris was denied the one missing element in its abundant musical life, a composer of the first rank. The reasons for this disappointing failure are many and complex: the Mozarts arrived too late to make any planned impact on the 1778 season, but early enough to become disillusioned; Mozart, rather than responding to the stimulus of the surroundings, became cynical about some of its pretensions; finally, in July, his mother died unexpectedly after a brief illness.

Mozart's letters to his father from Paris are full of ideas for compositions and hints of commissions (including an opera in French), but a symphony in D major was the most substantial product of the period. It was commissioned by the Concert Spirituel, the oldest and most important concert body in Paris. As the name suggests, the concerts had been devoted almost exclusively to sacred vocal music, but gradually instrumental and operatic music came to be played alongside. Mozart's symphony was first performed on 18 June as the first item in a concert that included music by Jommelli, J. C. Bach, Gluck and, as the 'spirituel' elements, a motet by Gossec and an oratorio by Bambini. The symphony was well received, but the undiplomatic Mozart did not stay for the remainder of the concert: 'I was so happy that as soon as the symphony was over, I went over to the Palais Royal, where I had a large ice, said the Rosary as I vowed to do – and went home.'

In the previous four years the only substantial orchestral work composed by Mozart had been the 'Haffner' Serenade (K250), and so the skill and corporate virtuosity of the Parisian players must have been a welcome challenge. Fifty-six musicians were engaged for the 1778 season and Mozart wrote for the full orchestra of double woodwind (including clarinets), two horns, two trumpets, timpani and forty-three string players (11, 11, 6, 9, 6). Mozart, rather cynically, had noticed the French predilection for '*le premier coup d'archet*', that is, a strong unison opening for full orchestra, and began his symphony in a similar fashion, though one doubts whether many Parisian composers could have integrated this cliché into the subsequent progress of the movement as well as Mozart does. In the finale Mozart teased the Parisians:

Having observed that all last as well as first allegros begin here with all the instruments playing together and mostly in unison, I began mine with 2 violins only, piano for the first 8 bars – followed immediately by a *forte*; the audience, as I expected, said 'hush' at the piano beginning – then, suddenly, the forte came – they heard the forte and clapped their hands at once.

Paris audiences preferred their symphonies to be in three rather than four movements (Parisian publishers often simply omitted the minuet from any four-movement symphonies that came into their hands), and Mozart duly obliged. However, he apparently misjudged Parisian taste in slow movements, which favoured the pleasantly tuneful rather than the profound or eloquent. Two were composed, the second after the indifferent reception accorded to the original in the first performance, and both have survived.

© David Wyn Jones

∾ Symphony No. 35 in D major, K385, 'Haffner' (1782)

1 Allegro con spirito
2 Andante
3 Minuet and Trio
4 Presto

When Mozart left the service of the Prince-Archbishop of Salzburg in June 1781, to begin a freelance career as a composer, performer and teacher in Vienna, the effects were more far-reaching than even he could have imagined. The Imperial capital offered him the kind of independence and cultured musical milieu he had not enjoyed back in Salzburg, and his response was to compose music of growing emotional and intellectual reach which, together with the music of his friend Haydn, was to help define the sophisticated and subtle expressiveness of the High Classical style.

That Mozart himself was aware of the new direction his music was taking is clear from a piece like the 'Haffner' Symphony, a Viennese work, but one which consciously looks back to the brilliant, plain-speaking orchestral style of the Salzburg years. It did so with good reason. In July 1782 Mozart received a letter from his father, Leopold, asking for a symphony to celebrate the ennoblement of a family friend, Sigmund Haffner. Mozart duly provided one, posting it to Salzburg in instalments accompanied by a correspondence which could not hide his irritation at the kind of paternal demand from which he must have thought to have freed himself. He sent the final package on 7 August, adding: 'I only hope that all will reach you in good time, and be to your taste.'

In its original form the symphony started with a march, and may well have had an extra minuet as well, thus making it similar to the type of multi-movement orchestral serenade that was popular in Austria at that time for grand public occasions. It was not uncommon, however, for these serenades to be cut down subsequently to form four-movement symphonies, and this is precisely what Mozart did when, having got Leopold to send back the score, he performed the 'Haffner' in Vienna for the first time in March 1783.

If Mozart's tetchy letters managed to give the impression that he was at all half-hearted about this work, there is little sign of that in the sparkling end result. He realised this himself when he saw the score again, remarking that it 'has positively amazed me, for I had forgotten every single note of it'. But then, he had by this time reached that stage in his career when, as he told his father, 'I am really unable to scribble off inferior stuff.'

© Lindsay Kemp

∾ Symphony No. 36 in C major, K425, 'Linz' (1783)

1 Adagio – Allegro spiritoso
2 Andante
3 Minuet and Trio
4 Presto

At the end of October 1783 Mozart and his wife Constanze were on their way back from Salzburg to Vienna via Linz, where their host for a few days was Count Thun, who was about to put on a private concert. He asked Mozart for a symphony, and on 31 October the composer wrote to his father: 'On Tuesday 4 November I'm giving a concert in the theatre here and, as I haven't a single symphony with me, I'm writing a new one at breakneck speed.' One's natural amazement that Mozart could produce a great symphony in a few days is not at all reduced by the thought that he had time to write letters as well!

In this case the speed cannot be explained even by the possibility that Mozart had it all in his head ready, so to speak, to be copied down quickly; he had to get to work with little warning. However one tries to explain these miracles, one is left with the music, which never loses its freshness and vitality and always astonishes by the subtlety of its organisation. Tovey remarked in one of his essays that this symphony has in the growth of Mozart's symphonic style 'much the same position as Beethoven's Fourth Symphony . . . both represent the supreme mastery and enjoyment of a sense of movement'. Whether in Mozart's case this enjoyment was a positive by-product of haste no one can tell; there is no sign of haste in the music, but every sign of perfectly controlled energy and fluency.

The 'Linz' Symphony is the first of Mozart's to have a slow introduction, a feature already made familiar by Haydn. It is at once grand and intense, darkening as it approaches the Allegro, which emerges with quiet, smooth power into the light, its phrases beautifully irregular as it grows. There is also some highly original scoring for the wind instruments. Mozart (as so often) does not indulge in elaborate thematic development, and the centre of the movement is mainly a fleet treatment of the florid violin passage that originally led back to the repeat of the exposition. The impressiveness of the movement lies not so much in the peculiarity of its themes or the weight of their development as in the unpredictable perfection of its inner proportions, resulting in the fine sense of movement of which Tovey spoke.

The slow movement blends grace with dignity and, sometimes, mysterious solemnity. It is in full sonata form, making imaginative use of a scale in its development. The trumpets and drums are not, as often in an Andante of this period, silenced, but contribute a quiet gravity from time to time. The Minuet and Trio are formal, depending more on proportion than on the unexpected, and the finale is one of Mozart's most exhilarating – his vivid sense of movement is here even more in evidence. Like that of the first movement and most of that of the Andante, the development treats a new element, now a striking skipping figure, possibly picked up from one of Haydn's early quartets (the finale of Op. 9 No. 1, also in C major).

© Robert Simpson

∾ Symphony No. 38 in D major, K504, 'Prague' (1786)

1 Adagio – Allegro
2 Andante
3 Presto

This symphony, Mozart's last before the final trilogy of 1788, was composed in Vienna in 1786. The finale seems to have been written first, in the spring or summer (it is possible that it may originally have been intended as a replacement finale for the 'Paris' Symphony, No. 31); the other two movements followed at the end of the year. The orchestral forces required are relatively large: strings, two flutes (rather than the usual one), two each also of oboes, bassoons and horns, two trumpets and timpani; and the work is of a richness and depth that demonstrate how much importance Mozart attached by this time to symphonic form.

The first performance of the symphony almost certainly took place in Prague, at a concert given by Mozart in the opera house on 19 January 1787. It was received with great enthusiasm, and remained a favourite in the Bohemian capital for many years. The chief purposes of Mozart's visit to Prague were to supervise the local company's production of his most recent opera, *The Marriage of Figaro* (which became a smash hit), and to make arrangements for a new opera – arrangements that resulted before the end of the year in the premiere of *Don Giovanni*.

The shadow of the Commendatore's statue in the forthcoming opera already seems to fall across the second half of the symphony's slow introduction, with its minor tonality, ominously marching bass lines, and eerie chromatic scales. And when the music emerges into the light of the Allegro, it is with a theme that parallels remarkably the main theme of the *Don Giovanni* overture; though its later intensive contrapuntal treatment, in the unusually eventful exposition section as well as in the development, looks some four years further ahead to another operatic overture, that of *The Magic Flute*.

The serene G major Andante, in 6/8 time, lacks any such specific operatic associations. But it does have some affinities with *The Marriage of Figaro*: technically, in the way it so often uses instruments as if they were characters in one of the opera's many ensembles; expressively, in its hints that the sentimental comedy played out on the surface masks deeper feelings underneath.

There is no minuet movement: an omission explained by some modern commentators in terms of a wish on Mozart's part to say all he had to say in three sonata-form movements, but perhaps due more simply to contemporary Bohemian, as opposed to Viennese, expectations of symphonic form. In any case, the symphony plunges straight into the finale, which again seems to belong to the world of *opera buffa*; in fact, the first four notes of the first theme echo the little duet between Susanna and Cherubino in Act 2 of *Figaro*. The offbeat start of this figure, of which great use is made throughout the movement, the syncopations that follow it in the first subject, and later the teasingly irregular phrase lengths of the second theme, all help to keep this one-in-a-bar Presto in constant, light-footed motion.

© Anthony Burton

✍ Symphony No. 39 in E flat major, K543 (1788)

1   Adagio – Allegro
2   Andante con moto
3   Minuet and Trio: Allegretto
4   Finale: Allegro

Mozart's last three symphonies, Nos 39 to 41, were written in the summer of 1788, three years before his death, in the incredibly short space of eight weeks (though this may have been preceded by a good deal of sketching). Together they form a perfectly balanced triptych reflecting complementary aspects of their composer's musical personality. Because of this, and because of the absence of specific evidence of performances in Mozart's lifetime, it has sometimes been assumed that he wrote them out of inner compulsion rather than for any external occasion. But, as Neal Zaslaw says in his study of Mozart's symphonies, this 'flies in the face of his known attitudes to music and to life, and the financial straits in which he then found himself'. Mozart probably intended these three last symphonies for a subscription series which he was planning for that year; but as far as we know (the Viennese records are far from complete) this never took place. However, he would have had opportunities to perform them on his visits to Leipzig in 1789 and Frankfurt in 1790, in charity concerts in Vienna in 1791, and probably on other occasions as well. The old myth that he never heard them played is unlikely to be true.

Another frequently repeated notion is that the three symphonies were intended as a triptych. If this means that they were meant to be performed together, the idea is a non-starter: concerts at the time rarely included more than two symphonies, and often even a single work was split into two instalments. But Mozart does seem to have set out to compose three symphonies of completely different and complementary characters, with a view to displaying his range of expression across his proposed concert series, and perhaps subsequently in a published set. And the character of each work is defined largely by his choices for two interrelated elements: key and scoring. No. 40, in G minor and without trumpets and drums, is intense and tragic; No. 41, in C major and without clarinets, is open and brilliant. As for No. 39, it is in the key of E flat major, which for Mozart implied warmth and solidity, even solemnity (in 1791 it was to be the home key of his 'Masonic' opera *The Magic Flute*). And these qualities are matched by the scoring for strings, with cellos and basses frequently separated and violas occasionally divided, and a wind section of flute, two clarinets (the newer instruments replacing the more usual oboes), two bassoons, two horns, and two trumpets with their associated timpani.

The full and warm sound of these instruments in this key is evident at once in the slow introduction, which opens with sonorous dotted rhythms, and includes some harsh dissonances before a quiet transition to the Allegro. One other significant feature of this introduction is the sweeping downward scales in the violins, which are echoed (consciously or unconsciously) in the Allegro, and in different forms in the slow movement and the finale. The Allegro itself is in 3/4 time, rather than the more usual 4/4, and after the imposing introduction the combination of this metre and the lyricism of the lightly scored first subject makes the movement seem initially rather slight. Its strength becomes apparent only with the strenuous tuttis which follow both the first theme and the group of ideas which make up the second subject.

Similarly, the A flat major Andante does not reveal all of its character at once: the serene surface presented at the opening is at first merely ruffled by two bars of minor-key colouring, and only then disturbed by a violent outburst in F minor, which later returns even more vehemently in the remote key of B minor.

The trumpets and drums, absent from the second movement, return to add weight to the Minuet. The Trio, in *Ländler* time (and apparently based on a traditional dance tune), is dominated by the clarinets, the first demonstrating the instrument's singing quality while the second plays an accompanying pattern in the low chalumeau register.

The closing Allegro is one of Mozart's most Haydnesque movements, resembling many of his older friend's finales in its perpetual-motion energy, with only occasional, telling halts, and in the way all its material is spun out of the opening idea – right up to the witty ending.

© Anthony Burton

∾ Symphony No. 40 in G minor, K550 (1788)

1 Molto allegro
2 Andante
3 Minuet and Trio: Allegretto
4 Allegro assai

The programme for a pair of charity concerts in Vienna conducted by Antonio Salieri in April 1791 included a 'grand symphony' by Mozart– probably one of the three he had written three years earlier, in the summer of 1788. The orchestra for these concerts included the clarinettist brothers

Johann and Anton Stadler (the latter soon to be the first soloist in Mozart's Clarinet Concerto). So this may perhaps have been the occasion for which Mozart added parts for two clarinets to the second work of the 1788 trilogy, the Symphony No. 40 – or rather, being the perfectionist he was, rewrote his original oboe parts completely for oboes and clarinets. His first version, however, has survived and remains a valid alternative; indeed, it is preferred by some conductors for its openness and astringency. The wind section also contains a flute, a pair of bassoons, and a pair of horns: to allow himself a wider range of notes on the valveless natural instruments of the time, Mozart wrote for one horn in G, and one in B flat. There are no trumpets, which would have been unsuited to the key of G minor, and therefore no timpani. But the relatively small size of the orchestra does not prevent the symphony from making an extraordinary impact.

Much of this impact is related to Mozart's choice of key. The type of the 'G minor symphony' was well established in the last third of the eighteenth century, through works by, among others, the Mannheim-trained Franz Ignaz Beck, the Bohemian-born Antonio Rosetti, Haydn and Johann Christian Bach. It was intense in expression, with sharp contrasts of mood; full of wide melodic leaps, powerful chromatic harmony and urgent propulsive rhythmic figuration; inclined towards lean contrapuntal textures: the epitome, in fact, of musical 'storm and stress'. Mozart was aware of the associations of the key from childhood, as a startling and very orchestral-sounding G minor movement (K15p) in his 'London Notebook' of 1764–5 demonstrates. Later he returned to it in his Symphony No. 25, K183, and in the magnificent String Quintet, K516. The particular achievement of the Symphony No. 40, though, is to match the surface intensity of the 'G minor style' with an equal intensity of musical thought, so that a profound logic – analysed by more than one commentator in terms of serial technique – underlies and even determines the work's harshest and most outlandish harmonic progressions.

Another striking feature of the work is the way in which its dark mood is sustained virtually throughout the piece. The first movement takes its urgent but subdued opening melody through some startlingly unexpected keys in the central development section, and converts its major-key second-subject group into the minor in the recapitulation. The E flat major Andante is clouded by chromaticism as early as its second bar, and its development is dramatic in the extreme. Even the Minuet is starkly contrapuntal – although its Trio does offer for the first time a moment of serenity in G major. And the finale intensifies the mood of the first movement, striking out into even more distant tonal regions in the development section, and this time not just recapitulating a major-key second subject in the minor, but recasting it completely with an uncomfortable new angularity – after which the minor key is maintained grimly to the end, to complete the first genuinely tragic symphony.

© Anthony Burton

∾ Symphony No. 41 in C major, K551, 'Jupiter' (1788)

1 Allegro vivace
2 Andante cantabile
3 Minuet and Trio: Allegretto
4 Molto allegro

'Haydn, in one of his newest and finest symphonies in C major [No. 95], had a fugue as a final movement; Mozart did this too in his tremendous Symphony in C major, in which, as we all know, he pushed things a little far . . .' This assessment of the 'Jupiter' Symphony, written in 1798, seven years after Mozart's death, is not at all untypical of its time. Its author was Carl Friedrich Zelter, a respected composer who, like many musicians, was happy to acknowledge Mozart's supreme ability while at the same time judging his music to be unnecessarily complicated and abundant in melodic material.

Whether or not Zelter was correct in assuming universal familiarity with the deluge of themes contained in the 'Jupiter' Symphony has long been a subject for conjecture. There are no records of any performances of the work during Mozart's lifetime, nor of the other two symphonies (Nos 39 and 40) that make up his last great trilogy, composed during the summer of 1788, though there were certainly occasions on which they could have been performed. That the 'Jupiter' should have attracted the (admittedly qualified) admiration of musically knowledgeable listeners such as Zelter while making little public impression is typical of Mozart's predicament in the last years of his life.

Although the symphony is traditional enough in many of its points of departure, there is enough that is radical about it to explain Zelter's mixed response. C major was a key usually associated with music for public ceremony, and the first movement's stately opening suggests that this will be the prevailing mood here. But Mozart's art had by now become a more all-embracing one than that; as in his greatest operas, he is able to inhabit more than one world at once, and so it is with surprising naturalness that there eventually appears a jaunty little tune (characterised by repeated notes) borrowed from an aria he had composed for a comic opera.

The Andante cantabile is eloquent and gracefully melodic, yet interrupted by passionate outbursts and haunted by troubling woodwind colours; while the Minuet and Trio have the courtliness and poise one would expect of them, even though the former is dominated by a drooping chromatic line that culminates in a delicious woodwind passage towards the end.

The most celebrated music of this great symphony is reserved, however, for the last movement. A vital and superbly organic combination of sonata form and fugal procedures in which melodic ideas fly at us in an exhilarating flood of music, it eventually finds its way to a coda in which five of those ideas are thrown together in a passage of astounding contrapuntal bravado. One can well imagine that this was where Zelter drew the line – if not, what else could there have been for him but to break his quill and take up some other profession?

For many years this symphony was known in German-speaking countries, somewhat analytically, as 'the symphony with the fugal finale'. The nickname 'Jupiter' appears to have originated in England around 1820, and how much more expressive it seems of this work's lofty ambitions! For the 'Jupiter' is not simply the summation of its composer's symphonic art; it is the greatest of prophecies of the genre's unlimited potential.

© Lindsay Kemp

Carl Nielsen (1865–1931)

Recognition, especially outside his native Denmark, came late for Nielsen. Born on the island of Funen, he joined a military band as a trombonist, aged fourteen. In 1884 he entered the Copenhagen Conservatory for four years, before beginning a sixteen-year career as a violinist in the Royal Danish court orchestra. During this time the orchestra premiered his First Symphony (1894), and he composed both his operas, *Saul and David* (1902) and the folk comedy *Maskarade* (1906), one of his greatest successes. The mainstay of his output was his six symphonies, which grew out of Brahmsian classicism, but developed a progressive approach, especially to tonality, that bypassed Romantic ideals. He wrote concertos for violin, flute and clarinet, contributed to a revival of Danish national song, and wrote a small number of programmatic orchestral works, including the 'nature scene' *Pan and Syrinx* and the *Helios* overture (a hymn to the sun), and the cantata *Springtime on Funen*. His love of nature is also apparent in his autobiographical book *My Childhood on Funen*.

❧ Symphony No. 4, Op. 29, 'The Inextinguishable' (1914–16)

1   Allegro –
2   Poco allegretto –
3   Poco adagio quasi andante –
4   Allegro

On 3 May 1914, Carl Nielsen wrote in a state of high agitation to his wife:

> I have an idea for a new work, which has no programme but which should express what we understand by the life-urge or life-manifestation; that's to say: everything that

moves, that craves life, that can be called neither good nor evil, neither high nor low, neither great nor small, but simply: 'That which is life' or 'That which craves life' – I mean, no definite idea about anything 'grandiose' or 'fine and delicate' or about warm or cold (powerful maybe) but simply Life and Movement, but varied, very varied, but holding together, and as though always flowing, in one large movement, in a single stream. I need a word or a short title to say it all.

The word he was looking for was 'Inextinguishable'. But he was not to find it until he had completed the symphony nearly two years after that semi-coherent outburst of enthusiasm. His thoughts crystallised in a short preface to the score: 'With the title "The Inextinguishable" the composer has sought to indicate in one word what only music has the power to express in full: The Elemental Will of Life. Music is Life and, like it, inextinguishable.' And in 1920 Nielsen sent his Dutch composer–conductor friend Julius Röntgen an explanatory note which further clarified his intentions: 'If the whole world was destroyed, Nature would once again begin to beget new life and push forward with the strong and fine forces that are to be found in the very stuff of existence . . . These "inextinguishable" forces are what I have tried to represent.'

In Danish *Det uudslukkelige* is a neuter noun. So we should think of this not as 'The Inextinguishable Symphony', but rather as a symphony whose subject-matter is 'that which is inextinguishable', i.e. the Life Force, as Bernard Shaw put it, or *élan vital*, in a formulation popularised around the time of the symphony by the philosopher Henri Bergson.

Nielsen's previous symphonies had been steadily expanding their horizons, to the point where No. 3 (1911) celebrated a conglomeration of positive values – freedom, creative energy, oneness with nature and, in the finale, what Nielsen himself dubbed the 'healthy morale' of the ordinary working man – all under the umbrella title of 'Sinfonia espansiva'.

The Fourth Symphony is in essence a defence of those same

values. By the time of its composition, Europe was racked by a war in which Denmark remained neutral but which caused Nielsen to question the 'national feeling' he had previously regarded as wholesome. There were conflicts, too, in his personal life: his marriage, to the prominent sculptress Anne-Marie Brodersen, was entering a period of turmoil, brought about by the revelation of his infidelities; and on 30 May 1914 he resigned his position as Assistant Conductor at the Royal Opera in Copenhagen, thereby becoming a freelance musician for almost the first time in twenty years. For all these reasons Nielsen felt compelled to re-examine his values as a composer and human being, and in these respects the 'Inextinguishable' is a classic mid-life-crisis piece.

The Fourth Symphony's four movements are played without a break. The turbulence of the opening bars immediately suggests how much is here at stake, as strings and woodwind vie with one another, and brass and timpani strive to maintain law and order. When this subsides, a long-drawn clarinet theme in winding Sibelian thirds seems to come from another world ('not really like me', as Nielsen remarked). Rather than remaining merely a haven for escapist reverie, this theme proves highly adaptable, marking out its Darwinian fitness for eventual survival.

In the pastoral–idyllic slow movement, the woodwind behave as an idealised village band, not quite sure whether they should be playing two or three beats to the bar. The tensely dramatic third movement begins with a passionate accompanied recitative for the violins, soaring over timpani and lower strings – 'like an eagle on the wind', according to the composer. Succeeding contrasts between passionate declamation and hymn-like serenity are eventually swallowed up in a radiant, affirmatory climax.

In the finale, launched by a torrent of scales in the strings, the element of antagonism resurfaces. Two sets of timpani, spatially separated, battle it out with the rest of the orchestra, before the triumphant return of the first movement's Sibelian theme.

© David Fanning

∾ Symphony No. 5, Op. 50 (1920–2)

1 Tempo giusto – Adagio
2 Allegro – Presto – Andante poco tranquillo – Allegro
   (Tempo I)

'Our work is a continual protest against the thought of death and an appeal to and cry for life.' That was how the Danish composer Carl Nielsen summed up his artistic vision in 1909, just before he began work on his Third Symphony, 'Sinfonia espansiva'. Within a few years, the carnage of the First World War was to add a terrible new intensity to Nielsen's thoughts of death. Although Denmark was neutral during the 1914–18 war, Nielsen, like most Danes, was acutely sensitive to the activities of his country's powerful neighbour to the south. In his Fourth Symphony, he had managed to find a hopeful message: life – symbolised by the first movement's ardent second theme – eventually re-emerges through onslaughts from two sets of timpani. It is not an outright victory – rather, as Nielsen put it, a depiction of how 'life was, is, and always will be in struggle, conflict, procreation and destruction; and everything returns'.

By the time he came to write his Fifth Symphony, however, Nielsen's faith in life's indestructibility and the inevitability of its return had been profoundly shaken, as he wrote:

> It's as though the whole world is in dissolution. The feeling of nationhood which hitherto was considered something high and beautiful, has become like a spiritual syphilis which devours the brains and grins out through the empty eye sockets in senseless hate . . . It's so unlimited and meaningless that life doesn't seem worth it.

Another cause for Nielsen's new pessimism could be found closer to home. The reunion he longed for with his estranged wife Anne-Marie was still in doubt, and separation from her left him feeling rootless and deeply depressed. That may have left an imprint on the emotional tissue of the Fifth Symphony.

Sir Simon Rattle is surely right, however, to describe the Fifth as Nielsen's 'War Symphony'. As Nielsen made clear, the theme of resistance to evil was central. The idea behind the Fifth Symphony, he told a friend, was – as in No. 4 – 'the division of dark and light, the battle between evil and good'. But the musical depiction of evil had become more sharply focussed. For the first time in a symphony, Nielsen used a battery of unpitched percussion, including an unmistakably militaristic side-drum. This comes to the fore in a hair-raising passage at the climax of the first movement, in which the side-drummer is directed to improvise 'in his own tempo, as though determined at all costs to obstruct the music'. The side-drummer's wild, anarchic invasion of the orchestral texture is all the more shocking as it comes after music of almost Brahmsian melodic warmth and radiance – an invasion of 'senseless hate' in the midst of 'something high and beautiful'.

At first, Nielsen considered giving his Fifth Symphony a title: the innovative two-movement structure was to be summed up as 'Dreams and Deeds'. But that, he eventually conceded, was just one way of summing up what he felt all his music expressed in one way or another: 'resting forces in contrast to active ones'. Nielsen was surely right to drop that title: the rather romantic-sounding 'Dreams and Deeds' doesn't give much indication of the Fifth Symphony's unsettling, exhilarating power.

The symphony's opening seems strangely calm – this could be what Nielsen called 'resting forces'. Violas play a quietly oscillating minor third, a neutral background against which bassoons, horns, flutes, then first violins unfold long, wandering phrases, as though trying to define a theme. A pattering repeating rhythm on side-drum sounds a note of warning, then the mood changes abruptly. Above a strutting two-note figure (timpani, and cellos and basses pizzicato), violins sing out anguished phrases, interrupted by wailing, shrieking figures from clarinet and flute. Gradually a kind of calm is restored; then the tempo drops to Adagio and violas begin a long aspiring melody – as warm and centred as the previous music was restless and inhuman. Then the mood darkens, and the side-drum begins its crazed assault. Through all this the orchestra struggles to keep singing the Adagio melody (led by horns and trumpets). At last it seems that order and melody have prevailed over anarchy. A hush descends, and a clarinet delivers an elegiac cadenza; but the side-drum's rhythms, now in the distance, continue to disturb the stillness – a memory, or perhaps a reminder that evil too will return.

In contrast to the first movement, the second begins (Allegro) with an explosion of 'active forces'. Initially the mood seems wildly joyous, but struggles follow, and then the energy seems to dissipate – are we returning to the first movement's unsettling initial calm? Instead, there follows what the Nielsen expert David Fanning has called 'a fugue from Hell' (Presto), punctuated by the shrieking clarinet from the first movement. The fury finally exhausts itself, and a slower, quieter fugue (Andante poco tranquillo) searches for a way back to the light. At its height, the opening Allegro music erupts again, this time leading to a long, gripping crescendo with whooping octaves from horns and trumpets and pounding timpani. The 'cry for life' intensifies, building to a brief, but defiantly positive conclusion.

© Stephen Johnson

Sergey Prokofiev (1891–1953)

An *enfant terrible* in his earlier years, Prokofiev entered the St Petersburg Conservatory aged thirteen, creating a stir with his early taste for rhythmic energy and grating dissonance. A rich period around the time of the Revolution brought the lyrical First Violin Concerto and the 'Classical' Symphony, before a spell in the USA, where his opera *Love for Three Oranges* and the Third Piano Concerto were badly received. He went on to Paris, drawn to the epicentre of the avant-garde, before moving his family to the USSR in 1936. Adopting a more direct, lyrical style in line with prevailing socialist-realist ideals, he produced the ballet *Romeo and Juliet* and the children's tale *Peter and the Wolf* (both 1936), the film music for Eisenstein's *Alexander Nevsky* (1938) and *Ivan the Terrible* (1945), and the epic opera based on Tolstoy's *War and Peace* (1943). Despite his compliant efforts, Prokofiev was denounced by Communist officials in 1948 ('the unfeeling essence of his music is alien to our reality'), though he had managed to placate them by 1951, when he won the Stalin Prize.

✄ Symphony No. 1 in D major, 'Classical' (1917)

1 Allegro
2 Larghetto
3 Gavotta: Non troppo allegro
4 Finale: Molto vivace

The year 1917 was perhaps the most productive in Prokofiev's career. Revolutionary turmoil notwithstanding, he made a start on a new opera, *The Love for Three Oranges*, resumed work on a new piano concerto (his third), and completed a whole series of disparate compositions: two more piano sonatas, the choral invocation *Seven, They Are Seven*, a set of *Visions fugitives* for piano, a (first) violin concerto and this 'Classical' Symphony (his official No. 1). Prokofiev's work in this period, as so often, can seem like a perpetual zigzag between incompatible means and conflicting goals. The aggressive innovator who delighted to offend was also a traditionalist who hankered after simpler, cleaner melodies. And yet how many of these works have turned out to be masterpieces! Prokofiev was a consummate professional who could turn his hand to anything.

Deliberately out of kilter with the spirit of its age, the 'Classical' Symphony is so familiar that we are inclined to take it for granted. Like Ravel's *Le tombeau de Couperin*, it predates Stravinsky's neo-classical project, not that its own crystalline surfaces betray any hint of cerebral calculation behind the scenes. The work is a good deal more than pastiche: it is full of those harmonic sleights of hand and uninhibited, wide-ranging melodies which, by 1917, delineate an unmistakable creative profile.

Prokofiev, whose usual practice was to compose at the piano, here chose to do without it:

> It seemed to me that, had Haydn lived to our day, he would have retained his own style while accepting something of the new at the same time. This was the kind of symphony I wanted to write: a symphony in the classical style. And when I saw that my idea was starting to work, I called it the 'Classical' Symphony: in the first place because that was simpler, and secondly, for the fun of it – to 'tease the geese' – and in the secret hope that I would prove to be right if the symphony really did turn out to be a classic.

There are the traditional four movements. The first is conventional in design, aerated in texture and extraordinarily fresh and bracing in effect. Its opening theme is snappy and athletic; the second, defying gravity and logic with its seesawing leaps, is more balletic, harmonically indebted to the

Ballerina's and Moor's waltz from the third tableau of Stravinsky's *Petrushka*.

The exquisite theme of the second-movement Larghetto floats in unforgettably (molto dolce – 'very sweetly') on stratospheric violins; the intervening episodes are serenade-like in their hopping and strumming.

The famous Gavotta, later co-opted into Prokofiev's *Romeo and Juliet* ballet, is utterly characteristic of the composer's quirky way with a tune. Whether negotiating the pitfalls of sentimentality or simply avoiding the obvious, he will often push his melodic line into a harmonic frame which seems arbitrary or disconnected on the page yet actually produces the feeling that a theme has been refreshed. The gentle, deceptive mockery of this movement is capped by its pianissimo farewell – in the olden style, as it were.

To cap it all, the joyous finale is a 'classical' essay in the avoidance of minor chords, sometimes delicate, sometimes cheeky. It is hard to believe that this carefree music was composed by a Slav between Revolutions, even if its peculiar charm derives from Rimsky-Korsakov and the great Russian ballet tradition quite as much as from Mozart and Haydn.

David Gutman © BBC

∾ Symphony No. 5 in B flat major, Op. 100 (1944)

1 Andante
2 Allegro marcato
3 Adagio
4 Allegro giocoso

The mid-1930s were harsh years for the Russian people, years in which no one could feel truly safe from the long arm of Stalin's regime. The Soviet Composers' Union contributed stringent guidelines for creative work as early as 1933, just when Prokofiev – the émigré contemplating permanent return – was granted the use of a Moscow apartment. Ideally, in this brave new world of Socialist Realism, the musician was supposed to look at contemporary problems from the perspective of a Utopian future, portraying today's defects as positive forces that would actually serve to push society towards the ultimate goal of Socialism. What could it all mean? Many composers simply ran for cover, reduced to writing what most of their colleagues had been writing for years: second-rate Tchaikovsky, or music that was nothing in particular and therefore presumably could not offend the Party boss, music that could not be 'wrong'. Prokofiev's answer was a tactical retreat into a universal, lyrical but, above all, fresher kind of idiom. Party demands for 'simplicity' served to stimulate as well as to stifle and they often accorded with his own instincts, his genuine patriotism, his willingness to tackle any given task with professional efficiency.

If his return home was a means of realising his true nature, the fifth of his seven symphonies marks another culmination, 'completing as it were a long period of my works. I conceived it as a symphony of the greatness of the human spirit.' Much was expected of it in war-torn Moscow, where the pianist Sviatoslav Richter attended the premiere on 13 January 1945:

> I will never forget the first performance . . . on the eve of victory . . . When Prokofiev mounted the podium and silence set in, artillery salvos suddenly thundered. His baton was already raised. He waited, and until the cannon fire ceased, he didn't begin. There was something very significant, very symbolic in this. A sort of common borderline had come for everybody.

A work of evident stature, yet immediate in its appeal, the Fifth Symphony received near-universal acclaim. The Soviets revelled in its theatrical and nationalistic qualities, while Western critics perceived a rejection of dramatic or programmatic schemes.

In the Fifth Symphony, Prokofiev integrates his material as seldom before in his orchestral music. Rhetorical devices and rhythmic motifs apparently designed to move the action along turn out to be closely interrelated; subordinate ideas are developed rather than dropped. In short, the 'prodigal son' (to borrow the title of his 1929 ballet) had acquired the discipline to attempt a real symphony within the traditional four-movement plan.

Taking a leaf out of Shostakovich's book, Prokofiev's first movement is more Andante than Allegro, although the second subject, marked 'poco più mosso', is more flowing. Much of the dramatic excitement is here achieved by harmonic means and the mood is elevated, worlds away from the gratuitous kinkiness of the younger Prokofiev. The grandiose coda draws together spiritual and musical threads. Thematically, it is rooted in a comparatively minor figure from the first group whose connection with the first subject proper is now made plain. Harmonically, the final cadence telescopes both chromatic tensions and diatonic resolution in a triumphant burst of glory. Prokofiev's dense orchestration contributes to the monumental effect.

Exploiting material once earmarked for the ballet *Romeo and Juliet*, the scherzo is launched by the strings' insistent quaver ostinato: its music is hard-edged and precise and even hints at ragtime. An invigorating contrast is provided by the trio section, the bright-eyed quality enhanced by Prokofiev's characterful harmonic sleights of hand. The return of the scherzo is unexpectedly sinister and macabre, but then the movement as a whole recalls the demoniacal wit of the younger Prokofiev without lapsing into shallow balleticism.

The F major Adagio introduces its haunting melody over the kind of 'pulsing' accompaniment Prokofiev so often favoured. If the forthright simplicity of its rhetoric looks forward to later scores, the introduction to the Allegro giocoso finale looks back to the work's opening theme: 'the theme of man's grandeur and heroic strength', according to Israel Nestyev, Prokofiev's Soviet biographer – he at least detects no irony. Whatever the intention, the main Allegro theme takes off with abundant good humour and Prokofiev avoids both empty nobility and naive optimism in its working out. Simple exuberance generates a fierce motoric energy and the denouement is certainly exhilarating. But is there not also perhaps a crack in the self-confident façade? Just before the close, Prokofiev suddenly reduces the dynamic level as if to make us confront the compromised and fretful quality of the rejoicing.

On a personal level, things would never be the same. A few days after the triumphant premiere, the composer slipped, struck his head and suffered severe concussion. Rushed unconscious to hospital, his blood pressure elevated dangerously. For some months he seemed barely able to hold on and he never conducted an orchestra again. Post-war Soviet cultural policies probably did in the end undermine the quality of his creative work, yet, in the words of the Soviet writer Ilya Ehrenburg, 'he never lost heart, never gave up the fight, and he died young in spirit, uncompromising, true to himself to the end.'

© David Gutman

Sergey Rakhmaninov (1873–1943)

For most of his life, Rakhmaninov led a triple career as pianist, composer and conductor. He graduated from the Moscow Conservatory with his first opera, *Aleko*, and took to conducting after the disastrous premiere of his First Symphony in 1897 directed by Glazunov. The resulting three-year compositional silence was overcome by hypnosis, and Rakhmaninov soon wrote his highly successful Second Piano Concerto (1901). He made a lucrative tour of America in 1909 (for which he wrote his Third Piano Concerto), and after the Revolution in 1917 he lived in self-imposed exile, largely in the USA. His richly chromatic, broadly lyrical and unashamedly nostalgic style has found many critics, but has ensured his music's popularity among audiences. In addition to his three symphonies and two piano sonatas, he wrote two sets of *Études-tableaux* and *Préludes* for piano, a mighty Cello Sonata, three evocative symphonic poems and a rich setting of the Vespers (*All-Night Vigil*, 1915).

❧ Symphony No. 2 in E minor, Op. 27 (1906–7)

1 Largo – Allegro moderato
2 Allegro molto – Meno mosso – Tempo 1
3 Adagio
4 Allegro vivace – Adagio – Tempo precedente

Rakhmaninov was one of the most prodigiously gifted musicians who has ever lived. As a virtuoso pianist his reputation remains second to none; before leaving Russia in 1917 he was almost as famous a conductor as he was a pianist; and as a composer his legacy includes some of the most enduringly popular works of this century.

Yet he was chronically insecure. Whether or not it was

childhood experiences that left their mark – his father squandered the family fortune, his parents separated, his sister died of diphtheria – he seemed to experience a recurrent longing to be somewhere other than where he was. Amid the hurly-burly of Moscow he longed for the tranquillity of his relatives' estate six hundred miles to the east beyond the Volga, or to travel abroad to compose in peace. Yet during his twenty-five-year exile he pined for the native soil which he regarded as his muse. In his composing scarcely a single major project was completed without agonising self-doubts on the way; often in performance he would make cuts in his own music, apparently fearful of boring his audience.

Yet it is the fusion of that colossal talent and that chronic dissatisfaction that makes his music unique. For the nostalgia and vulnerability are universalised thanks to the creative will-power which embodies them in massive and coherent structures; and in the end they always have to give way to waves of triumphant energy. In this way Rakhmaninov's self-conquest becomes our own, and we emerge invigorated.

The process is most dramatically symbolised in his four great piano concertos. But it is every bit as clear in his three symphonies, of which the Second, running to some sixty minutes, is the most imposing. He composed it in 1906 and 1907, for the most part in Dresden where he had taken refuge from the political and professional strains of life in Russia. Its massive dimensions, like those of the Third Piano Concerto of 1908, are in part a statement about creative power.

Rakhmaninov's First Symphony of 1895 had been a celebrated fiasco. Feebly conducted by Glazunov and likened in César Cui's review to 'a programme symphony on the Seven Plagues of Egypt', it was destroyed by the composer (the score was reconstructed from orchestral parts discovered after his death). The depression and creative paralysis which ensued were lifted in equally celebrated fashion when the hypnotist Nikolay Dahl managed to restore Rakhmaninov's spirits, unlocking the Second Piano Concerto from his blocked psyche. Operatic projects were soon to follow, but the prospect of another symphony was daunting. Rakhmaninov had something to prove to himself and to the world. He would have to lay to rest the sad ghost of his First Symphony.

He did so by drawing on the full arsenal of his technique, synthesising Russian symphonic trends with the glamour of the Lisztian symphonic poem. From Tchaikovsky he developed a vein of lyrical self-absorption and an obsession with fate, from Rimsky-Korsakov the notion of impregnable academic solidity in large-scale form, and from Taneyev (to whom the symphony is dedicated) the intricacy of motivic unity and of counterpoint. To all of these he added his own genius for expanding simple harmonic progressions from within, until they cover huge spans of accumulating or dispersing tension. And he kept one inspired ploy in reserve for the finale, a ploy which makes this work unique in his output.

The symphony's long slow introduction could just as appropriately be the conclusion to a slow movement, reflecting on past events with elegiac sadness. Placed as it is here, it sets the emotional tone for the entire first movement as a kind of pulling-itself-together. Heavy-heartedness is experienced to the full, then drawn upwards towards determination and energy, and finally transfigured into acceptance. This happens both in the introduction itself and repeatedly in the main body of the movement. The melodic material is spun from the stepwise turning figure heard in the opening bars, with almost all the interest in the long harmonic progressions on which it rides. So unobtrusive is the main theme of the Allegro that it features hardly at all in the development section or even the recapitulation. Instead the middle of the movement draws mainly on the introduction. It builds up a huge storm, very much in the manner of Tchaikovsky's 'Pathétique', eventually abating with the return of the consoling second subject before the final summons to defiance.

The second-movement scherzo is a muscular affair, relaxing into one of Rakhmaninov's great string tunes; the latter is supported by modal harmonies inspired by his love for Slavonic church music, and yet again it is restrained in its predominant stepwise movement. In a quid pro quo for this unscheduled lyrical effusion the traditionally relaxed trio section is replaced by an aggressive fugato on the scherzo's opening violin phrase.

Two memorable ideas provide the scaffolding for the slow third movement. The burgeoning violins with their opening arpeggio ascent soon peter out, but the clarinet tune they spark off is one of the most glorious melodies in the symphonic repertoire. Once again it moves almost entirely by step. In between the two statements of these ideas is a prolonged meditation on the introduction to the first movement, building inexorably towards a radiant affirmation of the ascending arpeggio. Violins restate the clarinet tune, as they do in the Second Piano Concerto.

As if in celebration of the psychological growth experienced in the slow movement, the finale opens in ebullient mood. This will be a movement which settles all previous scores. Its first episode takes on some of the unfinished emotional business from the scherzo in a threatening quiet march soon disposed of by a return of the opening theme. Then it is time for the masterstroke. A massive string theme breaks the mould of stepwise movement and takes possession of musical space with confident arching lines over pulsating triplets in the wind and brass. There is more coming to terms with the past to be done in this movement, but it is this theme, in even more triumphant guise, that will return to crown the entire work.

© David Fanning

∾ Symphony No. 3 in A minor, Op. 44
(1935–6)

1 Lento – Allegro moderato
2 Adagio ma non troppo – Allegro vivace
3 Allegro

Rakhmaninov began to compose his Third Symphony in the summer of 1935, two years after he had produced the

Rhapsody on a Theme of Paganini. He completed the first two movements at the villa he had built on the shores of Lake Lucerne (opposite the Villa Triebschen, where Wagner had completed *Die Meistersinger*), and in which he and his family had preserved something of the atmosphere of pre-revolutionary Russia. He had to suspend work on the symphony during the following autumn and winter, which were spent in arduous concert tours in the United States (Rakhmaninov's main source of income since his move to the West in 1917), and it was only in June 1936 that he was able to return to Switzerland to write the symphony's last movement. It was performed in America the following November. The composer was present at the first two performances and wrote:

> It was played wonderfully. (The Philadelphia Orchestra – Stokowski conducting.) Both audience and critics responded sourly. Personally, I'm firmly convinced that this is a good work. But – sometimes the author is wrong, too! However, I maintain my opinion.

Rakhmaninov recorded the work himself with the Philadelphia Orchestra in 1939.

The Second Symphony was a product of Rakhmaninov's early thirties, when he was at the peak of his triple career as composer, pianist and conductor. It is in every sense a big and rich work, with its saturated harmonies, orchestral opulence and melodic luxuriance. The Third, written some thirty years later, springs from the same sources that nourished all Rakhmaninov's music, but leaves a very different impression. It is, surprisingly, scored for a slightly larger orchestra than the Second (the contrabassoon, harps and some percussion instruments are absent from the earlier work), but is about twenty minutes shorter in performance, and far more concise in almost every respect.

Those first audiences who were disconcerted by the Third Symphony seem to have had this reaction for two quite opposite reasons. Listeners who expected Rakhmaninov to have changed with the times, to have developed a tougher style more in tune with the harsher climate of the 1930s, were disappointed to hear what appeared to be the same gestures, the same procedures. Others, perhaps more sympathetic to the composer's style, were dismayed by what they heard as the work's acerbities. One of these listeners was the composer and pianist Nikolay Medtner; after the London premiere of the symphony he is said to have lain awake all night, tormented by the thought that his old friend Rakhmaninov had fallen victim to 'modernism'.

Both views misjudge the work, but understandably so. The Third Symphony is an elusive piece, in which few things are quite what they at first seem to be. Consider, for example, what is usually referred to as the 'motto-theme'. This theme, a chant-like oscillation of three notes, is heard at the very opening, in the watery, strangled tone colours of solo clarinet, muted horn, and high solo cello. It reappears in various guises at salient points throughout the symphony, but only in the big fugal development of the finale does its latent significance come to the surface. Fleetingly, easily missed, appear passages where the motto is clearly heard to be a variant of the *Dies irae* – that melodic tag which stalks through Rakhmaninov's music as a grim *memento mori*, and which for once had seemed to be absent from a major orchestral work.

The broad outline of the first movement is a deceptively classical sonata form with clearly articulated introduction, exposition, development, restatement and coda; but the form's very clarity throws into relief a number of expressive contradictions. The introduction is brief: an unadorned statement of the motto, immediately swept aside by an outburst for the full orchestra which will return only at the beginning of the finale.

After this outburst, the Allegro moderato's main theme, scored for oboes and bassoons over a rocking violin figure, must sound at first hesitant and frail. Its sharp scoring, irregular phrasing and modally inflected harmonies give it an unmistakably Russian character, and despite its initial diffidence, it is this theme that contains the motifs for much of the symphony's material. In the development section it is fragmented and invested with a distinctly bitter flavour, inevitably suggesting the composer's sense of desolation at the loss of his Russian past.

The second theme, launched by the cellos, is one of Rakhmaninov's memorable 'big tunes': vocally phrased, sensual, capable of endless extension. It seems to inhabit a different world from the first theme, although the two are in fact closely related. It is absent from the long development, but when it returns in the recapitulation its expected stability is undermined by modulations into remote keys. Only a violent wrench from D flat to E major at its climax allows it to slide back into A major for the delicately scored coda.

At the centre of the symphony lies a single two-in-one movement combining Adagio and Scherzo, and juxtaposing, as it were, the two opposite areas of the work's emotional territory. This movement, like the first, opens and closes with the motto theme. The Adagio represents Rakhmaninov at his most succulent, with a controlled flow of expressive melody rising by degrees to an impassioned climax. The Allegro vivace, in complete contrast, is brittle, quirky, full of unexpected twists and bizarre orchestral sonorities. When it has run its course the Adagio returns, but as a tenuous memory of itself; much abbreviated, it cannot rise to its former level of intensity but gently fades away in a retrospective haze.

This central movement can be seen as a sort of pivot around which the symphony turns. The moments of nostalgic lyricism are now past, and it is the toughness introduced by the scherzo which nourishes the finale. It is in some ways the most straightforward movement of the three, with its sharp rhythmic impetus and orchestral virtuosity. But reminiscences of earlier themes, as well as the fleeting references to the *Dies irae*, cast disturbing shadows across its features.

© Andrew Huth

Camille Saint-Saëns (1835–1921)

The classical simplicity of Saint-Saëns's music, and the fluency with which he produced it, belies his more overtly intellectual pursuits as a scholar, editor, student of archaeology and natural history, and writer of poems, plays and criticism. A prodigy of Mozartian facility (aged ten, he gave a concert in Paris which included piano concertos by Mozart and Beethoven) he studied at the Paris Conservatoire before becoming organist at La Madeleine in 1857. He taught piano at the École Niedermeyer, where Fauré was among his students. A predilection for travel, especially to North Africa, influenced a number of musical references, as in his first opera *La princesse jaune* (1871), the 'Egyptian' Piano Concerto (No. 5), Persian songs and the *Suite algérienne*. Of his thirteen operas, only *Samson et Dalila* is regularly staged. In a bid to preserve his reputation as a serious composer, Saint-Saëns banned the publication of his *Carnival of the Animals* (1886) until after his death.

∾ Symphony No. 3 in C minor, Op. 78, 'Organ Symphony' (1886)

1 Adagio – Allegro moderato –
2 Poco adagio
3 Allegro moderato – Presto –
4 Maestoso – Allegro – Più allegro – Molto allegro

Commissioned by the Philharmonic Society of London for 1886, Saint-Saëns's 'Organ Symphony' marked a climax in its composer's international career and became, along with César Franck's D minor Symphony, one of the twin pillars of the French symphonic tradition. Saint-Saëns had by then already seen the hard-won success of his biblical opera *Samson et Dalila*, and toured as pianist in his own concertos.

He had led a revival of the nation's instrumental and orchestral music following France's defeat in the Franco–Prussian War of 1870–71, and had fought against the dominance of opera in France and of Austro-German music everywhere else. He had written symphonies before, but not since his early twenties. Cometh the hour . . .

This symphony has had its belittlers ever since, mainly people who can't take a vivid, prolonged and grand noise. That was not how his contemporaries heard it. Even from Vincent d'Indy, the composer and teacher who put Franck rather than Saint-Saëns on a Beethoven-like pedestal, it drew respect if not total admiration. In his textbook on composition, he asserted that the (in)famous end of the finale was the best part of the work. He did not explain why. He did have plenty to say about one of the symphony's innovations: constantly evolving themes. Beethoven, in his final string quartets, began to unify the movements with subtly related material. Schubert, in his 'Wanderer' Fantasy for piano, experimented with themes that transform from one movement to the next. But it was Liszt who, in his tone poems and his Piano Sonata, made metamorphosis the main formal basis of entire works; and it was to Liszt's memory that Saint-Saëns dedicated his Third Symphony.

The seed from which it grows consists of two kernels of melody in the short introduction, and the quicker theme that follows. These elements crop up at varying paces throughout the first movement, and they generate themes in the remaining movements (four altogether, linked in pairs, which Saint-Saëns himself rather misleadingly presented as two 'parts'). The languid melody of the Poco adagio; the gruff scherzo and its sparkling trio; the chorale and fugue and the successive waves of acceleration towards the end – each is transformed out of the same germinal elements, giving the music a character of constant striving towards its definitive form.

One of the main agents of change is time. The first-movement theme has a swaying ambiguity of pulse that

Saint-Saëns exploits purposefully as the symphony proceeds and quite brilliantly at its climax, foreshortening the rhythmic cycle and stretching it, finally running two cycles simultaneously under the time signature 3/1 with the result that the music seems to start spinning in two dimensions, like a planet that rotates on its axis while tracing out a larger orbit. It's as subtle a metrical game as anything in music outside India, and perhaps accounts for D'Indy's admiration.

Just as striking is the symphony's orchestration, in which the organ part is not so much a solo as an extra dimension of tone colour, along with a piano. When these are in play, the music's sound is as original as its form, and once heard is not forgotten. At one extreme are the extraordinary final moments, in which the organ first acts like the pedal section of the orchestra and then amplifies the overtones of the timpani. At the other are passages of great refinement. These include the mix of plucked strings and organ chords that accompanies the return of the slow movement's melody, and the beguiling combination of divided strings and four-handed piano that plays the finale's chorale – an effect which so pleased Saint-Saëns that he immediately adapted it for the 'Aquarium' in *The Carnival of the Animals*.

© Robert Maycock

Franz Schubert (1797–1828)

It used to be for his six hundred songs that Schubert was remembered, but his symphonies and piano sonatas have enjoyed greater attention in more recent times. His gift for lyrical melody and poetic expression gave rise to the bedrock of the Lieder repertory. Along with dances, marches and other piano miniatures, these songs would be performed in social gatherings, or 'Schubertiades'. Born in Vienna, Schubert was taught by Salieri while a chorister at the imperial court chapel. He worked initially as a classroom teacher to appease his father, but left after two years. Following the success of two Rossinian overtures, he spent one summer as a music teacher at the country estate of Count Johann Karl Esterházy. His aspiration to break into opera remained unfulfilled after a handful of unsuccessful efforts. He contracted syphilis in 1822. The last years of his life brought the 'Great' C major Symphony (1825), the song cycle *Winterreise* (1827), and the three great late piano sonatas (1828).

✎ Symphony No. 5 in B flat major (1816)

1 Allegro
2 Andante con moto
3 Minuet and Trio: Allegro molto
4 Allegro vivace

The amateur orchestra that gave the first performance of the Symphony No. 5 in B flat in the autumn of 1816 played an important part in advancing Schubert's reputation. It was a representative cross-section of musical officials, merchants and professional men, with a leaven of professional musicians like the leader, Otto Hatwig, who was a member of the orchestra at the Burgtheater. The orchestra's origins went back to the weekly practices held in the Liechtental schoolhouse during Schubert's schooldays. By 1816, however, it could muster twenty or more strings, woodwind, horns, trumpets and drums, and was able to explore the whole field of the classical symphony, including the first two symphonies of Beethoven. Schubert himself played viola, and his brother Ferdinand violin. The Fifth Symphony seems to have been written specially for it, and the work might stand as a kind of memorial to the resourceful world of private music-making in which Schubert grew up, and to which his genius was uniquely attuned. Though it was known at least in the Schubert circle in his lifetime, the symphony had to wait a long time for recognition. The first performance in England, inspired by George Grove and August Manns, took place on 1 February 1873.

The Fifth is the shortest of all Schubert's symphonies, the sunniest and the most wittily contrapuntal. The texture is light (there are no clarinets, trumpets or drums), the dynamic level is low, rarely rising above mezzo forte, there are no grand gestures, no slow introduction even. The cheeky five-note theme which enters unceremoniously at bar 5, marked pianissimo, is handled with assured invention, and neatly complemented by the lyrical second subject. The main theme of the Andante con moto, not perhaps very remarkable in itself, reveals unexpected depths as Schubert's mastery of melodic and harmonic elaboration gets to work on it; the conversations between strings and woodwind in the remote keys of C flat and G flat are splendid examples of his power to move the listener by the simplest means. The Minuet has the rhythmic drive of a true scherzo, while the Allegro vivace finale, based on one of Schubert's trotting four-quavers-in-a-bar tunes, is full of vivacity.

Like some other instrumental works of 1816 – the three piano and violin sonatas of March and April, for instance – the symphony achieves a classical consistency of style and formal perfection. It is the spirit of Mozart which broods over it, though the style and orchestration are Schubert's. In this, the last of his so-called 'schoolhouse symphonies', he reaches a kind of first-stage maturity, producing a work which is self-contained and self-consistent in Mozart's manner, yet full of its own Schubertian charm.

© John Reed

∾ Symphony No. 8 in B minor, 'Unfinished' (1822)

1 Allegro moderato
2 Andante con moto

Schubert wrote not one unfinished symphony but several: there are half a dozen surviving drafts or sets of sketches for incomplete symphonic projects, stretching from his teens to the very last weeks of his life. Paradoxically, the work known as the 'Unfinished' is so called because it is more finished than the other attempts, and thus capable of being performed. Schubert composed its first two movements in Vienna in October and November 1822, first in a two-stave score and then in a complete fair copy. He went on to draft a scherzo and trio on two staves, and even began writing an orchestral score of the scherzo; but both drafts peter out. Of the finale, no traces remain – unless it was used (or, perhaps, sketches for it were reworked) for the first Entr'acte in the incidental music for the play *Rosamunde*, which Schubert put together hastily in the last months of 1823. This piece is in the key of the Symphony, B minor, is scored for exactly the same orchestra, and is on a symphonic scale which seems to transcend its theatrical context.

In any case, Schubert seems never to have returned to the work. Late in 1823, he gave the score of the two completed movements to his friend Josef Hüttenbrenner. He probably intended that it should be passed to the Styrian Musical Society, in which Josef's brother Anselm was a leading light, as a token of gratitude for the Diploma of Honour which the Society had recently awarded to Schubert. Instead, the Hüttenbrenner brothers kept the score for many years, until in 1865 the conductor Johann Herbeck managed to get hold of it, and gave its first performance in Vienna.

But why did Schubert leave the symphony unfinished? We can dismiss the anachronistic idea that he felt it was complete as it was: however despondent he may have been at the thought of matching the high quality of the finished portion, he could never have considered a work of two movements in different keys as a completed symphony. Initially, it seems, he gave up work on the piece because he fell ill, with the first incidence of the syphilis which was to blight the remainder of his life and eventually cut it short. Then, when he made a temporary recovery, he urgently needed to concentrate on theatrical projects, in particular the opera *Fierrabras*. Perhaps, too, he felt unwilling to re-engage with a piece which reminded him of an especially painful time – which might explain why he gave away the score.

And there may be another reason. Schubert had begun the work with the intention of writing a full-scale symphony for public performance, as opposed to the private gatherings for which his first six symphonies had been composed. This intention is clear from the scoring, which includes a full woodwind section, trumpets and timpani as well as horns, and three trombones. But the music itself is so personal, even intimate, in its nature that it could hardly have been expected to receive a sympathetic hearing at any public concert of the time. Schubert may well have felt it would be a waste of effort to continue working on a piece which had no potential performers and no potential audience – though he must have hoped that his completed movements would one day find both.

One indication of the unusual nature of the 'Unfinished' Symphony is that all its principal themes, in both expositions and recapitulations, are marked pianissimo. In the first movement, there are three main ideas: the opening eight-bar theme on cellos and basses, unaccompanied – an unprecedented way of starting a symphonic Allegro; the ensuing melody for oboe and clarinet in unison; and the strings' major-key second subject. (The latter two themes are both preceded by their accompanying figuration, as if in a song – Schubert's melodic inspiration in this piece is essentially lyrical.) Although these themes are introduced quietly, there are nevertheless sharp stabs of dynamic contrast in the exposition, and in the development section the dynamic level rises to a furious, sustained fortissimo. This development section is dominated by the opening cello and bass theme; not surprisingly, this idea is then omitted from the beginning of the recapitulation; but it returns in the coda, to round off one of Schubert's most satisfying sonata structures.

The E major Andante con moto is another sonata movement, with two main ideas, the first principally for the strings, the second a long minor-key melody on solo clarinet (oboe in the recapitulation), which is remarkable for its unstable off-beat accompaniment and its equally unstable tonality. Here the dynamic contrast occurs not in the development section, which is a short, gentle exploration of the possibilities of the second subject, but in the outbursts for full orchestra which follow the statements of the two main ideas, to brutal, almost parodistic effect. All traces of these are expunged, however, by the coda, based on the first subject, which ends in a mood of almost unearthly serenity.

Anthony Burton © BBC

❧ Symphony No. 9 in C major, 'Great' (1825–6)

1 Andante – Allegro ma non troppo
2 Andante con moto
3 Scherzo and Trio: Allegro vivace
4 Allegro vivace

For many years it was thought that Schubert wrote his 'Great' C major Symphony in the last year of his life. It lay ignored, the story went, until Schumann rescued the score and persuaded Mendelssohn to conduct the symphony in Leipzig.

The truth is a little less romantic. Schubert wrote the symphony in 1825–6 and sent it to the Philharmonic Society (Gesellschaft der Musikfreunde) in Vienna with a suitable dedication. They acknowledged it with a token payment of 100 florins, organised the copying of the orchestral parts, and gave the work a run-through rehearsal, so Schubert did at least have the chance to hear roughly how it sounded.

Long symphonic works were often broken up for performance in the nineteenth century, and the first proper performance of any part of this symphony was of the finale only, in Vienna in 1836. Mendelssohn conducted all four movements, in Leipzig, in 1839 – an occasion that Schumann memorialised in a famous article, praising Schubert's 'heavenly length'. It also spurred him on to write his own symphonies. For some time there was continued resistance to Schubert's symphony from players, particularly string-players, who found it tiring and monotonous, and the symphony didn't win a secure place in the repertory until later in the century.

After composing his Sixth Symphony, also in C major (though a much breezier, lighter work than the 'Great'), Schubert made three attempts at symphonies that he never completed – one of them was the famous 'Unfinished' in B minor. In 1828 he made sketches for yet another symphony. So the 'Great' C major – described variously and with equal justification as No. 7, No. 8 or No. 9 – was not Schubert's 'final word' at all. Nor has it any of the disturbing darker moods of later works such as the String Quintet and last three piano sonatas. It does have their breadth, but it also has an unclouded spirit of optimism and a radiant sense of well-being and vigour. It's very much outdoor music, with a strong rhythmic impulse and an immense sense of confidence.

Conductors have often taken the 'slow' introduction (though Andante does not actually mean slow) at a gentle amble, as if the work opened in a romantic daydream before waking up abruptly. Some accelerate into the Allegro, though there's nothing in Schubert's score that tells them to do so. After hearing Mendelssohn's performance, Schumann said he was aware of no change of tempo at that point, but felt 'suddenly, without knowing how, we have arrived'. In fact, Schubert's introduction is marked 'alla breve' – with two main beats to a bar, not four as many faulty editions have printed – so he could not have meant it to be as slow as many conductors have thought; it is also thematically integrated with the Allegro, not only when the woodwind mark its theme out, complete, in the coda but, more significantly, because its second bar is used as a building block throughout the movement: the trombones give it a sense of stern purpose quite early on.

There is no real slow music in the symphony at all, for the second movement sets out at a brisk walk, the oboe introducing a tune that's simply begging to be whistled. The easygoing mood soon turns into grand emphasis, impersonal and just, while the second main theme is serene, mingled with the merest hint of sweet melancholy.

Very often, a scherzo is the shortest movement in a symphony. Schubert's is vast, and its vigorous drive is counterbalanced by swinging melody. The central Trio section, far from providing comfortable relaxation in lighter instrumentation, sails as on the full swell of the sea, the chorus of woodwind borne upon rocking strings.

The finale opens as it means to go on: with a vigorous upbeat. The movement is one of the most astonishing, apparently effortless, feats of sustained energy in music. Whether expressed in 'diddle-de-dum' patterns, or bouncing dotted rhythms, the galloping motion never loses its force, even when the music cruises, powered by its accumulated momentum. One of the suaver tunes – clarinets launch the central part of the movement with it – recalls one of Schubert's *Military Marches* for piano duet. Twice the orchestral forces seem on the point of disappearing in the distance, only to rally for a fresh onslaught. Yet this isn't a battle, and Schubert bypasses struggle altogether. What he achieves is a sense of endless vistas and the joyous freedom to explore them.

© Adrian Jack

Robert Schumann (1810–56)

After studying Law in Leipzig, Schumann intended to embark upon a career as a pianist, but an injury to his right hand compelled him to focus his energies on composition. During the 1830s he concentrated on works for the piano: largely character pieces, often literary-inspired, such as the *Papillons* (1831), *Carnaval* (1835) and *Kinderszenen* (1838). He founded the influential *Neue Zeitschrift für Musik* in 1834 and by the end of 1835 was in love with Clara Wieck, daughter of his piano teacher, Friedrich Wieck. The year of his marriage to Clara, 1840, saw a blossoming of song composition, including the cycles *Dichterliebe* and *Frauenliebe und -leben*, and the two sets of *Liederkreise*. Encouraged by Clara to explore larger forms, he wrote four symphonies, the concertos for piano (1845) and cello (1850) and the opera *Genoveva* (1852). In the 1840s his mental health declined; after an unsuccessful suicide attempt, he was admitted in 1854 to an asylum near Bonn, where he remained until his death.

∾ Symphony No. 1 in B flat major, Op. 38, 'Spring' (1841)

1 Andante un poco maestoso – Allegro molto vivace
2 Larghetto
3 Scherzo with two Trios: Molto vivace – Molto più vivace
4 Allegro animato e grazioso

The years that immediately followed Schumann's marriage saw a concentration on the symphony. Although he had composed a work in G minor at the age of twenty-two, this was put to one side and remained unpublished until 1972: for all its charm, it is not a mature symphony to set with the cycle of four that are among his finest works.

It took Schumann just four days in January 1841 to sketch

the B flat Symphony, Op. 38; it was scored a few weeks later, and given its first performance under Mendelssohn on 31 March. In a letter to his friend Wilhelm Taubert, who was due to conduct the work, Schumann later referred to the emotions that had possessed him when writing it. The inspiration had been a poem by Adolf Böttger, an author of verse romances, which ends with the line '*Im Tale zieht der Frühling auf*' (In the valley spring is approaching); the line fits the rhythm of the opening horn and trumpet fanfare. Schumann implored his friend:

> Try to inspire the orchestra with some of the spring longing I felt when writing the symphony. At the start, I should like the trumpets to sound as if from on high, like a call to awaken. In what follows in the introduction, there could be a suggestion of everything growing green, even of a butterfly taking wing, and in the following Allegro there's the gradual gathering of everything to do with spring.

The first movement was originally entitled 'Frühlingsbeginn' (The Beginning of Spring); the others were to be 'Abend' (Evening), 'Frohe Gespielen' (Cheerful Playfellows) and 'Voller Frühling' (Spring at its Height). Schumann later deleted these titles, however, as he preferred the work to be judged purely as a symphony, not a set of mood pieces, and he declared that he had in any case added them after finishing the music.

Whether or not the opening brass theme derives from Böttger's spring poem, it provides the forward thrust of the introduction, which gathers pace with inexorable force until the music bursts into the Allegro, with the theme now presented as the first subject and a brief contrasting second subject on woodwind. Certainly the opening theme is seldom absent, suggesting that a strong poetic idea is motivating the music, however logical the musical argument.

The slow movement is a reminder of Schumann's genius as a song composer; the rich depth of its orchestration shows how carefully he could plan his textures as part of his musical invention. Near the end, the trombones sound a new theme, which proves to be that of the ensuing Scherzo. The Scherzo itself is a powerful movement with two contrasting Trios, one march-like, the other dance-like.

The Allegro finale is again in sonata form, with a grandiose introduction leading to a noble first theme; the second is a version of the eighth of Schumann's *Kreisleriana* piano pieces (where it occurs, 'fast and playful', in the same key, G minor). This is the substance of a vigorous movement that finds room for cadenzas by the horns and a flute before driving to an exuberant finish.

© John Warrack

∾ Symphony No. 2 in C major, Op. 61
(1845–6)

1   Sostenuto assai – Allegro, ma non troppo
2   Scherzo with two Trios: Allegro vivace
3   Adagio espressivo
4   Allegro molto vivace

Lacking the picturesque elements of his First ('Spring') and Third ('Rhenish') symphonies, the formal innovations of the Fourth, or themes designed for instant memorability rather than intricate development, Schumann's Symphony No. 2 has never been his most popular. Yet it has never lacked admirers – Havergal Brian, for one, claimed it as the composer's 'most complete vision of the orchestra' – and it contains music of such power, formal decisiveness and character that it must be accounted one of the masterpieces of nineteenth-century symphonism.

Schumann wrote it during a long period of illness – the recurrent nervous exhaustion that some years later was to shade over into mental instability. He sketched it rapidly in December 1845, but took most of the next year to complete the orchestral score. Indeed, he felt the symphony symbolised his attempt to overcome physical and mental dejection, and the outer movements especially conform to the emotional pattern of struggle that finally issues in victory. This scheme inevitably evokes the example of Beethoven, and the Second is in many ways Schumann's most Beethovenian symphony – not least in its close-knit motivic working; but the archetypal plainness of its themes and the tremendous rhythmic energy of its fast movements may reflect the influence of Schubert's 'Great' C major Symphony (which Schumann had rediscovered and persuaded Mendelssohn to revive in 1839) as much as any of Beethoven's.

The first movement's impressive introduction simultaneously presents two elements: a brooding, undulating string theme and a starkly simple tonic–dominant fanfare in the brass. This latter idea, like a call to arms, is to be a motto theme for the entire symphony. The tempo quickens, and fragmentary anticipations of later ideas are heard along with the motto theme in a rhetorical build-up on full orchestra. This subsides, still increasing in pace, and the main Allegro bursts in. The first movement proper proves to be a concise, hard-driven sonata design with no real second subject; the principal subject, however, contains three main ideas, most noticeably the convulsive, insistent dotted-rhythm tune which begins it. Although the customary divisions of sonata form are clearly evident (with an exciting transition to the recapitulation), Schumann develops his ideas throughout in a remarkably organic display of motivic evolution.

A fiery Scherzo follows, full of quirky, capricious humour. If its running patter of violin semiquavers recalls Mendelssohn's scherzos, or its formal layout with two Trios resembles Beethoven, or if the Trios themselves seem to contain pre-echoes of Brahms, the piece as a whole is vintage Schumann, and as individual a symphonic movement as ever came out of the nineteenth century. By the end it has developed into a scintillating moto perpetuo, crowned in its final bars by the reappearance of the motto theme.

The C minor Adagio espressivo is an invention of considerable pathos, delicately scored and almost improvisatory in effect, although it is in fact very tightly organised. The cantabile main theme gives rise to a miniature three-part form whose central section is concerned with horn calls and arpeggios before the plaintive tune returns, elaborated by florid decoration and trills. A short fugato episode (deriving from the arpeggio figures) intervenes, and then the three-part form is repeated in more glowing colours, eventually attaining the major key.

An upward scalic flourish launches the finale in determinedly festive mood, soon passing into an ebullient march (whose persistent dotted rhythms act as a reminder of the first movement's main subject), treated with virtuoso orchestral skill. If this seems over-obvious finale planning, the movement evolves into one of Schumann's most original symphonic structures. Along with the march goes a subsidiary theme that is a major-key variation of the slow movement's main tune, and these materials are vigorously worked together in a highly compressed combination of development and recapitulation. The mood, however, darkens: the theme derived from the slow movement starts appearing in plangent inversion, and the tonality veers towards C minor. Imposing a semblance of peace, Schumann closes the section quietly on a succession of expectant triads.

He has in a very short time traversed a whole sonata movement except for its coda: yet the finale is only half over. A new, calmly lyrical theme strikes in (it derives ultimately from Beethoven's song cycle *An die ferne Geliebte*, 'To the Distant Beloved') and, in combination with previously heard elements (except the march, whose too-easy optimism never appears again), initiates a completely fresh development section. This grows increasingly dramatic, but eventually the music wins through to the major key; and in the real coda the lyrical melody and the motto theme combine triumphantly in a blaze of C major splendour.

© Malcolm MacDonald

∾ Symphony No. 3 in E flat major, Op. 97, 'Rhenish' (1850)

1 Lebhaft [Lively]
2 Scherzo: Sehr mässig [Very moderately]
3 Nicht schnell [Not fast]
4 Feierlich [Solemn]
5 Lebhaft [Lively]

By 1850 Robert and Clara Schumann had been married for ten years. After the unbearable tension of their unconventional courtship, the triumph of their union against her father's opposition, and an ecstatic honeymoon period which unleashed a flood of artistic creativity, the marriage – as even the most passionate of love matches is apt to do – had settled down to a more prosaic level, and had thrown up a few problems for both parties. Schumann's fragile ego had been badly dented by his wife's continuing success as a concert pianist, which all too often eclipsed his own renown as a composer – and he resented her frequent absences on concert tours; while she found practising difficult when he needed peace to compose, quite apart from coping with the exhaustion of almost continual pregnancy. Always prone to fits of severe depression, Schumann suffered several nervous breakdowns, which impacted badly on his career first as a professor at the Leipzig Conservatory, and latterly as a conductor at Dresden (where he held no official position, and had few friends or supporters). Life was made no easier by his technical shortcomings as a conductor, which often led to difficulties between him and the orchestras he attempted to direct.

It must have been with some relief then, that late in 1849, Schumann received an invitation to succeed Ferdinand Hiller as municipal music director at Düsseldorf. With some misgivings (since he had heard that the orchestra was poor) Schumann accepted the post in early April 1850, and took up residence with his ever-expanding family at the beginning of September.

Düsseldorf put on a gratifyingly warm reception for the Schumanns. They were greeted by Hiller, the retiring director, and other prominent musicians; entertained by a serenade from the *Liedertafel* (local glee club), and, a couple of days later, by a concert of Schumann's works, an official dinner, and a ball (which Robert and Clara were both too tired to attend). Schumann was still unwell from the upheaval of moving and distressed by the uncongenial atmosphere of their temporary apartment, which was cramped and noisy. Nevertheless, by the end of the month he had recovered sufficiently to enjoy a visit with Clara to Cologne, where they were particularly impressed by the magnificent Gothic cathedral. There, on 30 September, they attended a spectacular ceremony at which Archbishop Geissel of Cologne was elevated to the cardinalate.

By mid-October Schumann was feeling much better, and had started composing again. He began the Cello Concerto on 10 October, and completed it just a fortnight later. On the same day he conducted the first of the season's series of ten subscription concerts; the orchestra played well, and Clara was a great success as soloist. On 6 February 1851, at one of these concerts, Schumann introduced his own latest symphony, in E flat. It was to be his last – the one known as No. 4, in D minor, had been written in 1841, and was revised a decade later.

At the time of his marriage, Schumann's reputation was primarily that of a miniaturist – a fine craftsman of songs and piano music. Subsequently, under Clara's encouragement, he had begun to try his hand at the larger musical forms – orchestral music, and even opera – with varying degrees of success. By 1850 he had completed three symphonies, several overtures, the A minor Piano Concerto, the *Konzertstück* for four horns and orchestra, and the *Introduction and Allegro Appassionato*.

In several cases Schumann had attempted to cope with large-scale structures by experimenting with devices for structural unification, including motto themes and cyclic form. The E flat symphony, however, does not press the point. Instead Schumann took the opportunity of paying homage to his new home in the heart of the Rhineland by portraying, in a series of five contrasted tableaux, various aspects of local scenery, history and folklore. In this he was perhaps inspired by the programmatic nature of Beethoven's 'Pastoral' Symphony, while the symphony's epic nature is clearly derived from the same composer's 'Eroica', whose key it shares.

Although the E flat symphony was published without a title, Schumann himself referred to it as the 'Rhenish', and the name has stuck. The most overtly programmatic movements are the second and fourth, which both originally carried subtitles: the second was inscribed 'Morning on the Rhine' and the fourth 'In the manner of an Accompaniment to a Solemn Ceremony'– a clear reference to the archiepiscopal enthronement the Schumanns had witnessed in Cologne Cathedral in September 1850.

The 'Rhenish' is Schumann's only symphony that does not begin with a slow introduction providing the thematic kernel of the work. Instead the opening movement plunges straight into a long, majestic theme that is forcefully developed along Beethovenian lines, but with one notable Schumann fingerprint – the presentation of the second subject in the relative minor before it reappears in the expected dominant.

The second movement is a moderately paced, rustic-sounding scherzo, evoking the kind of peasant dance so beloved of German Romantics. The trio section is treated more as the second subject of a sonata form, rather than as an individual section.

The third movement is an intimate intermezzo in Romanze style; this is followed by the famous 'cathedral' evocation, marked 'Feierlich'. Here Schumann drew on his study of Bach's contrapuntal techniques to underline the religious associations – in a stroke of inspiration – with the sombre main theme presented on dark-hued trombones.

In contrast, the finale returns us to the bright sunshine outside: this is a rather large-scale movement of driving energy, whose coda attempts to draw together the threads of some of the previous themes of the symphony.

Barely a month after the premiere, relationships between Schumann and the Düsseldorf orchestra had become strained, and before another year had passed he had begun to suffer the first physical and mental symptoms of his fatal decline. But the 'Rhenish' Symphony – the product of his first optimistic months in his new post – remains as one of his finest orchestral works.

© Wendy Thompson

∾ Symphony No. 4 in D minor, Op. 120 (1841, rev. 1851)

1   Ziemlich langsam [Rather slow] – Lebhaft [Lively] –
2   Romanze: Ziemlich langsam [Rather slow] –
3   Scherzo and Trio: Lebhaft [Lively] –
4   Langsam [Slow] – Lebhaft [Lively]

On 1 September 1841 Clara Schumann gave birth to a baby girl – the Schumanns' first child, Marie. Schumann was delighted with the new arrival, writing to his mother-in-law of 'great rejoicing in our house'. Clara was equally delighted when, less than a fortnight later, on her own birthday, her husband presented her with the score of his second symphony, in D minor. Clara had actively encouraged Robert to turn his attention from the small-scale forms – mainly songs – that had preoccupied him during the previous year of their marriage, and to concentrate instead on orchestral music. Such was her influence that within the space of a few months he had completed a Symphony in B flat (the 'Spring') which was performed at the end of March 1841, followed by the *Overture, Scherzo and Finale* in May and, in the same month, the Fantasie in A minor for piano and orchestra (later expanded to become the Piano Concerto).

Schumann then immediately began work on another symphony, his second, finishing it in just over three months.

Although the Schumanns would have been pleased enough to stay at home with their new daughter during the autumn of 1841, Clara was invited to play in Weimar and Leipzig, and when performances of Robert's music were guaranteed into the bargain, they accepted. The new symphony was premiered in Leipzig on 6 December by the Gewandhaus Orchestra. Unfortunately Mendelssohn, who was to have conducted, withdrew, and the performance was unsatisfactory. It was about as well received by the audience as the arrival of Marie had been by her grandfather, the irascible Friedrich Wieck, who must have viewed the baby as the final cementation of his beloved daughter's unsuitable marriage.

Shocked by the symphony's poor reception, Schumann withdrew the work, and it lay untouched for a decade. In the meantime his self-confidence as a symphonic composer had evaporated, and he wrote only two more symphonies, including the E flat (the 'Rhenish'), which was completed in 1850. In that year the Schumanns moved from Dresden to Düsseldorf, where Robert took up the post of municipal music director. The appointment was to prove disastrous: conducting was not his forte, and he was beginning to suffer from the aural and mental disorders of his terminal disease (now generally thought to have been tertiary syphilis). Yet, although his early enthusiasm for the new job had largely waned by the end of 1851, he summoned up enough energy to revise the abandoned symphony in December of that year.

Schumann at first wanted to call the revised piece 'Symphonistische Fantasie' (Symphonic Fantasy), but shortly before the first performance on 30 December 1852 he changed the title back to 'Symphony', giving it the number 4. Briefly, the revision consisted of a few improvements to the structure and notation of the piece – slight extensions and contractions of phrases (mostly in the first and last movements); the tightening of the overall structure, involving the running together of all four movements (a relative innovation); revision of passages to clarify thematic links between the movements; translation of tempo indications from Italian into German; the halving of note values in the outer movements to double the length of each bar, presumably in an attempt to speed up the tempo in performance; and a complete overhaul of the scoring. Schumann was pleased with the result. 'I have orchestrated the symphony afresh altogether,' he wrote proudly to the Dutch conductor Johannes Verhulst five days after its successful performance at the Lower Rhine Music Festival in May 1853, 'and it is certainly better and more effective than it used to be.'

Schumann's revision of the orchestration has, however, generally been considered unfortunate. He may not have been the Cézanne of the orchestral palette, but his earlier works show that he was far from incompetent: the 1841 version of the symphony demonstrates an admirable lucidity of scoring. Sadly, most of his technique was developed subsequently through his practical experience as a conductor. The violinist Joseph Joachim, who often had the thankless task of leading for Schumann, said acidly that he 'never could conduct'. 'At a performance of one of his symphonies', Joachim recalled, 'he stood dreamily with raised baton, all the players ready, and not knowing when to begin.' Rather than risk an instrument not coming in on cue (partly owing to his own faulty conducting technique) Schumann chose to play safe by doubling the important parts to such an extent that the entire orchestra played all the time. It is also possible that the tinnitus that afflicted him in his later years literally prevented him from hearing what he was doing.

Despite these criticisms, Schumann's Fourth Symphony has been described as a 'landmark in the history of the symphony'. Although Beethoven's Fifth is clearly its starting point, Schumann here introduced revolutionary structural devices that were to influence the future course of the form. It is one of the earliest successful cyclic symphonies. Not only is it intended to be played without a break, but all four movements are inextricably linked by a subtle process of thematic transformation later taken up in the symphonies and tone poems of Liszt, Tchaikovsky, Sibelius, Franck and Elgar.

Schumann may have borrowed from Berlioz the idea of presenting the basic motivic material of the whole work in the slow introduction to the first movement. The first of these motifs – a triplet stepwise figure heard immediately after the opening chord (on second violins, violas and bassoons) – provides (in inverted form) the material of the third-movement Scherzo, while the second – a rising arpeggio figure followed by a turn (which originally appears on first violins, punctuated by woodwind chords) – dominates the more or less monothematic first movement, and goes on to permeate the entire structure in one form or another.

The enchanting A minor second-movement Romanze, offering a moment of repose from the intense rhythmic drive of the other three movements, was barely touched at all in the revision. In 1841 Schumann wrote in his diary: 'My next symphony [the D minor] will be called "Clara" and in it I will paint her picture with flutes and oboes and harps.' Instead, she is perhaps here embodied firstly in an oboe and cello tune, but more certainly in the exquisitely graceful violin solo of the luminous D major central section.

This shapely theme itself returns in altered form in the third movement to temper the Trio section of the powerful Beethovenian Scherzo, characterised by driving cross-rhythms and sudden sforzandos; and its return and gradual disintegration forms a bridge passage to the brass chorale that prefaces the assertive finale.

© Wendy Thompson

Dmitry Shostakovich (1906–75)

Shostakovich won early fame as a pianist and composer at the Petrograd Conservatory, graduating with his First Symphony (1925). His modernist tendencies were halted by Stalin's socialist policy on the arts, and following the damning *Pravda* editorial in 1936 on his opera *Lady Macbeth of Mtsensk*, Shostakovich offered his Fifth Symphony ('A Soviet Artist's creative reply to just criticism') as a rehabilitation piece. He was condemned again (along with Prokofiev) in 1948, and for five years until Stalin's death published only patriotic cantatas and small-scale works. But he continued to compose, and completed fifteen symphonies, fifteen string quartets, six concertos (two each for piano, violin and cello), and scores for around thirty films. His final works – such as the last two symphonies, the last four string quartets and the Viola Sonata – are characterised by their sparse textures and their deep intensity and gravity.

∿ Symphony No. 1 in F minor, Op. 10 (1923–5)

1 Allegretto – Allegro non troppo
2 Allegro
3 Lento
4 Allegro molto – Lento – Allegro molto

The First Symphony of Shostakovich represents perhaps the most precociously brilliant symphonic debut in the history of music. Shostakovich had begun to sketch the work on 1 July 1923, when he was not yet seventeen. Then came the death of Lenin on 21 January 1924, which fired the young composer to attempt a symphony dedicated to the memory of the great Revolutionary leader, but the project was soon abandoned as lying beyond his powers. In October of that year work began in earnest on the First Symphony, with the second, scherzo movement; by February 1925 the first three movements were complete in piano score. After a creative block, due more to sheer physical exhaustion than to compositional inability, the finale began to take shape; it was ready by May. The whole symphony was completed in full score on 1 July. In April of the following year (not without some minor reservations on the part of director Glazunov and his colleagues) the work was accepted as qualifying Shostakovich for admission to postgraduate studies in composition at the Leningrad Conservatoire. It had meanwhile been programmed for inclusion in the Leningrad Philharmonic's concert under Nikolay Malko, and was given its first performance on 12 May 1926 – a performance at which the scherzo had to be repeated.

Within two years the work had established an international reputation – in Berlin under Bruno Walter and in Philadelphia under Stokowski, after which Klemperer and Toscanini took it up. In Soviet Russia the success of the symphony launched Shostakovich as that country's leading young composer (a commission for a symphony celebrating the tenth anniversary of the Soviet regime followed almost immediately); in the West it proved a success less easy to follow, and notwithstanding the breakthrough of the widely acclaimed Fifth Symphony in 1937, a critical view of young genius warped by political controls began to gain currency. As time passed, the First Symphony became a favourite with the composer himself; he alluded to it in his autobiographical Eighth Quartet and, as if bringing the symphonic wheel full circle, in the no less autobiographical Fifteenth Symphony (his last).

By any standards the First Symphony remains a remarkable work – youthfully exuberant, yet strangely dark and menacing in many of its pages. The first movement, with its lively yet enigmatic introduction in search of a theme (and key), establishes an almost theatrical style of soloistic exchange among the individual members of the orchestra. The *Allegro non troppo* follows in the miniature sonata form. Its mood of ironic playfulness (twice breaking out into a quickly smothered street rampage) anticipates by just over four decades the mood of the Eleventh String Quartet in the same key.

The second-movement scherzo (in A minor) introduces an unexpected soloist – the piano. Although joining in the revels, this impertinent newcomer finally plays the role of detached, ironic commentator on what has proved to be a kaleidoscopic sequence of events, both humorous and grotesque, in the orchestra. (This is a role that the young Shostakovich was accustomed to play as pianist for the silent movies in Leningrad, while he was actually working on the symphony.)

The fun is now over. Taken together, slow movement and finale come to grips with serious questions for which the two previous movements have not prepared us. The build-up of unrelieved tension in the slow movement is considerable – through the anxious oboe melody (a derivative of the main theme of the first movement) accompanied by claustrophobic string harmonies, the menacing trumpet and side-drum leit-motif, and the mournful funeral-march theme on the solo oboe, which could be the echo of some revolutionary song. The finale (in which the piano returns) is all alarm and panic, shot through with exuberance – another of Shostakovich's revolutionary inspirations.

The introduction to the finale, which emerges threateningly out of a crescendo side-drum roll, establishes organic links between the two movements. Janus-like, it both anticipates the fugitive main theme of the Allegro and, in the cellos, looks back to the anguished rising sevenths of the slow movement's oboe melody. It is, moreover, destined to return more than once in the main body of the finale. Having groped its way to an angry assertion of F minor, the Allegro now surges forward in three crashing waves towards a second subject. This is where Shostakovich, through an exact intervallic inversion, transforms the melodic shape of the preceding funeral-march theme into the 'big tune' of the movement – a tune which manifests itself in both a positive and a negative guise. In what now becomes the central 'meno mosso' (slower) section of the movement, we are concerned with lyrical reminiscence rather than development. The frantic activity returns: in a destructive climax of transformed restatement (trombones in a massive augmentation of the first theme) the rhetoric of the solo timpani, inverting the menacing leitmotif of the slow movement, leads into a magnificently worked Largo coda. This brings together the main thematic material of the movement (both second subject and, in due course, the first) in a great rising current of melody that surges towards the final thunderous torrent. Elated yet anxious, tragic yet not without hope, this is already the authentic voice of Shostakovich, which all the subsequent years of Stalinist intervention were unable to exorcise.

© Eric Roseberry

‽ Symphony No. 4 in C minor, Op. 43 (1935–6)

1 Allegretto poco moderato
2 Moderato con moto
3 Largo – Allegro

For 25 years, Shostakovich's Fourth Symphony was effectively non-existent. Like the many victims of Stalin's purges in the 1930s and 1940s, it too had 'disappeared'. Only the composer, a few friends and colleagues, and the members of the Leningrad Philharmonic Orchestra who had rehearsed it in 1936 knew what was in the score. Why did the planned first performance never take place? Official Soviet sources offered an explanation. After sweeping condemnation of his opera *Lady Macbeth of Mtsensk* in the state newspaper *Pravda* (in an article headlined 'Chaos instead of Music'), Shostakovich had decided to withdraw the symphony. On reflection, he had realised that the *Pravda* allegations were right. In response, he had written a new symphony, No. 5 – heralded as 'A Soviet Artist's creative reply to just criticism'. The triumphant premiere of the Fifth Symphony had set the seal on the whole business. On the rare occasions when Shostakovich referred to No. 4 in public, his remarks were dismissive: it suffered from 'grandiosomania', he claimed. The score remained on the shelf until 1961, eight years after the death of Stalin, when a relatively liberal political climate made reappraisal of past 'mistakes' possible – at least in theory.

But after the Fourth Symphony began to be heard in Russia and in the West, doubts began to accumulate. True, the symphony was grandiose – it lasts about an hour in performance and the orchestral forces are vast; certainly there were manic elements in its make-up – the ferociously fast fugue that brings about the first movement's violent climax, the weird fairground music at the heart of the finale and its sudden emotional plunge into tragedy in the coda. But the quality of the musical invention was phenomenal – as the conductor Otto Klemperer had realised when Shostakovich played him the symphony at the piano in 1936 (strange that Klemperer never said anything about it in later years). The sequence of events might sometimes be bewildering – at least on first hearing – but it was never, never dull.

Perhaps the real problem with the Fourth Symphony was that its emotional message was dangerous – particularly in that bleak minor-key ending, with low pulsating bass rhythms clearly invoking the end of another great Russian tragic symphony: Tchaikovsky's 'Pathétique'. Russian art in the mid-1930s was dominated by the official ideal of 'Socialist Realism' – art which affirms 'the ultimate rightness of reality' (in other words, Stalin's policies). This was not the time for agonised confessions or desperate protest.

In 1979, a book appeared in the West entitled *Testimony: the memoirs of Shostakovich as related to and edited by Solomon Volkov*. In spite of issues about its authenticity, *Testimony* had valuable things to say about the Fourth Symphony, and how it grew out of Shostakovich's, and his country's, experiences of Stalinism at its most vicious – a time of terror, when friends and families denounced each other in frantic efforts to save their own necks: 'The mass treachery did not concern me personally.

I managed to separate myself from other people, and in that period it was my salvation. Some of these thoughts you can find, if you wish, in my Fourth Symphony. In the last pages it is all set out rather precisely.'

One of Shostakovich's closest friends, Isaak Glikman, confirms that the Fourth had special personal significance for Shostakovich. Glikman tells how he sat next to Shostakovich at the symphony's 1961 premiere:

> When the devastating music of the introduction resounded around the Hall, it seemed to me that I could hear his heart knocking audibly in agitation. He was in the grip of an unconquerable anxiety which only subsided at the start of the superb coda. Under the fresh impression of what he had just heard, [Shostakovich] told me, 'It seems to me that in many respects my Fourth Symphony stands much higher than my most recent ones.' He identified totally with the overwhelming musical force of this lost child.

Overwhelming musical force is right. The long first movement opens with a sledgehammer march, introduced by shrill high woodwind and xylophone. After a while, the martial music gives way to a lugubrious slow section, beginning with a long bassoon theme, later brutalised by tubas, basses and contrabassoon, with jagged, dissonant interjections from trombones, horn and xylophone. The march returns in barrel-organ-like scoring for woodwind, then the ferocious fast string fugue builds to the movement's main climax, underlined by pounding rhythms for four percussionists. The main themes return, but in new guises, leading finally to a quiet, sullen coda – fury has only temporarily abated.

The second movement is much shorter, cast in a broadly conventional scherzo–trio–scherzo form. But the writing is as imaginative as anywhere in the first movement – near the climax of the movement there is a breathtaking rapid crescendo in which all twenty woodwind instruments slither in one by one. The movement ends to an accompaniment of eerily clicking percussion – a passage Shostakovich returns to in the closing pages of his last symphony, No. 15.

The finale is as long as the first movement, and still more powerful. A sombre funeral march (with more than a hint of Mahler) leads to a furious Allegro. In turn, this gives way to the weird fairground episode mentioned above. Eventually this seems to be trying to sink to rest in a quiet C major (strings); but with an ominous crescendo for two sets of timpani and bass drum, the coda turns the mood on its head. The funeral-march theme returns (trombones and tubas, *fff*), provoking a massive climax, then all is quiet: a long-held chord of C minor, with throbbing low strings and harp, bleak echoes of earlier themes, and finally the sad, liquid chimes of a celesta. Not since Tchaikovsky had a Russian symphony ended in such unrelieved darkness.

Stephen Johnson © BBC

✎ Symphony No. 5 in D minor, Op. 47 (1937)

1 Moderato – Allegro non troppo – Largamente – Moderato
2 Allegretto
3 Largo
4 Allegro non troppo

From its very first performances, given at the height of Stalin's Great Terror in November 1937, Shostakovich's D minor Symphony has seldom failed to move an audience. Tagged 'A Soviet artist's creative reply to just criticism', it is at once the most popular and the most mysterious of twentieth-century symphonies, its precise intentions hotly debated by commentators of all ideological persuasions and none. Everyone agrees that the Fifth was a make-or-break work for the composer, the first piece in which he squared the circle, writing music of obvious integrity and frank emotional appeal while at the same time effectively remaking himself as composer laureate to a totalitarian regime.

This was an astonishing achievement in context, but then Shostakovich had few options left. In January 1936, after Joseph Stalin himself had attended a performance of Shostakovich's successful (but dangerously erotic) opera *Lady Macbeth of Mtsensk*, there appeared the notorious *Pravda* editorial 'Chaos instead of Music', with its threat that things could 'end badly' for Soviet musicians – and for Shostakovich in particular. Compelled to engage with contemporary problems from a Utopian perspective that held today's defects to be positive forces pushing society towards the goal of socialism, Shostakovich nevertheless contrived to win official recognition as the Soviets' 'optimistic tragedian'. Hence, while the Fifth might still be read as the progress of an intellectual from a state of individualistic error to a nirvana of self-transcendent solidarity with the masses, that is not what it means to us today. Nor, Shostakovich appears to have believed, would it ever have been so interpreted by his own people. The veteran conductor Kurt Sanderling was at the first Moscow performance of the work in January 1938 and remembers that 'after the first movement, we looked round rather nervously, wondering whether we might be arrested after the concert'. After the third movement, many wept openly. And yet, in the long run, the extent to which such music embodies an anguished debate with a regime that dispensed both the highest awards and the deepest humiliations may matter less than how well it works as a piece of absolute music in the great tradition.

Although the Fifth is a more conservative, less colourful symphony than its immediate predecessor, which was suppressed by the composer himself until the high noon of Khrushchev's Thaw, its idiom is foreshadowed in the Cello Sonata that pre-dates *Pravda*'s outburst by more than a year. Like many of his Left-leaning contemporaries in the West, Shostakovich was already fining down his musical language because he *wanted* to, reverting to more orthodox models, making his music easier to follow. While Stravinsky and Mahler continue to loom large in the score, the norm of dissonance is lower and there are the traditional four movements.

The Fifth Symphony's opening movement is clearer in outline than the corresponding movement of the Fourth, even if it is by no means merely simple. Indeed, the angular contour of its main material rang alarm bells with sympathetic colleagues anxious to secure the composer's rehabilitation with the Party. The easeful balm of the long-limbed second subject, with the violins in the upper register, is distinctly provisional too, its spaciousness and tranquillity born of suffering. The development process is characteristic, brutalising these ideas into a malevolent march, and peaking with a climactic resolution in D minor and a determined unison declamation of first group material. The icy, contemplative coda offers no consolation.

The Allegretto, a heavy-footed Mahlerian *Ländler* embracing a contrasting 'ironic' trio section is similarly straightforward in layout. The ending is Beethovenian: the trio naively wanders into the path of the oncoming coda and is knocked flat by it.

The emotional heart of the symphony is the meditative, at times frankly Tchaikovskian, Largo which so moved contemporary audiences. It is certainly the finest music Shostakovich had composed up to that time, moving from serene detachment to the kind of direct outpouring of tragic emotion rarely found in the sophisticated products of Western culture and effectively outlawed from Russian art at that time by the sheer unfeelingness of the Terror. There are echoes of traditional Russian orthodox chant and of Mahler's *Das Lied von der Erde* in the melodic writing. Significantly, Shostakovich divides his violins into three and the violas and cellos both into two sections: he obtains rich and varied string textures, but also deploys the expressive resource of a small body of strings playing really quietly.

The brass instruments, silent throughout the slow movement, are back with a vengeance in the sometimes brutish finale, long excoriated by Western highbrows for its supposed shortcomings in terms of technique and structure. Few performances would nowadays set out to evoke the euphoria of a successful party congress – an approach rendered more plausible by a confusion over metronome marks. But even if we doubt the evidence of *Testimony*, the composer's much-disputed memoirs, it is apparent that Shostakovich had other ideas. Seemingly by design, the music refers us back to the song 'Rebirth' (*Vozrozhdeniye*), the first of the *Four Pushkin Romances*, Op. 46 (1936–7). This is obvious in the movement's elegiac central episode, less so in the swaggering march theme, which alludes instead to a setting of the words '*khudozhnik–varvar*', the 'barbarian–painter' who ignorantly daubs over a masterpiece: in time the pigment will flake away to reveal the truth of the original inspiration. After so many obsessively repeated As on the high violins, the mood at the symphony's close can scarcely be described as either submissive or jubilant. The business of rejoicing sounds forced in some of the symphonic finales of Mahler and Tchaikovsky. What Shostakovich encodes here is not sarcasm but rather the determination to survive.

David Gutman © BBC

∾ Symphony No. 8 in C minor, Op. 65
(1943)

1 Adagio – Allegro non troppo
2 Allegretto
3 Allegro non troppo
4 Largo
5 Allegretto

Shostakovich's Seventh Symphony – the 'Leningrad', composed in 1941 during the Nazi siege of that city and premiered under wartime conditions in Russia the following year – made the composer's name famous throughout the Allied world within months. Toscanini and Henry Wood were among the many conductors to take it up, indispensable as its more than musical message seemed at the time. The composer's face appeared, wearing a fireman's helmet, on the front of *Time* magazine. He and the piece were an emblem.

Shostakovich is not the only composer whose music has been treated as an emblem, of course. Tchaikovsky, Mahler and Beethoven have all at times been listened to more for what their music seems to tell us about fate and suffering, than for the intrinsic truths that are the music itself. But when faced with a masterpiece it is good to pay attention to the notes, to hear them as music, and not only to bathe in a hot steam of stimulation. We must not forget that we are listening to someone *thinking musically*. And thinking musically is certainly what Shostakovich is doing in his Eighth Symphony.

Some idea of what this means may be gauged from a simple comparison. It is well known (and often obvious in the music) that Mahler was an important influence on Shostakovich. One of the ways in which this influence operated was in the construction of melodies unusual for a symphony. A distinctive feature of many of Mahler's melodies is the way they manage to combine the memorably self-contained qualities of a tune (often quite a long tune) with the dynamic freedom and openness of more compact symphonic 'material'. So too with Shostakovich's melodies. It is true that with both composers the tunes are never quite as self-contained as we might think – they are actually bound to the rest of the symphonic structure with links of steel – but the point is that we *hear* them as tunes.

There is another quality in Mahler's melodies on which Shostakovich also built, a quality much in evidence in this Eighth Symphony. One of Mahler's most magical tricks is to offer us melodies that change, develop and transform themselves apparently beyond recognition, and yet, as we listen, we know that we are still listening to the same melody. The result is a dramatic intensification of the fundamental tension between music that is the same and music that is different. There's a wonderful example of this in the main melody that runs through the first two movements of Mahler's Fifth Symphony.

Shostakovich, in his Eighth, pushes this question of musical identity almost to the limits. The entire work abounds in ideas that constantly remind us of other ideas, the most violently contrasted musical images suddenly startling us with unexpected qualities of similarity. A motif here, a chord there, sometimes a single note or instrumental colour, can make a connection in our memory with something that we had earlier thought quite different.

It is interesting, too, that the cumulative effect is no Germanic revelation of fundamental unity, but quite another feeling – of the constant shifting of the ground beneath our feet. Someone once described Schoenberg as 'the poet of anxiety'. In Shostakovich, perhaps, we have the poet of uncertainty. Of course, we know from history that this uncertainty is rooted in terror; but if we listen to the uncertainty musically, we will often hear terror answered or confronted by something else very different but equally unfixed – something that just as constantly changes and slips from our grasp.

Take the first movement of Shostakovich's Eighth. About ten bars from the opening, the first violins enter with a melody over a pulsing accompaniment. More than fifty bars later, at a slightly faster speed and in a new time signature (5/4 as opposed to 4/4), we hear another melody, also in the first violins, also over a pulsing accompaniment. Any half-attentive listener will feel that we are in a sense coming back to the same idea. And yet it is not the same tune. The curious feeling we have of knowing and yet not knowing where we are is one that occurs again and again throughout this piece.

Shostakovich wrote this symphony, one of the largest structures in his entire output, in just forty days stretched over a couple of months. Maybe it was the sheer speed of composition that enabled him to hold in his head relationships of this kind, so clear and yet so fluid, and on this enormous scale.

The original piano sketches of this symphony appear to have been written in a single day – 2 July 1943 – and cover no fewer than twenty-six pages of manuscript. Yet by 3 August – despite the intervention of his duties in the search for a new Soviet national anthem – Shostakovich had completed the symphony's first movement. A few days later he left Moscow with his family to visit Ivanovo, a new 'House of Creativity' for composers just opened in a country district a few hundred miles north-east of Moscow.

By 18 August Shostakovich had finished the second movement, and the famous third movement was written in a week. At the start of September, Shostakovich had to go back to Moscow to meet his mother and other relations. Yet despite this interruption, by 5 September the entire score was complete.

It seems astonishing, given the pressure Shostakovich was under during these few weeks, that the Eighth Symphony, if by no means his longest, is one of the most powerful proofs of the degree to which he possessed what Schoenberg called 'the breath of symphonists'. Phrase after phrase propels us forward with the most natural physical confidence that we will arrive at the next stage. The individual lines are clearer and cleaner even than in the Fifth Symphony, without their yet having become thin and starved with anguish. This is still a young man writing at the height of his powers.

Perhaps this work's most impressive quality lies in the relationships between its movements, in the relative weight that Shostakovich assigns to each part of the structure. All his middle-period symphonies, from the Fifth (1937) to the Twelfth (1961), explore in different ways this idea of shifting the balance between the parts that make up the whole.

In the Eighth, we seem to be offered too many movements: five, which nevertheless make several claims to be considered as the more familiar four. Is the third movement, for example, a second scherzo or a finale *manqué*? Does it belong to the first two movements, or to the last two? And what about the fourth movement passacaglia? Is it the real slow movement, the heart of the work, or just an introduction to the last movement (that's to say, the real last movement – after a failed attempt to end in the third movement)? And what about the famous first movement? What sort of a movement is it anyway, with its enormous slow introduction and its brutally truncated fast section in the middle?

It may be that you do not like asking questions like this about a piece of music, but my point is that it is not you or I asking the questions, but the music itself. As with a sculpture by Henry Moore or a building by Le Corbusier, it is the very distortions and disproportions of the forms within this music that bear the greatest weight of meaning. And one of the most powerful and distinctive of these distortions is exposed at the very moment in the first movement when the fast music that we had expected to continue and develop is brutally cut off at the climax.

This climax, a shattering repetition of a single chord, is very reminiscent of a particular moment in Mahler – the famously dissonant chord near the end of the first and last movements of the Tenth Symphony. Shostakovich's chord is far less complex than Mahler's: it consists, at first, of only three notes (albeit orchestrated with ear-splitting violence). But these three notes are of crucial importance: they are in fact the central idea of the work, the one that holds the rest together. Nearly every other idea has clear connections with this motif. Its sound saturates the second movement, provides the ending of the third movement, the starting point of the fourth, and – just as in Mahler's Tenth – returns in the fifth movement in more or less its original form (a climax all the more terrifying because it has gathered into itself the accumulated experience of the previous hour or more of music).

After the original appearance of this chord in the first movement, the music continues with probably the most famous episode in this whole work, a solo for the cor anglais so long, so agonisingly drawn out, that it can seem almost unbearable to listen to. Here is another marvellous example of this composer stretching to the limits our sense of what could possibly be appropriate, what could possibly be in proportion.

At the time of the Eighth Symphony's first performance, Shostakovich gave an interview in which he described the second movement as 'a march with elements of a scherzo'. Since the rediscovery around 1998 of the sketches for the lost, three-movement *Jazz Suite* No. 2 of 1938, we now know that he had a specific 'Scherzo' – that *Jazz Suite*'s absurdly jaunty opening movement – in mind. Marked Allegretto, the movement begins and ends as a wild march but slips into popular dance music at several moments in its course.

The third movement, by contrast, must be one of the most naked creations even in this composer's unadorned output: few symphonic movements in the repertoire have been driven so far and so fast on so little material, used to such shocking and relentless effect. The end of this third movement is joined to the next, a broad and spacious passacaglia, by a melodramatic, even cinematic, roll and crash of percussion. It is a gesture deliberately at odds with the incantatory inwardness of the music that follows – a twelvefold statement of a mysterious ground bass in the lower strings. The strictness of this twelvefold structure is masked by the almost improvisatory freedom of the music above it, unfolding a structure and a line all of its own. This line begins in the strings, passes in turn to the horn, to the piccolo, to the rest of the flutes, and finally to the clarinets.

The last movement gathers together the threads of all four preceding movements. For example, it answers and reverses the sense of experience of the second, the *Jazz Suite* 'Scherzo' movement. Both have the same tempo marking, Allegretto, and nearly the same metronome mark. The second movement is in a march-like 4/4 that keeps dancing into 3/4; the last begins and ends in 3/4, but slips back several times into a 4/4 march rhythm. And the parallels don't end there. There is a whole mass of thematic resemblances between the two movements, above and apart from the general tissue of cross-references that holds the whole symphony together. But it is not only the second movement that Shostakovich revisits in this finale. At the climax (which is the climax not only of this movement, but of the whole symphony) he plunges back into an almost exact recapitulation of the agonising and grinding dissonances of the first movement's climax. We relive a wealth of earlier experiences, but with a wholly new understanding of their significance.

Some people would have us listen to this great work (and to most of Shostakovich's music) as almost exclusively a monument to the appalling times in which he lived. It certainly is that (for like any artefact, this symphony inevitably tells us something of the circumstances under which it was made) but it is not only that. It is also a tribute to, and proof of, what survives beyond those times, the continuing revelation of meaning that lies not outside, but within the very notes themselves.

© Gerard McBurney

∾ Symphony No. 10 in E minor, Op. 93 (1953)

1 Moderato
2 Allegro
3 Allegretto
4 Andante – Allegro

Like the Fifth Symphony, the Tenth proved to be a watershed in Shostakovich's career. But if the Fifth was the brilliant outcome of creative perestroika in the light of threatening Party criticism in 1935, the Tenth was, if anything, a remarkable expression of the 'thaw' which was to follow the death of Stalin in February 1953. Shostakovich wrote the symphony quickly in the summer of that year, but it had been stirring in his mind for some time, and the pianist Tatyana Nikolayeva recalled that Shostakovich played excerpts from it to her in 1950–1, when he was working on the Twenty-Four Preludes and Fugues. Indeed, some of the thematic–motivic ideas of the Tenth had already been anticipated in such works as the withheld First Violin Concerto (1947–8) and Fifth String Quartet (1952), and the 'songfulness' of the symphony was to some extent prepared by the vocal music and film scores – much of it making extensive use of Russian folk-song material – which the composer had produced during the difficult years following the Zhdanov decree of 1948.

The time gap between the 'little' Ninth (1945) and the epic Tenth is the longest between any of Shostakovich's fifteen symphonies. His symphonies of the war years had come under attack, and it seems reasonable to suppose that the Tenth quickly took its final shape as a direct result of the sense of release brought about by Stalin's death; indeed, the Shostakovich–Volkov memoirs go so far as to suggest that the second movement – a baleful scherzo in 2/4 time – was 'a portrait of Stalin, roughly speaking'. (But this is an over-simplification of a movement which contains all sorts of semantic puzzles, beginning with the quotation of a theme identified with the Russian people in Musorgsky's *Boris Godunov*.)

The Tenth Symphony, following its first performance in Leningrad under Evgeny Mravinsky on 17 December 1953, was the subject of an important debate organised by the Composers' Union in 1954. Soviet composers and critics were still deeply conscious of Shostakovich's official disgrace as a symphonist, and were all too familiar with the problems of interpretation his conflict-laden music presented to Party ideologists. The so-called 'tragic' and 'isolated' elements of his style, the question of how successfully he had solved the problem of providing an acceptably happy ending to his symphony (certain critics considered that the work needed a fifth, triumphant, movement!) – all these 'erroneous tendencies' were mulled over in speeches and exchanges, for Shostakovich the condemned 'formalist' had yet to be rehabilitated by the decree of 1958 which finally put paid to the excesses of the Stalin period. Some kind of agreement seems to have been reached as to the work's ideological acceptability under the term 'optimistic tragedy', for it was clear that the composer – ideology apart – had produced a musical masterpiece. At this conference Shostakovich refused to be drawn on the subject of what his symphony was about. He contented himself with modest self-criticism about a possible miscalculation of the proportion of slow to fast music and blamed himself for writing it so quickly; on the question of meaning he said simply that he had 'wanted to portray human feelings and passions'.

Much of the fascination of the symphony lies in the composer's Chekhovian use of certain *idées fixes*. For example, the
personal motto theme DSCH (the German names for the
notes D, E flat, C and B natural, taken from the spelling of
Shostakovich's name in the German transliteration), which
emerges in the third movement and asserts itself triumphantly at the end of the finale, or the enigmatic horn call
E–A–E–D–A repeated twelve times in the third movement, a
movement which also brings back the introductory theme of
the first movement. (Recent research has established that the
E–A–E–D–A motif was, in fact, derived from the first name
of the Azerbaijani pianist and composer, Elmira Nazirova,
who had studied with Shostakovich and with whom he carried on an intense correspondence during the summer of
1953.) Like Tchaikovsky's Fourth Symphony, the initial thematic material of each movement is unified by a scale-wise
motif of a minor third (Tchaikovsky's falls, Shostakovich's
rises) and this motif is eventually absorbed into DSCH in the
third movement.

The dramaturgical scheme is, likewise, splendidly carried
through. The first two movements are diametrically opposed:
the long, questioning lyrical flow centring on E minor which
breaks out of its introspection and mounts to a towering climax before returning to its starting point is set against a
scherzo of the utmost violence and brevity in B flat minor.
The martial 'scherzo' – biting, aggressive, mechanical, cruelly
satirical – was something of a Shostakovich speciality. In his
'war' symphonies, Nos 7 and 8, the composer had already
introduced such music. There had been the notorious
episode of the goose-stepping 'invasion theme' in the first
movement of the 'Leningrad' Symphony (shades of Ravel's
Boléro!) and the grim marches of the second and third movements of the Eighth – a kind of expression that occurs also in
the scherzo movements of the Third and Eighth string quartets. In the symphonies they introduce an ironic note of evil
triumph that – as in Berlioz, Liszt and Mahler – runs counter
to the idea of the scherzo as a joyful, life-affirming dance.

Both Mahler and Tchaikovsky had introduced sinister, grotesque elements into their scherzo movements and in his Sixth Symphony Tchaikovsky had given his martial third movement an ironic twist in the context of the desolate finale. Here in the second movement of his Tenth Symphony, the concentrated fury of Shostakovich's blistering, spitting march knows no bounds.

The third movement in C minor introduces the author himself with his calling card, DSCH. It may suggest relief in the more traditional form of a dance-scherzo in 3/4 time, but its mood is suppressed and unstable. It alternates hesitant, even stealthy steps with a more confident assertiveness. A clear horn call suggests a lightening of mood, and there is a rare vision of peace. But it also brings back a dark reminiscence of the first movement, and there are darker things to come with further intensive development of the main theme. DSCH enters with a new vehemence of expression. The ending of this movement is tonally enigmatic, with the 'freezing' of the horn call's notes into a string chord set against DSCH on the upper woodwind. We seem poised between darkness and light.

The finale begins darkly, with a searching recitative (cellos and basses) that heralds sorrow and anxiety. Cries are heard in the response of flute, piccolo and bassoon to the long oboe melody – cries which are to be heard again in the tense development of the Allegro, with its return to the evil scherzo at the climax. But now they lead on to the apparent merriment of the 'jolly' main theme of what proves to be an emotionally very complex dance finale in E major. It is all very well to talk about a 'lightening of mood' here; but there are contradictory forces in this movement which appear to be at work right to the very end, with its manic assertion of DSCH, first high on the horns, and then in a frenzied tattoo on the timpani. There is much agitation in the middle of this finale, out of which DSCH suddenly towers in awesome unison. A Romantic dawn seems to be breaking in the return of the introduction's cello/bass theme, first on the cellos, then on the violins. But it ushers in an entrance of the main theme on solo bassoon in a grotesque march. And throughout there is a subversive tension in the many tonal twists that never seem to settle for a positively unequivocal E major. True, we have moved from minor to major, but all is not clear. It becomes possible to understand why critics at its first performance felt the need for a fifth, openly triumphant movement. Perhaps the composer–critic Andrey Volkonsky was glossing over the disturbing aspects of this finale with the oil of Socialist Realism when he referred in 1954 to 'a line from darkness to light'?

All this is borne out in a penetrating study of the symphony by David Fanning. He suggests – and argues cogently – that it is possible to detect the old satirical spirit breaking out in the language of 'double-speak'. Yet is it possible to doubt that Stalin's death and the composer's personal survival gave Shostakovich grounds for optimism and self-assertion in this symphony? Certainly the recording made in 1954 by Shostakovich and his colleague M. Weinberg in the composer's version for piano duet brings out the latent mordancy in the humour of the finale. But does that lessen its high spirits? The answer must, in all honesty, be yes and no.

© Eric Roseberry

∾ Symphony No. 11 in G minor, Op. 103, 'The Year 1905' (1957)

1   Palace Square: Adagio
2   The Ninth of January: Allegro
3   Eternal Memory: Adagio
4   The Alarm Bell: Allegro non troppo – Adagio – Allegro

When Shostakovich's Symphony No. 11 first appeared, in 1957, there was nothing about it that was likely to offend the Soviet authorities – provided they didn't probe too deeply. Written for the fortieth anniversary of the October

Revolution, the symphony's title and musical content invoked a suitably revolutionary theme: the failed Russian uprising of 1905, which had been brutally put down by the troops of Tsar Nicholas II. The unmistakably tragic character of the work might have aroused suspicion in another context, but Shostakovich's use of revolutionary songs from the time of that abortive first revolution was apparently enough to dispel official doubts. This was a good socialist theme: the impoverished, humiliated people rise up against the imperial oppressor; their action fails horribly, but defeat only makes the survivors hungrier for freedom and vengence – the determination that will lead to the successful revolution of 1917 is born here.

The Soviet powers were delighted, and greeted the new symphony with hymns of praise. In private, though, some of Shostakovich's admirers were bitterly disappointed: their hero had sold out – politically and musically; the use of communist-approved political songs was tantamount to capitulation. But there were others who heard a different message in the Eleventh Symphony, among them the great Russian poet Anna Akhmatova. After the Leningrad premiere, a friend asked her privately what she thought of the work; Akhmatova told her, 'Those songs were like white birds flying against a terrible black sky.'

What none of Shostakovich's detractors appeared to notice was that the songs quoted in the symphony were all anguished in tone. They expressed despair, rage against tyranny, grief for sufferings past – but no consoling hope, no looking forward to the glorious revolutionary dawn. When the choreographer Igor Belsky used the music of the Eleventh Symphony for a ballet, Shostakovich told him, 'Don't forget that I wrote the symphony in the aftermath of the Hungarian Uprising.' It was in 1956, the year before Shostakovich wrote the work, that Soviet troops had crushed the popular revolution in Hungary – in the process destroying hopes that the Soviet Union might turn into a significantly more liberal regime in the wake of Stalin's death. Bear that in mind, and the words of the songs, and the manner in which Shostakovich treats them, take on a wholly new meaning.

The symphony's opening is wonderfully atmospheric. Hushed, icy harmonies for strings and harp evoke the mood before the uprising – tense, still, expectant. The feeling of anticipation intensifies as drums beat a quiet tattoo, and a muted trumpet sounds distant, ominous fanfares. In this powerful musical scene-painting we may hear the influence of Shostakovich's experience in writing for the cinema: one can imagine a long, slow tracking shot, taking in the immensity of the Palace Square before the arrival of the revolutionaries. Later, two flutes introduce the first of the songs, 'Listen': 'The autumn night is black as treason, black as the tyrant's conscience. Blacker than that night a terrible vision rises from the fog – prison.'

Suddenly, without break, the tempo increases. Violas, cellos and basses introduce a low, scurrying figure, which is then sung out in slower note-values by clarinets and bassoons. This is another revolutionary song: 'O Tsar, our dear father! Look around you; life is impossible for us because of the Tsar's servants, against whom we are helpless.' Excitement builds in two great waves; then, after a brief recollection of the first movement (the icy harmonies now sounded by woodwind), the final crescendo begins with a transformation of the drum tattoo from the opening of the symphony. This reaches its peak in an outburst of unprecedented violence: savage martial rhythms for full orchestra, with timpani and five percussionists – the uprising is crushed.

Abruptly the violence ceases and, as our ears adjust, we become aware that the strings are playing the icy 'Palace Square' chords again, now with ghostly trills – again a very cinematic touch: suddenly we are transported from the thick of the violence to its aftermath, the vast square filled with the bodies of the victims. A slow, quiet processional begins: pizzicato cellos and basses at first, then with the elegiac song 'You fell as a victim' on violas. This builds gradually to an impassioned climax, with timpani and percussion recalling the recent massacre. Bleak calm descends, 'You fell as a victim' is heard once more, then the finale erupts, with a protest song on brass and timpani: 'Rage, you tyrants – mock at us, threaten us with prison and chains. We are strong in spirit, if weak in body! Shame, shame on you tyrants!'

Eventually more memories are heard: 'O Tsar, our dear father' (full orchestra), the icy string-and-harp harmonies from the opening of the symphony, then a solo cor anglais broods plaintively on motifs from the third movement. Deep bell sounds then ring out from bassoons, contrabassoon, drums, gong, harp and pizzicato cellos and basses. Shostakovich was almost certainly thinking of the deep bell in Musorgsky's opera *Boris Godunov*, which he had reorchestrated in 1940. In *Testimony*, he explains what this bell sound meant to him: 'When the bell tolls, it's a reminder that there are powers mightier than man, that you can't escape the judgement of history.' The message is underlined in the work's final pages: angrily lamenting wind and brass, more pounding militaristic percussion, and the drum-tattoo figure from the opening of the symphony sounded out threateningly by bells.

Stephen Johnson © BBC

∾ Symphony No. 15 in A major, Op. 141 (1971)

1   Allegretto
2   Adagio –
3   Allegretto
4   Adagio – Allegretto

What is it about last symphonies? Do they really have a special aura, or is it just sentimentality that makes us think so? Certainly we can imagine a composer summoning up his creative resources to bid a conscious farewell to this most demanding of genres. And yet, with the very much disputed exception of Tchaikovsky, there is rarely any evidence to support such a notion. Rather the contrary. Beethoven's hymn to brotherly love in his Ninth Symphony was not so conclusive as to stop him sketching a Tenth; Schubert's 'Great' C major (No. 9, as we know it) turns out to pre-date the 'Unfinished' (No. 8); and Mahler was in far more positive spirits composing his apparently valedictory Ninth than popular biography would have it – high-minded expostulations, such as Schoenberg's, on its finality have been toned down since the full revelation of Mahler's work on his Tenth Symphony.

But what of the symphony since Mahler? Is it just coincidence that the last symphonies of Nielsen, Bax, Prokofiev, Vaughan Williams and Shostakovich all feel like new departures, that all of them are more intimate and enigmatic than their predecessors, and that they are all less often heard? Maybe part of the answer is that all these composers happened to die in peacetime, and that their last symphonies reflect the uneasy tranquillity of a post-conflict era. Having each embodied the experience of war in one or more of their symphonies, it is hardly surprising that they should then seek to rest from their labours and turn inward. And if there is a disturbingly ambivalent quality, that may be because infirmity or disillusionment deflected those aims in mid-course.

Take Nielsen's 'Sinfonia semplice' (No. 6) of 1925. It was supposed to be a cheerful work, in conscious distinction with his conflict-torn Fifth. But illness and cynicism soured the tone, producing something altogether more frightening and more powerful. Coincidence or no, precisely the same is true of Shostakovich in his Fifteenth. He certainly knew Nielsen's work by this time, as he once told the Danish conductor Ole Schmidt; and like Nielsen's Sixth, Shostakovich's Fifteenth starts with innocent-sounding repeated notes on the glockenspiel. If we are to believe his favourite pupil, Boris Tishchenko, Shostakovich had also intended his Fifteenth Symphony to be a cheerful work, a deliberate turning away from the themes of death and oppression which had dominated his Thirteenth and Fourteenth. But his health had been in progressive decline for more than a decade. In 1967 he had been diagnosed as suffering from a form of polio (that diagnosis is still contested incidentally), and during the composition of the Fifteenth he experienced acute eye-strain. Given all that, and the fact that Russia was in the middle of Brezhnev's Era of Stagnation (as it is now known), an intended cheerfulness was always going to be difficult to maintain. All the same, in the hands of a genius the discrepancy between intention and reality is precisely what produced one of the most elusive and fascinating masterpieces in symphonic history.

The facts are easily told. Shostakovich was sixty-four when he composed the piece between April and July 1971, four years before his death. It was first performed in Moscow on 8 January 1972 under the composer's son, Maxim. Coming after two symphonies commemorating the 1905 'Bloody Sunday' demonstration and the 1917 Revolution (Nos 11 and 12), and two based on texts (Nos 13 and 14), the Fifteenth is Shostakovich's first non-programmatic symphony since the Tenth of 1953.

Virtually everything else has to be couched in terms of hypothesis, speculation and rhetorical question. Above all there are the notorious quotations, which call into question the symphony's 'non-programmatic' status, laying down tempting trails for those who like to narrow down the 'message' of music to a synopsis or a manifesto.

The game of quotations begins a couple of minutes into the first movement. The trumpet announces the second-subject theme in the academically correct dominant key (E major) beginning with a repeated-note short–short–long rhythm and artfully covering all twelve notes of the chromatic scale. After counterstatements in the wind and strings the trumpet makes as if to repeat its theme; but instead the repeated notes go straight into the main theme of Rossini's *William Tell* overture. On one level this is easy to account for. Anyone who has sat at the piano as a teacher or a student must have been tempted to have fun 'bending' a theme into some well-known variant thereof. For a composer like

Shostakovich, with his avowed interest in 'all music from Bach to Offenbach', and his decades of experience in composing for the theatre and the cinema, it was almost second nature (remember the Offenbach can-can, for instance, in *The New Babylon* of 1929). Forget the depth psychology and the musicological sleuthing. This is simply wry humour. Or at least it could be.

But would anyone dare say the same of the opening of the finale? Here the muted brass intone the 'fate' motif from Wagner's *Ring* cycle, and the timpani answer with a rhythmic tattoo which identifies the quotation as *Götterdämmerung* Act 3, immediately after the death of Siegfried. Aha! – so it's all about the death of the hero . . . Then the pizzicato cello and bass notes crystallise into the first three notes of the *Tristan* Prelude. Aha! – it's the death of the hero's love . . . !

And we're still not finished with quotations. In a Chicago Radio interview Shostakovich mentioned that the last movement quotes a Glinka song. This can only be an early romance whose first three notes duplicate the *Tristan* quotation and whose main theme is paraphrased by Shostakovich's. The text goes 'Do not tempt me needlessly with the return of your kindness; to the disappointed one all the blandishments of past days are foreign'. Well, that chimes in with Shostakovich's various amorous affairs, laid bare since glasnost by his Soviet biographer Sofiya Khentova. Ahhaah! It's the death of Shostakovich-the-hero's love.

Any more evidence for disguised autobiography? Well, the connoisseur of Shostakovich's output will notice any number of allusions to his own works, so could this be a more cryptic version of the Eighth String Quartet with its unmistakable self-quotations?

So there we have it. The first movement must have been the young hero (at the entry of the Rossini theme Maxim Shostakovich always thinks of Tell's assurance to his son that he will shoot straight); and the finale must be his death and commemoration. So the Adagio second movement, with its Stygian brass chorales, lamenting cello and lugubrious trombone, must be the funeral oration. And the twisted Allegretto third movement must be the Dance of Death. The twelve-note themes in the inner movements would support that; for Shostakovich such themes had already come to symbolise the ineluctability of death. So in fact it is another 'death symphony', just like the Fourteenth but without the texts, and somehow drawn into this realm in spite of its good intentions. And maybe the composer's own commentary, to the effect that the first movement represents a toy shop at night and that the whole symphony is a birth-to-death piece, should be given more credence than it often is. After all, toy shops, in the world of horror movies, can easily take on associations of malevolence . . .

The 'musical meaning' of the piece refuses to be pinned down. Whatever extra-musical images a composer may have in mind, in practice, once the compositional process is under way, it unfolds a world of meaning all its own, not obliterating those extra-musical elements, but transmuting them, transcending them. Similarly an author's personal life experiences may trigger off a novel or a play, but once the characters begin to live their own lives, the autobiography becomes largely immaterial. Let's look at the finale of the Fifteenth from a different angle.

Just suppose that Shostakovich's first idea for the finale was the wistful violin tune, the one that starts with the *Tristan* motif. That would be a reasonable starting point, given that it follows the same contours as the first movement's playful opening motif, but with an entirely opposite rhythmic character. Suppose that he then noticed that the midway cadence of this theme would go rather nicely with the harmony of Wagner's 'fate' motif, just as the first movement trumpet tune neatly diverted into *William Tell*. Letting such quotations into a symphony was, after all, nothing new; it was all the rage for Western composers in the 1960s, and Shostakovich's pupil Boris Chaykovsky had put in a whole medley of unexplained quotations in his fine Second Symphony of 1968. Then suppose that Shostakovich realised that this 'fate' motif progression would do rather nicely as an elliptical introduction too, deliberately placing the whole movement on a wobbly pedestal. Suppose that he then decided to follow the 'fate' motif with the rhythm from Siegfried's death, aware that he could easily transform this rhythm at the end of the work into the haunting tick-tock semiquavers he had previously used in his Fourth Symphony and Second Cello Concerto, thereby supplying an effective counterpart to the 'wobbly' introduction. Suppose that he then allowed the repeated notes to punctuate the movement midway (again on the timpani); suppose that this could overlap into a passacaglia, paraphrasing another of his earlier works (the 'Leningrad' Symphony's invasion theme); and suppose he could then plant a pizzicato version of the *Tristan* motif in the introduction as the seed for this passacaglia.

This is, of course, a conjecture, no more than another plausible scenario for Shostakovich's thought processes. He was not one to verbalise about his compositional practices, except perhaps to throw others off the scent. Whatever the truth in this instance, the important thing to acknowledge is that a composer may make quotations and allusions as much for musical as for semantic reasons.

A further puzzle is presented by some references in *Testimony*, Shostakovich's notorious ghost-written memoirs, to Chekhov's short story 'The Black Monk'. This is the melodramatic tale of a psychology lecturer whose marriage to a childhood friend is counterpointed with visions of a hooded monk – an alter ego, in fact, who exhorts the lecturer to believe in his own greatness and ends up driving him insane. You can see the attraction for a man with a life story like Shostakovich's, and he considered writing an opera on the subject. But does it have anything to do with the Fifteenth Symphony? Or is it just a mischievous false trail? Certainly no commentator yet has succeeded in making any detailed parallels between the story and the music.

So all this gives us is pieces of a puzzle, the greater part of which has been withheld. We try to connect the pieces as best we can, but we only have fragments to go on and may even be looking at some of them upside-down. We sense that the whole 'picture' is complex and mysterious and that fragments may be all that one person can hope to perceive. Yet the mastery of the composition leads us to accept and wonder at the results, even when they defy explanation.

And finally, when the C sharp octaves on glockenspiel and celesta that end the piece have died away, what impression are we left with? Of course, that is in the hands of the conductor and the orchestra as much as the composer. Maybe we go away with the thought that the percussion writing echoes Shostakovich's Fourth Symphony, the work that lay banned for twenty-five years in the Stalinist freeze; and maybe we think of all the other Shostakovich pieces the Fifteenth has alluded to. If each of his mature symphonies is a tombstone, then this one is an entire graveyard. Or maybe we marvel at how the pulsating semiquavers echo the death-of-Siegfried rhythm at the beginning of the finale, and how the final octave C sharps on glockenspiel and celesta echo the first two notes of the entire symphony, in short how an extraordinary range of images is united in one process – which is the proudest boast of any traditionally minded symphonist. Or again, maybe we hear echoes of another octave C sharp on the tuned percussion at the end of another composer's ambivalent last symphony – Prokofiev's Seventh. At any rate we surely come away with the feeling that the spiritual echoes of Shostakovich's symphonic swansong will haunt us long after the acoustic ones have faded into applause.

© David Fanning

Jean Sibelius (1865–1957)

Sibelius established himself early in his career as Finland's national composer, helped by his ability to convey the austere beauty of his country, his passionate adoption of themes from the Finnish folk epic the *Kalevala*, and his patriotic music such as *Finlandia* (1900). Born north of Helsinki, he initially intended to become a violinist, but studied composition in Vienna and Berlin between 1889 and 1891. His choral *Kullervo* Symphony and the tone poem *En Saga* (1892, both inspired by the *Kalevala*) preceded seven purely orchestral symphonies, ranging from the Tchaikovsky-influenced First (1900) to the enigmatically brief Seventh (1924). Supported by a government pension from the age of 32, he effectively retired for the last thirty years of his life, writing no major works (though he at least started an Eighth symphony, which he destroyed). His Violin Concerto, by turns introverted and highly virtuosic, remains among the most popular in the repertory.

✸ Symphony No. 1 in E minor, Op. 39
(1898–9)

1   Andante ma non troppo – Allegro energico
2   Andante (ma non troppo lento)
3   Scherzo: Allegro – Lento (ma non troppo) – Tempo primo
4   Finale (Quasi una fantasia): Andante – Allegro molto

The four *Lemminkäinen Legends* were premiered in April 1896, four years after the *Kullervo* Symphony. Sibelius's reaction to these works was characteristically self-critical. Two of the *Legends* were withdrawn and were not performed again until 1935, while the other two (*The Swan of Tuonela* and *Lemminkäinen's Return*) were subjected to revision. *Kullervo*, meanwhile, was completely withdrawn shortly after its premiere and was not heard again in its entirety during the composer's lifetime.

Sibelius's evident dissatisfaction with these works may have been fuelled by a feeling that they came close to abstract symphonic statement but fell short of that supreme goal because of their avowed programmatic content. The *Legends* so nearly constitute a four-movement symphony, but they ultimately lack the overall structural coherence that distinguishes a truly symphonic design.

By mid-1898, Sibelius could avoid the symphonic challenge no longer. Throughout the autumn, a new work gripped him with increasing intensity, making him largely oblivious to the political and cultural turmoil that had suddenly exploded around him.

As one of Russia's annexed countries, Finland had long been allowed to go its own way, but the accession to the Russian throne of Tsar Nicholas II in 1898 saw a change in Finland's political climate. A process of 'Russification' was swiftly introduced, culminating in the so-called 'February Manifesto' of 1899 in which draconian measures were announced, curbing free political expression. Emerging from his symphonic labours in early 1899, Sibelius was swept along by the rising tide of national protest. During the following months he contributed several musical works to the Nationalist cause, including *Finlandia*.

On 26 April, the First Symphony was premiered to great acclaim. However, the applause paled in comparison with the ovation accorded another new Sibelius work on the same programme, *The Song of the Athenians*. Listening nowadays to this almost comically feeble piece of agitprop, it seems beyond belief that its success should have eclipsed that of the symphony at the time. It is perhaps less surprising to learn that the symphony was immediately tarred with the same political brush and that various nationalist programmatic interpretations were attached to it – interpretations that also saddled subsequent Sibelius symphonies and which he refuted with increasing irritation.

If those nationalist commentators had only listened to the music itself, they would have heard a work steeped in the Russian tradition, with Tchaikovsky as its most conspicuous model. Nevertheless, these influences never entirely stifle the already intensely personal and highly original voice of Sibelius himself.

Although the first movement's haunting introductory clarinet solo is also quoted at the start of the Finale, its function is more one of mood-setting than providing important material for later development. Considerably more significant is the quietly sustained accompanying drum roll. This is the first of many long-held notes (pedal points) that dominate the symphony and which form such an important feature of Sibelius's musical style. When the main Allegro energico gets under way, the pedal points help to create a sense of vast slow motion deep below the agitated surface. The ability to shift imperceptibly between these extremes of speed is one of the great mysteries of Sibelius's music and this movement is a truly impressive example.

The slow movement is perhaps more consciously indebted to Tchaikovsky, though the fearsome central climax and stormy return of the opening melody are unmistakably Sibelian. Bruckner, meanwhile, has often been cited as the major influence on the pounding rhythms of the Scherzo. While superficially true, this tends to distract from the great originality of this vital and dramatic movement. The structure is most ingenious: the main Scherzo section is a fully worked-out sonata-form movement. However, a few bars into the recapitulation of the opening, a slow trio suddenly interrupts the flow, before the sonata–scherzo resumes exactly where it left off.

The Finale, marked 'Quasi una fantasia', is sometimes criticised for being too diffuse and for allowing the heart-on-sleeve Romanticism of the central 'big tune' to take over. But a sensitive performance makes one aware of the extraordinary bass line accompanying this melody. It is in fact another pedal point, utterly implacable, holding the melody and harmony in check and generating huge tension. This is only discharged at the very close – a dramatic stroke of immense originality and daring.

© John Pickard

∾ Symphony No. 2 in D major, Op. 43
(1901–2)

1 Allegretto
2 Tempo Andante, ma rubato
3 Vivacissimo – Lento e suave
4 Finale: Allegro moderato

In 1907, the composers Mahler and Sibelius met in Helsinki. They took walks together, during which, Sibelius tells us, they 'discussed all the great questions of music thoroughly' – a pity no one was on hand to take notes. Fortunately Sibelius did recall something of their discussion on the subject of the symphony:

> I said that I admired its severity of style and the profound logic that created an inner connection between the motifs . . . Mahler's opinion was just the reverse. 'No, the symphony must be like the world. It must embrace everything.'

Statements of belief are one thing; practice is another. Certainly no twentieth-century symphonist is more supremely logical than Sibelius at his best. But it is equally clear that symphonic writing meant more to him than 'sounding form'. On one occasion he described his symphonies as 'confessions of faith from the different periods of my life'; and even such a seemingly abstract process as the 'arrangement of themes' could reveal a mystical dimension: 'It is as if God the Father had thrown down the tiles of a mosaic from heaven's floor and asked me to determine what kind of picture it was.'

In the case of the Second Symphony, those God-given 'tiles' seem to have arrived in a striking variety of ways. The Finale's lamenting second theme (woodwind over ominously murmuring string figures) was apparently written in memory of Sibelius's sister-in-law, Elli Järnefelt, who had committed suicide. In contrast, the glorious transformation of the main Finale theme in the coda was, Sibelius said, a musical impression of the Finnish painter Akseli Gallén-Kallela's villa in the Karelian forests. Ideas for the slow movement began life as sketches for a tone poem about Don Juan; Sibelius's programme for the opening of that work can be fitted without much difficulty to the first section of the symphony's slow movement: 'Sitting in the twilight in my castle. A stranger comes in. I ask him more than once who he is. Finally he strikes up a song. Then Don Juan sees who he is – Death.' Twilight, ghostly footsteps, a sombre bassoon tune, anxious repeated questionings, crescendo, then the revelation of 'Death' on full brass, *fff* – it's all there if you wish to hear it. But the theme that follows, a warm major-key melody for strings, *ppp*, has a very different label in Sibelius's sketches: 'Christus'.

Could Sibelius have intended the Second Symphony's slow movement as a kind of tone poem: a musical dramatisation of a battle for the soul between Life/Christus and Death? Interestingly, this is the movement some critics have found least satisfactory from a purely symphonic point of view. Perhaps we need an extra-musical programme here to make absolute sense of the music. It is certainly tempting to interpret the coda as the inevitable bleak outcome of the Life/Death contest: shrill woodwind and brass raging impotently against the dying of the light.

The first movement, however, needs no programme: its musical logic is absolutely self-explanatory at every turn – which is not to say that it can't also be vividly atmospheric and ardently expressive. But it is the profound, organic logic of this movement – the 'inner connection between the motifs' – that ultimately makes it such an overwhelmingly impressive experience. Virtually everything derives in some way from the opening string figure, in particular from the simple, three-note motivic outline F sharp–G–A. Turn it upside down and you have the oboes' and clarinets' answering theme; run it downwards and then back up again, and you have the beginning of the violins' forte unaccompanied tune that emerges a little later; play it backwards and you have the basis of the woodwind's urgent 'second subject'.

This process of transformation – intellectual and powerfully intuitive at the same time – gives the music an almost Beethovenian energy; it allows Sibelius to build a thrilling climax at the beginning of the recapitulation. At the end of the movement the opening string figures return, rising as before, then falling to the tonic: F sharp–E–D. The effect of 'full close' is as inevitable and satisfying as a mathematical QED.

The influence of Beethoven is clearer still in the third movement, which follows the archetypally Beethovenian plan of scherzo–trio–scherzo–trio–transition to finale (the recurring trio section being in a much slower tempo). Echoes of the first movement's three-note germinal motif can be heard in the tearing string figures of the scherzo, and in the second phrase of the oboe's chant-like trio tune. But in the transition to the Finale one can sense that a new, elemental transformation is under way.

We don't have to wait long for the result. After a massive crescendo the Finale theme emerges in full splendour on strings, the brass responding with heroic fanfares. In essence it is unmistakably a version of the rising three-note string figure that opened the symphony, and yet it feels like a new creation. The sense of epic struggle in this last movement inspired some Finnish commentators (who presumably knew nothing of the Don Juan project) to interpret Sibelius's Second Symphony as a political statement: a 'Liberation Symphony', portraying the Finns' determined resistance to Russian imperialism. Sibelius denied this repeatedly and emphatically, and given his remarks to Mahler about 'severity' and 'profound logic', one can understand why. Still, it is a token of the Second Symphony's dramatic and expressive power – not of musical weakness – that it invites interpretations. It is also evidence that Sibelius's artistic embrace could be wider than he was sometimes prepared to admit.

© Stephen Johnson

∾ Symphony No. 3 in C major, Op. 52
(1907)

1 Allegro moderato
2 Andantino con moto, quasi allegretto
3 Moderato – Allegro (ma non tanto)

In 1907, the year the Third Symphony finally saw the light of day, Sibelius met Mahler in Helsinki and duly recounted the nub of their conversation to an early biographer, Karl Ekman. Mahler famously thought the symphony should be 'like the world' and 'embrace everything', a concise retort to Sibelius's 'admiration for strictness and style in a symphony and the deep logic which unites all the themes by an inner bond'. At one time, they had seemed to be travelling along the same path: Sibelius completed his epic five-movement *Kullervo* Symphony for soloists, chorus and orchestra in 1892, at the same time as Mahler's massive Second Symphony, the 'Resurrection', hung fire. Yet when Mahler composed the whole of the even more massively affirmative Eighth in the summer of 1906, the symphony that hung fire was Sibelius's Third – a work that, when completed, ran for less than half an hour and was scored for double woodwind, a modest brass department, strings and timpani. It was the first symphonic manifesto of those qualities he outlined to his fellow composer, although some of his tone poems – especially *En Saga*, composed in 1892 and revised in 1902 – already fitted the bill.

The refining process had begun with the elliptical first movement of the Second Symphony. Constant Lambert in *Music Ho!* praised its one-off originality in the context of the symphony. Yet in his hurry to wax superlative (and rightly) over the Fourth as a supremely unified masterpiece, Lambert was surely wrong to label the Third 'transitional' and to praise its finale for supreme originality at the expense of previous movements. The 'power of sustained musical thinking' that Lambert so admired begins here with the opening bars of the work, and from there until the emphatic end of the adventure there are no superfluous gestures.

Without a hint of a prelude, the cellos and basses launch us on a bracing first-movement journey that effortlessly flows to embrace other striking ideas clearly defined by the wind and brass respectively. A broader, more epic theme straight from the world of *En Saga* gives a wider perspective; on its return it will be the only major stretch of the work until the finale to demand the full orchestra's attention. Shadowy wisps of familiar themes and disquieting hints at that 'devil in music' interval of the tritone, the augmented fourth destined to dominate the Fourth Symphony, lead the traveller through stranger terrain in the development, steered back to sanity by the epic theme as it passes upwards through the woodwind. A new but seemingly organic hymn of thanksgiving, again scored with care, ends the movement with utter naturalness.

What follows might be mistaken for an interlude as one simple ballad passes from woodwind to strings and back. Yet the nuances of the spare accompaniment and the spaces around help to give it the character of a mysterious incantation against disquieting powers of darkness; and the spirits are ready to jump again as the finale begins with fragmentary but potent reminiscences, direct or merely suggested, of the first two movements. This, surely, is why a new and noble song needs to appear halfway through the movement. It seems an unlikely candidate at first as it steals in on the four horns, but sustained by nervous energy it forces its way through a field of bristling figurations and fearlessly yanks the lurking tritone into the daylight. In a symphony where full ensembles are kept to a minimum, the last twenty-four bars of brass cavalcade cannot fail to provide the most persuasive of symphonic perorations.

© David Nice

❧ Symphony No. 4 in A minor, Op. 63
(1909–11)

1 Tempo molto moderato, quasi adagio
2 Allegro molto vivace
3 Il tempo largo
4 Allegro

Sibelius began his Fourth Symphony towards the end of 1909 and finished it only just in time for the first performance, which he himself conducted in Helsinki in April 1911. It is often described as his most austere symphony, his darkest – and also his greatest. Many non-lovers of Sibelius's music find this the hardest to belittle of his symphonies. After the clear-cut decisiveness of the Third Symphony, in which Sibelius is supposed finally to have shed romantic nationalism for a new-found classicism – though a classicism still strongly coloured by picturesque Nordic feeling – the Fourth represents something withdrawn, aloof and elusive. During the period of its composition Sibelius wrote that the 'strong atmosphere' of his music was 'born from solitude and pain'. Following an operation for throat cancer he had renounced smoking and drinking, which gave him grounds enough to feel something of a martyr. Despite his famous exchange with Mahler in 1907, in which Sibelius declared his belief in the 'severity of form' and 'profound logic' of the symphony as a genre, he was to write in his diary three years later that 'a symphony is not just a composition in the ordinary sense of the word; it is more of an inner confession at a given stage of one's life'.

What did Sibelius mean by 'inner'? Merely 'intimate', or had he in mind a reality independent of consciousness? In any event the music of the Fourth Symphony seems to rebel against intention, just as Sibelius insisted that his basic themes and motifs must determine the form of a composition, not the reverse. Only at one point in the Fourth Symphony, towards the end of the third movement, when the strings break out in a rash of emotion, is an idea brought to

predictable fruition. The opening movement is like a prologue, wary of the home key, though there is a brief, sunny
glimpse of A *major* just before the music peters out on a wintry unison. The second movement relaxes at once into F
major, but quickly plunges into gloom and a slower tempo
from which it never recovers; again, it withers away on a key
note which is only nominal. The ending of the slow third
movement, in C sharp minor, echoes that of the first, with a
related motif, reaching up to and over the tonic by way of
chromatic notes that weaken rather than confirm it. Only the
final movement ends with something like a conventional
cadence, yet even here the effect is of an uneasy truce. The
first three movements end softly, the last no more than mezzo
forte, and, Sibelius adds, dolce.

Yet the work as a whole embraces a wider range of moods
and styles than its reputation for bleakness suggests. In the
slowest sections of the first movement chains of brass fanfares
appear like beacons, their strong, simple harmonies reassur-
ing in a landscape of uncertain horizons. But they are not part
of the main current – to follow that we have to listen to the
slow-moving bass line, which is briefly removed altogether,
to alarming effect, during the stormy central section of the
movement. If those brass passages suggest Bruckner, there
are glimmers of Wagner's *Parsifal* in the string writing of the
third movement. But stranger than these is the wide arc of
violin melody with which Sibelius launches the finale.
Spanning a major ninth plus a tritone, it sounds like nothing
so much as the acidulated tonality of neo-classical Stravinsky;
it is possible to hear in this a parody of the overripe melody at
the climax of the preceding movement.

In a diary entry for 13 May 1910, Sibelius admonished
himself. 'Don't let all these "novelties", triads without
thirds and so on, take you away from your work. Not everyone can be an innovating genius.' By triads without thirds
Sibelius might have been referring to Scriabin, whose
Prometheus was to have had its first British performance in
1912 at the same concert as Sibelius's Fourth Symphony.

(Scriabin withdrew because of lack of rehearsal, and never met Sibelius.)

Yet if Sibelius felt unable to compete on the level of novelty (the 'circus', he called it), he must have known that the pursuit of novelty brought dangers, at least to him, of self-limitation. There is, in fact, no lack of stylistic audacity in the Fourth Symphony, but it does not exclude more familiar elements. 'Your struggles with form. Concessions to tradition', he jotted in his diary later in 1910. Anyone who speaks of concessions to tradition is set on finding his own path. Listeners can be reassured by the fact that analysts have not found agreement in charting it, leaving us free to discover.

© Adrian Jack

ꙮ Symphony No. 5 in E flat major, Op. 82
(1915, rev. 1916, 1919)

1 Tempo molto moderato – Allegro moderato (ma poco a poco stretto) – Presto – Più presto
2 Andante mosso, quasi allegretto
3 Allegro molto

Throughout his working life Sibelius kept diaries. For anyone who cares about his music, and particularly about how it came into being, they are packed with revelations. The years 1914–15 – the period when Sibelius began making extensive sketches for the Fifth Symphony – are especially interesting. Sibelius writes about how he composes: 'Arrangement of the themes. This important task, which fascinates me in a mysterious way. It's as if God the Father had thrown down the tiles of a mosaic from heaven's floor and asked me to determine what kind of picture it was.' And he reflects on the broader meaning of his symphonies: 'To me they are confessions of faith from the different periods of my life. And from this it follows that my symphonies are all so different.'

Then, in an entry dated 21 April 1915, Sibelius relates one of the new symphony's themes to an event which stirred him to the core:

> Today at ten to eleven I saw sixteen swans. One of my greatest experiences! Lord God, what beauty! They circled over me for a long time. Disappeared into the solar haze like a gleaming, silver ribbon. Their call the same woodwind type as that of cranes, but without tremolo. The swan-call closer to the trumpet . . . A low-pitched refrain reminiscent of a small child crying. Nature mysticism and life's angst! The Fifth Symphony's finale-theme: legato in the trumpets!

It took Sibelius another four years of hard work (including two extensive revisions) to bring the Fifth Symphony to its final form. The musical tiles had to be moved around again and again before Sibelius was satisfied he could see the overall picture clearly. But one important feature is common to all three versions of the symphony. That finale theme – which Sibelius continued to refer to as his 'Swan Hymn' – doesn't actually appear on the trumpets until near the end of the symphony, where it is marked 'nobile' (noble). It heralds the beginning of a long, arduous crescendo, clearly evoking 'life's angst' in grinding dissonances and hard-edged orchestration. There are other passages in the Fifth Symphony where shadows fall across the music – the sombre, plaintive bassoon solo at the heart of the first movement (emerging through nervous, whispering string figures) is another point at which the music seems to look back to the pain and dark introspection of the Fourth Symphony (1911). Certainly the Fifth isn't all solar glory. But that only makes the final triumphant emergence of the 'Swan Hymn' all the more convincing: the symphony has had to struggle to achieve it.

A quiet, pregnant horn motif sets the first movement (Tempo molto moderato) on its course; this is the musical seed from which the music grows in two huge crescendo waves, each one topped by a blazing two-note trumpet-call.

Then the splendour fades, and we the hear the long, plaintive bassoon solo mentioned above. For a while, the music seems to have lost its sense of direction. In the symphony's first version (1915) the movement petered out soon after this, to be followed by a faster scherzo. But then Sibelius was struck by a stunning new idea – why not make the scherzo *emerge* from the Tempo molto moderato? The result is one of the most gripping transitions in symphonic music. It begins with another elemental crescendo; the original horn motif shines out on trumpets; then – almost imperceptibly at first – the tempo begins to quicken. The music goes on getting faster and faster; by the time we arrive at the 'Più presto' closing pages it's hurtling forward with tremendous energy – the nearest thing in music to a depiction of white-water rafting. It's hard to believe that this apparently seamless organic process wasn't conceived in a single inspiration – harder still to accept that it could have been achieved by moving around and exchanging musical 'tiles'.

At first, the next movement (Andante mosso, quasi allegretto) appears to offer a relaxing contrast. Broadly speaking, it is a set of free variations on a folk-like theme heard at the beginning (pizzicato strings and flutes). But things are going on under that seemingly calm surface, creating tensions which emerge in troubled string tremolos or in the brief but menacing brass crescendos towards the close.

The tension is released as action in the finale (Allegro molto), which begins as a rapid airborne dance for high strings. This sweeps on into the first appearance of the 'Swan Hymn' (swinging horn figures and a chant-like melody for high woodwind – more bird cries, perhaps). The whole process is repeated, but with telling variations – for example: the 'Swan Hymn' now appears in a different key, on woodwind and muted strings. Then the tempo drops and the mood becomes tense and expectant – until the 'Swan Hymn' returns quietly but radiantly on trumpets, initiating the long final crescendo. For a moment, 'Life's angst' seems to prevail, but at last the first swinging phrase of the 'Swan Hymn' re-emerges in full orchestral splendour. The end is remarkable: six sledgehammer chords separated by long silences – the music seems to hold its breath; then, suddenly, almost brusquely, Sibelius brings the symphony to a close.

Stephen Johnson © BBC

❧ Symphony No. 6 in D minor, Op. 104 (1923)

1 Allegro molto moderato
2 Allegretto moderato – Poco con moto
3 Poco vivace
4 Allegro molto – Allegro assai – Doppio più lento

Sibelius wrote down themes which ended up in his Sixth and Seventh Symphonies as early as 1914 and 1915, the period in which he composed the first version of his Fifth Symphony. It would take an awful lot of detective work, and some inspired guessing, to reconstruct the story of how he arrived at the final forms of two such different works, but they became unrecognisable from his descriptions in advance. The Sixth, he told a friend, would be 'wild and impassioned in character. Sombre, with pastoral contrasts. Probably in four movements, with the end rising to a sombre roaring of the orchestra in which the main theme is drowned.' As for the Seventh, it would have three movements, the last a 'Hellenic rondo'. He did, however, say that these plans might possibly be altered according to the development of the musical ideas, because 'as usual, I am a slave to my themes and submit to their demands'.

After Sibelius had actually finished the Sixth, he changed his description completely, and said it was 'very tranquil in character and outline'. As for the Seventh, three movements became one. No two symphonies by Sibelius are alike, and this was the composer's conscious decision, but the Sixth and Seventh, his last two, are even further from preconceived or academic forms – more 'mobile' – than any of their predecessors.

Once he settled down to composing the Sixth in earnest, Sibelius worked quite quickly, beginning in October 1922, and finishing it shortly before the first performance, in Helsinki, which he conducted the following February. The Seventh took another year and was first played in March 1924, in Stockholm, also with Sibelius conducting.

The Sixth is still probably the least often played and the least known of all Sibelius's symphonies. It is also held in particularly high regard by the most knowledgeable Sibelius enthusiasts, partly, perhaps, because it is undemonstrative and invites the most varied personal responses from listener to listener.

The serene opening is certainly one of the most unusual and beautiful ways to begin a symphony that anyone could imagine, evoking trees stirred by the wind, in the unsullied Dorian mode (the 'natural', or white-note, scale on D), until it crescendos into a grinding chromatic discord from which emerges, on the brass, C major. At this juncture the music sets out more playfully, against a simmering accompaniment on harp and strings.

Having established the harmonic and modal home ground of the movement (and the entire symphony), Sibelius tries his hardest to destabilise it, with a particularly decisive plunge into B minor when the cellos propose something at last resembling a melody (though it's marked 'mezza voce', so the listener should have to search it out) amid the almost casual surrounding figuration. A terse, heroic flourish (the old Sibelius helping us to get our bearings) breaks out in F major, but proves a red herring as a tide of ascending and descending scales washes it away. The penultimate moments are darkly threatening (shuddering cellos), if not downright weird, before a D flat major scale climbs upwards, giving way to a bold C major chord. Then, more quietly, the peace of the Dorian mode to end.

Sibelius himself said that the Sixth Symphony was built on linear rather than harmonic foundations. But although a composer has privileged knowledge of his own work, we are not obliged to accept what he says about it as the whole truth.

Sibelius may have been thinking of the strange modal patterns that are such a feature of this symphony, and he loved scales just as much as Mozart did, but harmony plays a powerful role, too, and the opening woodwind chords of the second movement are as piquant as passages in Richard Strauss's *Ariadne auf Naxos*. These thread their way through the major part of the movement, to distinctly anguished effect (and ambiguities of key centre), while the violins outline phrases with a defiant, if fractured, cast. Quite unpredictably, the latter part of the movement (Poco con moto) is entirely taken up with subdued oscillating patterns on the strings and louder woodwind interjections. Is this a kind of naturalistic reverie? Note the quietly shocking cadence (the chords of D major, C major, G minor).

After the unsettling effect of the second movement, the third is more definite, firmer. It is a frozen scherzo, with long, harmonically static passages over pedal points connected by accented chords on the brass which serve as hinges. They also provide splashes of heightened colour. Melodic, or thematic, interest is reluctant to emerge, and the atmosphere is subdued until the rollicking final chorus, horns braying.

With the final movement, we have more definite themes than anywhere else in the symphony, and for the first time, regular phrases which answer each other. The opening antiphonal exchanges between woodwind and strings are abruptly replaced by a more playful, mobile style and then a more purposeful mood, which eventually works up into a howling storm, cut short by a modified return to the opening dialogue. The home stretch (Allegro assai) is reached with a sense of relief, as if to anticipate a resolution, which comes, finally (Doppio più lento), at a slower pace. In a sense, this final movement can be regarded as a set of free variations on the opening phrases, though people have described it in all sorts of ways, and we might as well rest content with the composer's assertion that, like the other movements, it was 'formally completely free'.

Adrian Jack © BBC

❧ Symphony No. 7 in C major, Op. 105 (1924)

Adagio – Vivacissimo – Adagio – Allegro molto
moderato – Vivace – Presto – Adagio

Sibelius's Seventh is very different from his Sixth Symphony
– much more positive, easier to understand (hence its relative
popularity) and more broadly conceived. The three separate
movements the composer at one time envisaged became one:
fluid, various but unified, like an ocean which may be calm or
storm-tossed, but is always in motion. Save for a few bars, the
whole work is written in 3/2 or 6/4, a constant unit that fluc-
tuates only up to a point, beyond which it is subdivided to
make faster music. The harmony is not modal, unlike that of
the Sixth: there is as dramatic a battle for the home key as in
any symphony by Beethoven. It takes no fewer than sixty bars
for C major to assert itself for the first time, and at the very
end of the symphony, its achievement is stressed by prolonged dissonances which resolve only reluctantly.

Perhaps the experience of writing the Sixth released a more
relaxed and expansive melodic style in the later work, which
is punctuated at three salient moments by a noble statement
on a solo trombone: it clinches C major after the long, richly
scored opening section; then, following a series of playful
exchanges between woodwind and strings, it steadies a gathering storm; and, towards the end, it marks a point of arrival.

Adrian Jack © BBC

Richard Strauss (1864–1949)

Strauss composed from his early years (his first two published works were written when he was ten), and also developed a conducting career alongside his success in composition: 1886 saw not only the premiere of his First Horn Concerto, but also a conducting post at the Munich Court Opera. In the same year, influenced by Liszt, he produced *Aus Italien*, the first of a string of brilliantly orchestrated tone poems extending through the 1890s, among them *Don Juan*, *Till Eulenspiegel* and *Also sprach Zarathustra*. Strauss was also inspired by Wagner, and went on to write some of the 20th century's finest operas: in 1905 he shocked the operatic world with *Salome*. *Elektra* (1909, another fiercely powerful portrait) marked his first collaboration with the poet Hugo von Hofmannsthal, a partnership that bore four further operas, including the comedy *Der Rosenkavalier* (1911). Towards the end of his life, he returned to a more conservative style, with works such as the Second Horn Concerto (1943). He died on 8 September 1949, several months before the first performance of his *Four Last Songs*.

∾ *An Alpine Symphony*, Op. 64 (1911–15)

Night – Sunrise – Ascent – Entry into the forest – Scene by the brook – Waterfall – Apparition – Flowery meadows – Mountain pasture – Thickets, briars, erring tracks – On the glacier – Dangerous moments – Summit – Vision – Rising mists – The sun gradually hazes over – Elegy – Calm before the storm – Storm and descent – Sunset – Dying away – Night

Behind the obvious up/down trajectory of the *Alpine Symphony* lies an inner programme of great importance to its composer: a Nietzschean hymn to the oneness of humanity and nature that makes the work a sequel to *Also sprach Zarathustra* rather than to the autobiographical *Ein Heldenleben* and *Symphonia domestica*. Strauss originally wanted it called *The Anti-Christ* after the first instalment (1888) of Nietzsche's 'revaluation of all values'. The symphony, he said, 'contains moral purification through one's own strength, freedom through work, worship of nature eternal and magnificent'. Though this might have been a welcome clarion call to the offensive/defensive spirit of wartime Germany (the piece was completed, and first performed, in 1915), his publishers were understandably reluctant to sanction such an explicit affront to orthodox Christianity, and the current title prevailed.

Since the scheme of an ascent and descent is of its nature allegorical, emblematic, *moralisé*, this decision surely accords best with Strauss's genius for the actual rather than the metaphysical. And the *Alpine Symphony* is certainly centred in actual experience – boyhood holidays, a teenage adventure prophesying the eventual narrative (its immediate outcome was a fantasia for solo piano), a mooted orchestral piece around the turn of the century, returned to in 1911 while awaiting a further operatic text from Hugo von Hofmannsthal to follow up the success of their *Rosenkavalier*. The attitude then, however, was disconcertingly flippant; Strauss told his librettist that the interim symphony gave him less amusement than swiping insects.

By 1914 it had matured into high seriousness. Minor irritation with hot-weather bugs evolved into a major expression, via Goethe and Nietzsche, of man's relationship with nature, evinced by his own powers of creation and re-creation. This must explain the tone of that on-the-face-of-it puzzling remark, 'Now at last I have learnt to orchestrate', as well as his concern in later life to programme the Alpine Symphony in preference to the earlier symphonic poems, all of them more popular, some to the point of being hackneyed.

Since his conspicuous orchestral mastery had been universally acknowledged from *Don Juan* onwards, what can he have meant? His own term for his earlier technique was 'alfresco', meaning (perhaps) a kind of safety-in-numbers brilliance, bustle, sheen, allure; the *Alpine Symphony*, by comparison, handles its colossal forces with prime-of-life comprehensiveness. One remarkable feature is the extraordinary sense throughout its first half of rising into ever higher altitudes without crass literalness. This demonstrates rare mastery. Yet there is little doubt that the work's actual material is less distinctive – often bland, sometimes banal – than in those unforgettable early stunners, and the operas that followed. Perhaps another notorious remark associated with this work – 'I wanted to compose it as a cow gives milk' – has applications beyond the merely metaphorical.

Definitely not for the opening and close, a magnificent evocation of 'Night' with the majestic mountain contour (brass chorale) soft yet firm through the thick blanket of shimmering blackness (multi-divided strings sustaining all the notes of the B flat minor scale over four octaves). The darkness begins to sift and disperse, the mountain contour grows more distinct, and with a single glockenspiel note the first splinter of light strikes the summit; 'Sunrise' ensues with a marvellous whoosh.

The 'Ascent' sets out the symphony's main theme, vigorous, energetic, upward-tending, all hope and aspiration. Soon we encounter a hunting party – sixteen off-stage brass players (twelve horns, pairs of trumpets and trombones) have a good time. The 'Entry into the forest' (the main theme manfully confronting nature turned suddenly threatening, before mitigation into birdsong and lovely solo-string passages) prepares the ground for the 'Scene by the brook', which soon builds up to an iridescent 'Waterfall' containing an 'Apparition' – perhaps an Alpine Fairy as in Byron's *Manfred* (previously rendered in music by Schumann and Tchaikovsky). For 'Flowery meadows' and 'Mountain pasture' Mahler inevitably comes to mind – cowbells, birdsong, nostalgic yodelling. An echo resounds into the resonating spaces.

The music presses on and up into more rarefied elevations, is soon entangled in 'Thickets, briars, erring tracks', and aghast at their culmination, 'On the glacier'. After 'Dangerous moments' (closely recalling the nightmare between heated bedroom and bustling breakfast in the *Symphonia domestica*), gleaming exposed textures without comfort lead to the 'Summit' which, after the expected fanfaring brass, yields to a shy, wavering oboe solo, before bathetic triumph in C major – Strauss's most dangerous key – sweeps all doubts away.

'Vision', the symphony's still centre, is achieved by masterful diminution of volume and density – a soft supplicatory celebration tinged with ambiguity and questioning (and a marvellously agile solo for the first trumpet), leading to an area of dark perplexity, the mountain contour reappearing, choked in riffles of 'Rising mists'. 'The sun gradually hazes over'. 'Elegy' (eloquent massed string lines supported by the organ), then 'Calm before the storm' (combining snatches of the elegiac music with the tentative view from the summit, now on clarinet, intertwined with the intermittent prickle of a high, soft, repeated oboe-note). The opening curtain of thick-clustered B flat minor returns, with lurid onomatopoeia for distant lightning and thunder, precipitating 'Storm and descent' in all its furious closeness, vividly and naively rendered in wild flailing and rushing, underpinned by massive organ chords and a whirling wind machine, while the main ascent-theme scrambles precipitately downwards as best it can. This, the symphony's recapitulation, revisits some of the places along the upward climb in reverse order – the wildly agitated waterfall is especially memorable.

The sound and fury abate: when they wholly cease, the mountain contour is revealed again, naked and plain. 'Sunset' (with elements of the 'Elegy'): the organ re-emerges redomesticated as background support, coming to the fore in its own right, then in 'Dying away' accompanying a solo horn, then solo trumpet, then a bank of woodwinds (whereupon the horn soloist falls silent, the player's rest marked by the composer 'in gentle ecstasy'). As this paragraph closes, the strings re-enter in a long, rapt descant over the final putting-to-rest of the aspiring main theme. The *Alpine Symphony*'s secret message – 'purification through strength, freedom through work, reverence for nature eternal and magnificent' – has been uttered. The echo heard earlier resounds again into the darkening spaces. All doubts as to over-protraction in this final stretch are resolved when the opening haze descends and 'Night' settles over the whole huge panorama; the mountain contour, more subliminal than actual, is seen/heard once more through the dense darkness, and the closing phrase (on violins) sketches the complete ascent/descent trajectory in five summative bars.

© Robin Holloway

Igor Stravinsky (1882–1971)

Stravinsky's unrivalled impact on the course of twentieth-century music was originally brought about by the complexity and originality of his first ballets, on Russian themes, for Diaghilev's Ballets Russes: *The Firebird* (1910), *Petrushka* (1911) and *The Rite of Spring* (1913), though we now know how much they owe to the Russian folk-music tradition. With his move to Paris and another ballet, *Pulcinella* (1920), came a shift to the sharp-edged clarity of the neo-classical style, which also characterises the Octet (1923) and the Piano Concerto (1924). In the eight months to June 1939, Stravinsky suffered the loss of his daughter, wife and mother in turn and, with war impending, decamped to the USA, where he undertook numerous conducting tours, and composed *The Rake's Progress* (1951). In the 1950s, ever in tune with the times, Stravinsky made another compositional change, in which he embraced serialism (the ballet *Agon*, 1957; the cantata *Threni*, 1958). He made many recordings of his own music, as both conductor and pianist.

∾ Symphony in C (1939–40)

1 Moderato alla breve
2 Larghetto concertante
3 Allegretto
4 Largo – Tempo giusto, alla breve

My new symphony is going to be Classical in spirit, more concise in its form than Beethoven . . . Instead of all chords gravitating toward one final tonic chord, all notes gravitate toward a single note. Thus the symphony will be neither a Symphony in C major nor a Symphony in C minor, but simply a Symphony in C.

So Stravinsky described his new work in an interview with a Boston newspaper in October 1939. Only the first two movements were then complete. He had just arrived in the USA for what he had planned as his fourth visit, but would in fact remain there for the rest of his life. He later suggested that he could feel some disparity between the symphony's first two 'European' movements and the third and fourth 'American' movements, but no other commentator has been able to detect any such break in style.

The symphony took shape during the most disturbed and unhappy period of Stravinsky's life. By the autumn of 1938 the outbreak of war was inevitable; his eldest daughter died in November 1938, and then his wife and mother died within three months of each other in the spring of 1939; Stravinsky himself became seriously ill, and the symphony's first two movements were composed in the sanatorium where he was convalescing. These public and personal disasters are not, of course, reflected in the music (Stravinsky's aesthetic of music as something 'supra-personal and supra-real' would naturally forbid that) but they may well have acted in an opposite direction, leading Stravinsky to plan his work on the purest classical lines – a challenge, as it were, to the disorder and disintegration that surrounded him.

The instrumental works from the decade preceding the Symphony in C (notably the Violin Concerto, the Concerto for Two Pianos, the ballet *Jeu de cartes* and the concerto *Dumbarton Oaks*) are largely articulated through techniques deriving from the Baroque, in particular ritornello and concertante principles. The *Dumbarton Oaks* concerto (1938) is Stravinsky's 'Brandenburg', and really marks the end of his fruitful re-examination of Baroque methods. Now began a period when he was to refer back to the Viennese classical tradition, with which he had always had an ambiguous relationship, largely because in his youth he had reacted so strongly against music which he saw as representing its decadence and exhaustion. He had certainly had Beethoven in mind in 1924, when he composed his Piano Sonata, and now it was to be the classical symphony of Beethoven and Haydn that served him as a background and cultural reference point for his own.

To the names of Beethoven and Haydn should also be added that of Tchaikovsky. The relationship between Stravinsky and Tchaikovsky is only superficially incongruous. Both composers were intensely conscious of their Russianness (and for all his displacement, Stravinsky thought in Russian until the end of his life), and both sought to cross-pollinate their innate national characteristics with the best of Western techniques and styles. A further link between the two is their devotion to ballet. When Tchaikovsky's pupil Taneyev observed that passages in the Fourth Symphony sounded like ballet music, the composer's reply was essentially, 'And why shouldn't they?' Stravinsky would have defended the balletic gestures of his symphony in much the same way.

The outward shape of the Symphony in C, as well as its general proportions of time and density, follow classical patterns. The four movements, which last around twenty-five minutes, comprise a sonata allegro, a slow movement, a quick dance movement and a finale with slow introduction. There are close thematic links between the movements, the most important being the various permutations and transformations of the three-note figure B–C–G with which the symphony opens, and which returns in augmentation at the end of the finale.

A remarkable feature of the first movement is that for all its rhythmic vivacity, everything is contained within the initial 2/2 time signature. As the composer pointed out, 'the first movement is the only large one in the whole inventory of my mature works with no change of metre, whereas the third movement's rhythmic irregularities are among the most extreme in any of my compositions.'

Although its form and lineaments refer to a long-established symphonic tradition, Stravinsky's music does not and cannot aim at the sort of dialectic that we generally associate with the word 'symphonic'. When the work first appeared, there was considerable discussion as to whether or not it was a 'real' symphony. What is beyond question is that it is 'real'

Stravinsky. The traditional elements of syntax – modulations, transitions, developments – are all to be found where they might be expected, but frequently behave in very unexpected ways. We are often made to feel that we are faced with the *idea* of a symphony, but that the actual processes are refracted beyond recognition through Stravinsky's unique sensibility. The past is absorbed, broken up and then reassembled to create a new vision of order and clarity.

The Symphony in C was informally commissioned by the Chicago Symphony Orchestra in 1938, but this was only confirmed in April 1940; almost until the outbreak of the war Stravinsky believed that the first performance might be given in London by the BBC Symphony Orchestra. When the symphony was finally completed in August 1940, Stravinsky wrote on the title page: 'This Symphony, composed to the Glory of God, is dedicated to the Chicago Symphony Orchestra on the occasion of the Fiftieth Anniversary of its existence.' Stravinsky himself conducted the premiere in Chicago on 7 November 1940, and the first British performance was given by the BBC Symphony Orchestra under Adrian Boult in 1943.

© Andrew Huth

ᕽ Symphony in Three Movements (1942–5)

1   ♩ = 160
2   Andante
3   Con moto

Usually so sure of his artistic direction, Stravinsky experienced three periods of obvious stylistic anxiety in the course of his long working life. The first, at the end of the First World War, reflected the prevailing insecurities of the time, magnified by the problems of exile. The third, after *The Rake's Progress* (premiered in Venice in 1951), was also, in its way, Stravinsky's reaction to the crisis of modernism after the Second War. The second, during his initial years in the USA in the early 1940s, had no such general cause, but was apparently a symptom of disorientation in his personal life: new country, new friends, new wife. Stravinsky's music of the time reflects his unsettled state. For the first time he accepts frankly commercial work; he starts pieces then puts them aside; he makes works out of unrelated fragments. He becomes, for a time, more devout, as well as (perhaps consciously) more Russian. Creatively, this is possibly the most confused period of his whole career. That it should somehow have given birth to a masterpiece like the Symphony in Three Movements proves only that, where genius is concerned, ordinary standards do not apply.

Stravinsky's own account of the origins of this work is bizarre. He regarded it as in some sense a war symphony. The violent outer movements, he confessed, were inspired by war documentaries of 'scorched-earth tactics in China', newsreels of goose-stepping Nazis, and (at the end) the rise of the Allies. As for the central movement, this is supposed actually to have been written as film music, to accompany the scene of the 'Apparition of the Virgin' in *The Song of Bernadette*, the 1943 Oscar-winning Hollywood adaptation of the 1941 novel by Stravinsky's fellow émigré (and Alma Mahler's third husband), Franz Werfel. The film score itself was never written, for the characteristic Stravinsky reason that 'the conditions, business and artistic, [were] entirely in favour of the film producer'. In fact, most of the early 1940s film projects mentioned by Stravinsky in his conversations must have been word-of-mouth affairs, since little relevant business correspondence survives in the composer's archives – a fairly sure sign that not much existed. Vera Stravinsky's diaries report only 'visits' by film moguls, and there are oblique references in letters to publishers. The truth probably is that any accommodation to the real musical needs of the silver screen would have been out of the question for Stravinsky, as we can gauge from the rumpus he later made about Stokowski's adaptation of *The Rite of Spring* for the Disney film *Fantasia*. It would certainly be hard to imagine anything less cinematic than the middle movement of the present symphony. The other programmatic suggestions are hardly any truer to Stravinsky's music, and perhaps the most interesting thing about them is that he ever let them slip out at all.

Whatever its precise origins, the symphony was composed over a period of time, and its movements were combined at a late stage. The first movement was written in 1942, at a time of intense anxiety about the political situation in Europe, and when the west coast of the USA was itself under threat of war (Vera's diaries record being woken in Santa Barbara by air-raid sirens). Even so, the movement was composed as a coherent whole, in Stravinsky's usual highly focused manner, and its aggression is buoyant, not anguished. The slow movement followed in 1943, and the finale (apart from a brief notation among the 1942 sketches) not until the early summer of 1945.

According to Robert Craft, the composer's assistant and chronicler, Stravinsky often described the first movement as a piano concerto, even though the sketches suggest that the piano was a late addition to the score. The piano, in any case, does not feature in the second movement (where the solo role is taken by a harp), while the combination of piano and harp in the finale is a natural – and very Russian – solution to the problem of combining the two unrelated movements, as perhaps is the use of material belonging in origin to the first movement.

But are they unrelated? Certainly the tone of the Andante is in drastic contrast to that of the outer movements, its neo-rococo ornateness seemingly at odds with their Dionysiac frenzy. There are, nevertheless, significant similarities. The most audible is the way the slow movement picks up the bass clarinet's repeated quaver figure at the end of the first movement, including its occasional silent downbeat, and treats it as the basis of the new main theme. There are also thematic similarities. For instance, the curious dotted melody for low flute which forms the basis of the Andante's middle section is clearly related to material in the first movement, while the harp accompaniment uses an arpeggiated idea fundamental to both the outer movements. Finally there is important common ground in the area of harmony. In all three movements, Stravinsky uses a modal scale made up of alternating tones and semitones (the so-called octatonic scale, or Messiaen's Mode 2), which yields features like the clashing major and minor thirds in the first subjects of the Andante and finale respectively, the grinding triads an augmented fourth apart in the first movement, and the association between the opening C major and closing D flat major in the finale, which answers the dramatic minor ninth with which the work opens.

On the other hand, something episodic in the writing as a whole belies the work's description as a symphony. No doubt its long-range connections (including those mentioned above) are symphonic. But the underlying character of Stravinsky's writing is as always sectional and concerto-like (he himself says in *Expositions and Developments* that he 'thought of the work then as a concerto for orchestra'). This may recall Messiaen's 'personnages musicals'. Particularly in the outer movement, one has the feeling of ideas intercut with one another, in the character of a film montage. If you want a cinematic association with Stravinsky, this is probably the most suitable one you could find.

© Stephen Walsh

Pyotr Ilyich Tchaikovsky (1840–93)

After study at the School of Jurisprudence and four years working in the Ministry of Justice, Tchaikovsky enrolled at the newly founded St Petersburg Conservatory (1862–5). He came into contact with the 'The Five', whose leader, Balakirev, supervised the younger composer's *Romeo and Juliet* overture (1869), which already displayed a gift for tragic lyricism. Despite his homosexuality, he married a young admirer of his music in 1877, which proved disastrous after a matter of weeks. That year also saw the beginning of a fourteen-year relationship with Nadezhda von Meck: though they never met, she acted as Tchaikovsky's benefactress and soulmate by correspondence, and the ballet *Swan Lake*, the Fourth Symphony and the opera *Eugene Onegin* were the results of her support. A fallow period followed the successful Violin Concerto (1878), lasting until the *Manfred* Symphony (1884). Between 1890 and 1892 he wrote two further ballets, *The Sleeping Beauty* and *The Nutcracker*, demonstrating a skill and seriousness of purpose in the medium unusual for a composer principally renowned for his symphonies. He died, possibly through suicide, within ten days of conducting the premiere of his Sixth Symphony.

∾ Symphony No. 2 in C minor, Op. 17, 'Little Russian' (1872–3, revised 1879)

1 Andante sostenuto – Allegro vivo
2 Andante marziale, quasi moderato
3 Scherzo and Trio: Allegro molto vivace
4 Finale: Moderato assai – Allegro Vivo – Presto

Although Tchaikovsky never became a fully fledged member of Balakirev's group of Russian nationalist composers, 'The Five', he gained associate membership, as it were, by means of

the Finale of this work. It was at a musical evening arranged at
the house of Rimsky-Korsakov in December 1872, after a
piano performance of this Finale, that the enraptured company
'almost tore me to pieces', as Tchaikovsky put it in a letter
written shortly afterwards to his brother Modest. V. V. Stasov,
chief ideologue and propagandist of 'The Five', was in close
touch with Tchaikovsky during the period of the symphony's
first complete public performance (Moscow, 7 February 1873)
and never forgot it. Later in 1873, he was to write:

> Tchaikovsky has not always been successful in handling
> folk material, but he has created one masterpiece in this
> idiom – the Finale of his Symphony in C minor, based on
> the Ukrainian folk song 'The Crane'. In terms of colour,
> structure and humour this movement (in C major) is one
> of the most important creations of the entire Russian
> School.

Of the first three symphonies, it was the Second that came
to overshadow its no-less-worthy neighbours in public
esteem, less perhaps on account of any intrinsic superiority
than through this rousing Finale, with its several echoes of
Glinka's *Kamarinskaya* and *Ruslan and Lyudmila*, and its kinship with such things as the great '*Slava*' choral scene
(Prologue, Scene 2) of Musorgsky's *Boris Godunov* and 'The
Great Gate of Kiev' that ends *Pictures at an Exhibition*. And
perhaps the publicity the Finale received has tended to push
into the background the fact that Tchaikovsky, conscientiously
self-critical as always, subjected the work to a very thorough
revision in 1879. (As Gerald Abraham has observed, the critics seem not to have noticed the alterations at the first performance of the revised version in 1881.) It is fascinating to
discover, for instance, that the yearning second subject of the
first-movement Allegro originally served as the opening
theme and that, replacing it with the familiar martial theme
in repeated notes, Tchaikovsky completely recomposed the
first movement, leaving only the introduction and coda in
their previous form. (Not all Tchaikovsky's colleagues, by the

way, felt that this revision was an improvement on the original, and that view has since been endorsed in David Brown's authoritative study of the work in his critical biography.)

Such considerations apart, the work in its present form surely deserves its lasting popularity. It is not just the Finale, of course, that uses folk material from the Ukraine ('Little Russia'). The first movement begins with a folk tune on the solo horn which – both here (as a theme for variations) and in its subsequent incorporation into the development section of the Allegro – recalls not only Tchaikovsky's own practice in *Romeo and Juliet* but suggests the influence of Schubert in the first movement of his Ninth Symphony. Another folk tune makes its appearance (flute and oboe) in the middle section of the second movement; marking an allusion to the symphony's main key (C minor) and sharing the melodic contours and treatment of its big brother in the first movement; it can be interpreted as an *idée fixe* in the larger context of the symphony as a dramatic whole. The Scherzo's dance Trio is also folk-like, with its insistent anapaestic rhythms (short–short–long) and splendidly characteristic retransition to the Scherzo, via urgent antiphonal dialogue between wind and strings. There is no slow movement: instead we have a droll little march with a contrasting second tune of great tenderness. Following the large-scale symphonic march of the first movement with its grand passions, there is a touch of dramatic irony here as if we were listening to a gentle parody of what has just taken place. This movement had started life as a wedding march taken from a destroyed opera, *Undine*, of 1869; possessing neither the rapt contemplation of its second-movement counterpart in the First Symphony nor the agitated feeling of the fourth-movement Andante in the Third Symphony, it is nonetheless a pointer towards the more pungent transformation of march idioms that took place in the inner movements of the Fourth and Sixth.

Both the splendidly Russian Scherzo, with its charging iambic metre and clashing major seconds, and the brilliant Finale, reveal Tchaikovsky's instinctive feeling for rhythm and orchestral timbre. As Stasov pointed out, Tchaikovsky was by temperament an orchestral composer and his inimitable sense of instrumental character is always part and parcel of the themes and their treatment. As a small but significant example, take the way in which Scherzo and Trio are united in the epigrammatic little coda of the third movement. Here is the same kind of linkage through antiphonal exchange that was to make the coda to the Scherzo of the Fourth so exciting. In the fleeting cavalcade come woodwind, strings and horns, then the cutting edge of the trumpets is unleashed in the swift build-up to the final gesture. At the other end of the scale, the sheer physical élan of the Finale's crowd scene presents that public face which made him a man of the people. At the time of the Second Symphony, however, he could still mingle with the crowd without self-pity, and that gives the Finale its own unclouded exuberance.

© Eric Roseberry

✺ Symphony No. 4 in F minor, Op. 36
(1877–8)

1 Andante sostenuto – Moderato con anima
2 Andantino in modo di canzona
3 Scherzo (Pizzicato ostinato): Allegro
4 Finale: Allegro con fuoco

By early 1877, when Tchaikovsky began sketching his Fourth Symphony, he had reached the height of his powers. He had just completed his first great opera, *Eugene Onegin*, following on from his first balletic masterpiece, *Swan Lake*, and his grandiose First Piano Concerto. He had just started to benefit from the regular allowance sent to him by the wealthy, eccentric widow, Nadezhda von Meck.

On the other side of the balance, he was about to enter a marriage, with disastrous consequences not unconnected to his homosexuality. The reasons for this move, and the nature of the ensuing events, have been much mythologised, and recent scholarship reveals them to have been rather more mundane than was once believed (there is no evidence, for instance, that Tchaikovsky was moved to attempt suicide). Nevertheless, it is true that he himself considered the Fourth Symphony to be at some level a reflection of his recent emotional strife.

Tchaikovsky's benefactress has to be thanked for more than just her generous material support. Following the first performance of the Fourth Symphony in February 1878, she asked her protégé whether the work had any kind of programme. And this innocent query elicited one of the most famous letters ever penned by a composer: one that hardly any commentator has since been able to resist.

Tchaikovsky referred to the symphony's blood-curdling opening fanfares as 'the kernel of the whole symphony': 'This is Fate, the force of destiny, which ever prevents our pursuit of happiness from reaching its goal . . . It is invincible, inescapable. One can only resign oneself and lament fruitlessly.' And he duly wrote out the theme of 'fruitless lament', which is the quiet, breathless idea on violins and cellos, after the fanfares have ebbed into silence. This agitated music ebbs and flows with all the instability we would normally expect from a symphony's development section. But ultimately it achieves nothing, ending up in the F minor tonic where it began. Almost as though there has never been a problem, the clarinet and bassoon hit on a friendlier version of the lamenting theme, the tempo slows, and suddenly a new idea is upon us, lilting and balletic in its motion, on a solo clarinet, with the flutes echoing. As Tchaikovsky more poetically put it: 'Would it not be better to turn from Reality and immerse oneself in Dreams?' Even the lamenting theme can now return with a smile on its face.

But this easy solution to the problem of malign destiny is premature, and at the peak of exaltation the opening fanfares burst in, on snarling trumpets and horns. 'This was only a dream, and Fate awakes us,' as Tchaikovsky hardly needed to confirm. Laments and the ghastly summons of fate continue to alternate in the development section, to increasingly desperate effect, and the recapitulation again plays out the drama of Dreams and Reality. An inspired, multi-sectioned coda drives home the message that 'All life is the ceaseless alternation of bitter reality with evanescent visions and dreams of happiness.'

This first movement is almost as bulky as the other three put together, and it casts a long shadow. Tchaikovsky's letter sets the scene for the slow movement, referring to 'that melancholy feeling that arises in the evening as you sit alone, worn out from your labours'. As in the first movement, there are contrasting themes that Tchaikovsky describes as memories of 'blissful moments when our young blood seethed and life was good'. Note the past tense. Happiness in this symphony is almost never in the here and now. Finally the opening song-like theme returns, with added decorative figures in the woodwind, very reminiscent of their contributions to the first movement's 'Dream' theme.

There are three main ideas in the Scherzo, all of them sharply characterised. The first is a dancing pizzicato in the strings; the second is a folksy tune on the oboe, over a drone bass in the bassoon, for which Tchaikovsky suggested the image of a drunken peasant; the third evokes a far-off military parade. These three themes are shuffled around, superimposed and cunningly spliced. For Tchaikovsky they were 'fugitive images that pass through one's mind when one has had a little wine to drink and is feeling the first effects of intoxication'.

Then comes a rude awakening, with the rushing unison theme of the finale. Here Tchaikovsky's description tells only one side of the story: 'If you can find no impulse for joy within yourself, look at others. Go out among the people. See how well they know how to rejoice and give themselves up utterly to glad feelings. It is a picture of a popular holiday festivity.' The finale's second theme – first heard on the woodwind punctuated by rushing scales on violins and violas – seems to confirm that description, since it is a folk song, famous to all Russians: 'In the field stood a birch-tree.'

But there are other resonances in Tchaikovsky's words, not least in his phrase 'Go out among the people.' That echoes the celebrated injunction of Alexander Herzen, the spiritual founder of the Russian revolutionary movement: 'Go to the People,' he declared – and that is just what the so-called Populists did in 1874 and 1875, just three years before Tchaikovsky was composing his symphony. What the Populists encountered, however, was widespread indifference, if not downright hostility. As one Russian commentator later put it, 'Socialism bounced off people like peas from a wall.'

Tchaikovsky himself was a staunch Tsarist and at one with his patroness in despising Communism. Though his views on the Populist movement are not recorded, it is entirely possible that his use of the phrase 'Go out among the people' was ironic and that he was aware that Going to the People might not be as fulfilling as it promised to be. If so, that would account for his finale's increasingly panicky attempts at affirmation, eventually halted by the dire summons of the first movement's fate theme. After that, it is very much up to the conductor whether to interpret the coda as straightforwardly triumphant, or to push it over the edge into hysteria.

© David Fanning

∾ Symphony No. 5 in E minor, Op. 64
(1888)

1 Andante – Allegro con anima
2 Andante cantabile, con alcuna licenza
3 Valse: Allegro moderato
4 Finale: Andante maestoso – Allegro vivace

In Leipzig in January 1888, at an intimate luncheon, Tchaikovsky first met both Brahms and Grieg. He took immediately to the latter, promptly deciding that his next symphony would be dedicated to him. Brahms was more problematic, proving to be easier company after they had been drinking a little. But the real difficulty was Brahms's music; it was not to Tchaikovsky's taste, though he never questioned the German's stature or integrity. Tchaikovsky was on his first foreign tour as a conductor, and Brahms attended a rehearsal of his First Suite, though without being impressed except by the opening Introduction and Fugue.

Then in Hamburg, a fortnight later, Tchaikovsky met a certain Theodor Avé-Lallemant, an old man of very conservative tastes who struggled to Tchaikovsky's rehearsals – but then told him frankly, though with great embarrassment, that he disliked his music, especially its noisy percussion. But, he added, if only Tchaikovsky would settle in Germany and accept the Western classical tradition, there was hope for him. The two men parted cordially, for Tchaikovsky recognised the criticism was honest and based on a real acquaintance with his music. Nevertheless, the encounter seems to have stirred him to take on the implied challenge. He would show them by composing a symphony in which his own Russian voice was uncompromisingly clear, yet which would also exhibit that balanced structure and expressive control which Avé-Lallemant valued so greatly and which Brahms exemplified so ideally. And having composed the symphony, in a charmingly mischievous spirit he dedicated it to Avé-Lallemant. (Grieg would be compensated with the dedication of the fantasy-overture *Hamlet* instead.)

Like the Fourth and Sixth Symphonies, the Fifth is programmatic – in some way concerned with fate – and pointedly quotes a piece of existing music: in this case a phrase setting the words 'Turn not into sorrow' in the trio of Glinka's opera *A Life for the Tsar*. A fragmentary programme also exists for the first movement: 'Introduction. Complete submission before Fate – or (what is the same thing) the inscrutable design of Providence. Allegro: 1. Murmurs, doubts, laments . . . 2. Shall I cast myself into the embrace of faith?' This also helps clarify the role of the Glinka-derived motto or 'fate theme' which opens the symphony and which recurs in all the later movements, twice erupting brutally in the slow movement, but by contrast slipping almost benignly into the end of the Valse, then pealing out reassuringly in the introduction to the Finale and triumphantly at the end. Tchaikovsky's programme shows that fate is now to be identified with the divine will, and thus gives promise of ultimate redemption – so we are surely justified if we feel that all ends in a spirit less of defiance than of determined optimism.

The Fifth Symphony is a work whose content is totally characteristic of Tchaikovsky, yet which heeds the older classical tradition, deliberately rejecting the kind of structural innovations so boldly exploited in the Fourth and Sixth. To have created a symphony which is both profoundly programmatic yet perfectly viable when heard simply as music is a remarkable achievement.

So what did Brahms and Avé-Lallemant think of the symphony? In 1889 Tchaikovsky returned to Hamburg to conduct the new piece, arriving to find Brahms installed in the neighbouring hotel room. The latter delayed his departure by a day so that he could hear the symphony, and reportedly approved of everything except the Finale. Sadly, it seems that Avé-Lallemant never heard the piece. But one thing would certainly have pleased him: unusually, Tchaikovsky had restricted his percussion writing to include only timpani.

The first movement is the most poised of sonata structures, though the exposition does contain three, rather than two, subjects. The middle movements play a different role to those of the Fourth and Sixth Symphonies: there, they provide respite from the weightier matters of the corresponding first movements. Not so in the Fifth; after the relatively concise first movement, the slow movement reveals itself as the emotional heart of the symphony, with its meltingly melancholic horn theme, more impassioned second melody, and the rough intrusions of the fate theme. The movement's centre is more relaxed, however; the engaging Valse that follows yet more so.

Nor does the Finale return to weightier matters. Like many classical finales, it is bright and buoyant, though in length it nicely balances the first movement. After the Glinka-derived theme has returned for the last time in the grandiose coda, all is brought full circle in a recall of the first movement's main theme.

© David Brown

∾ Symphony No. 6 in B minor, Op. 74, 'Pathétique' (1893)

1 Adagio – Allegro non troppo
2 Allegro con grazia
3 Allegro molto vivace
4 Finale: Adagio lamentoso

Tchaikovsky would not disclose the secret programme of his Sixth Symphony, composed in the last year of his life at the height of his international fame and recognition. (There had been a Cambridge honorary doctorate that very year.) Tantalisingly, he had thought of calling it simply 'Programme Symphony' until his brother Modest came up with the suggestion of 'Pathétique'. 'Capital,' said Tchaikovsky and, bearing that title, to his Moscow publishers it went, with all the connotations (Beethovenian and otherwise) of an adjective meaning many things to many people.

We know that Tchaikovsky considered that he had put more of himself, more sincerity (to use his own word), into this symphony than into anything he had previously written. And the word 'sincerity' sets up immediate connections with his two previous symphonies, for he had been worried about the lack of it in the noisy march Finale of his Fifth. That symphony had been a sort of sequel to his 'fateful' Fourth, in whose Finale he had sought (but clearly did not find) consolation in popular rejoicing.

If we accept that, in the Sixth, Tchaikovsky once more confronts the Dostoyevskian 'questions of existence', addressing himself to the problems of suffering man and his struggle with fate, then we can see that this symphony attains its goal with a starkness, a complete honesty of expression, that somehow evaded him in the Finales of both the Fourth and the Fifth. The Sixth, then, becomes the crowning achievement in a trilogy of symphonies about fate in which total submission – that is, acceptance of death – becomes the only way out.

Among all the great swansongs in the history of music, this work has a peculiar human poignancy. Within ten days of its first performance in St Petersburg on 16 October 1893, its lonely, suffering composer, at the height of his fame, was dead – possibly by his own hand. Tchaikovsky's fear of death was intense. What premonitions and presentiments lay in the Stygian gloom of the Sixth Symphony's opening, to which the Finale returns? What private terrors found expression in the shattering outburst at the beginning of the development of the first movement? What bitterness lay concealed in the proud arrogance of the march? And yet we know that Tchaikovsky was happy in the creation of this work, that it took possession of him completely, and – for all the difficulties of orchestrating it – he was absolutely confident of its worth. It certainly will not do to regard this symphony as a kind of suicide note, for here was a composer at the zenith of his powers in a mood of creative exultation. His death at the age of fifty-three was a tragedy for music; but, were it not for the hand of fate, there could have been more masterpieces – and not necessarily tragic ones – to come.

Unique though the Sixth is, its first movement is clearly a child of the same parent that fathered *Romeo and Juliet*, the composer's real 'Opus 1'. And thinking about the content and musical language of that fate-obsessed work – its key (B minor), its form (slow introduction–sonata-allegro–coda), its material (short, highly charged motivic development versus broad love theme) – there is a musico-dramatic prototype here. But the theatricality of the symphonic poem is replaced in the symphony by a deeper subjectivity of expression. For one thing, the love theme is not in the remote key of D flat major (as in the tone-poem) but emerges in D, the relative major of B minor. Here is classical orthodoxy put to a new psychological power of expression! Human love seems to represent an alternative state of being rather than a drastic change of scene. Here is hope as an alternative to restless anxiety and despair, and when we hear the ascending scales of the quiet 'aftersong' duet on the woodwind, we gain an insight into Tchaikovsky's creative method in this symphony. For Tchaikovsky's Sixth uses simple rising and falling stepwise motion as a leitmotif of hope and despair. Can they be reconciled after the events of the development, with its shattering outburst, its awesome intonation of the Orthodox funeral service plainchant on the brass, and the overwhelming cry of the climax? Tchaikovsky seems to think so, when he leads the return of the love theme into the calmly measured tread of the (B major) coda with its ascending brass chorale over a stepwise descending pizzicato bass.

The second movement is a waltz intermezzo like that in the third movement of the Fifth. But here – again in the consoling key of D major – is a waltz in 2 + 3 time which (despite what some see as the limping uneasiness of its gait) is surely the very antithesis of despair in its gently rising motion. Only the 'trio', with its falling appoggiaturas in the minor, offers slight feelings of regret that the return of the waltz effectively dispels. And in the coda how clearly again does Tchaikovsky spell out a feeling of hope and despair held, as it were, in the balance! Falling scales in the woodwind, rising scales in the strings, and all in the purest D major. Despite the shadowy return of the trio's falling motif in halting sighs at the end, we may take hope.

So far there has been no scherzo as such. The classical tradition of Haydn and Beethoven established this as a dance movement within the sonata cycle expressing – usually in 3/4 time – the positive, joyful side of life. But Tchaikovsky has a surprise in store. Here is a march, a genre that the composer had made his own in a whole range of works that extends from children's pieces, toy marches (such as the one in *The Nutcracker*) to the fantastic visions of the 'Pizzicato ostinato' movement in the Fourth Symphony. There is often more than a hint of the grotesque in Tchaikovsky's marches. And so it is here, in a kind of march-cum-scherzo. A long, even fussy introduction – possibly too long to be quite normal – presents motifs that have something of the mechanical about them. The angular theme in fourths, for instance, is not exactly a human, vocal theme. The falling scales – recognisable for the fateful role they have already played – have an air of menace as the crescendo mounts. (The rising scales, on the other hand, now seem a mockery.) And there is something unstable about the tonality – G major finally slewing round to E major for the full statement of the theme that repeats itself in a rather hectic crescendo. A short trio section polarises assertive chords and further toyshop grotesquerie. When all this comes round again to lead into a full-blown assertion of G major plus coda, there is a ring of hollow triumph which the heavy descending scales at the end only reinforce. Could it be that all this exciting noise represents more of an evil grimace than a shout of triumph?

The Finale (in which we return to B minor) confirms these fears. (And how strange to think that, in the early days of Soviet Russia, they sometimes used to reverse the order of these two movements so that the symphony could end 'positively'!) With the overwhelming force of falling stepwise motion, the whole movement is dragged down into the depths of despair. Its smooth descent is actually the result of two angular parts divided between first and second violins, so beneath the sorrowful surface lies a hidden turmoil. Formally speaking, this lament is simplicity itself in its alternation of two lyrical themes, minor and (relative) major. But unlike in the first movement, the major key brings no relief and in the end it, too, is pulled down into the minor in a final gloomy descent. Tchaikovsky spoke of this movement as having something of the spirit of a Requiem. He was not necessarily to know that future generations would come to think of it as his own.

© Eric Roseberry

Ralph Vaughan Williams (1872–1958)

Unlike Elgar before him, Vaughan Williams received a traditional musical education at the Royal College of Music in London, but he also studied abroad – in Berlin with Bruch and in Paris with Ravel. Soon after his return came the *Fantasia on a Theme by Thomas Tallis* and *A Sea Symphony* (1910); he became active as a collector of folk music and edited *The English Hymnal* (1906). After completing his second symphony, *A London Symphony* (1913), he joined the army. As well as choral works such as *Sancta civitas* (1925) and *Serenade to Music* (1938), he wrote a Mass and made many choral arrangements of English folk songs. Apart from *The Lark Ascending* for violin and orchestra, his concerto-type works – for viola (*Flos campi*), piano, oboe and tuba – remain rarely performed. After the death of his first wife, he remarried aged eighty, and produced two more symphonies before his death.

~ ***A London Symphony* (Symphony No. 2)** (1912–13, rev. 1920, 1933)

1 Lento – Allegro risoluto
2 Lento
3 Scherzo (Nocturne): Allegro vivace
4 Andante con moto – Maestoso alla marcia (quasi lento) – Allegro – Maestoso alla marcia – Sostenuto – Lento

The decade before the outbreak of the First World War was a vintage period for the British symphony: indeed, it saw the emergence of the four earliest examples of the genre which remain in the repertoire. Elgar's First Symphony was first performed, with enormous success, in 1908; his Second, to a much cooler reception, in 1911. Meanwhile, Vaughan

Williams's *A Sea Symphony* had had its premiere at the Leeds Festival in 1910. And while that work might well be considered more cantata than symphony, there could be no such doubts about the classification of its purely orchestral successor, *A London Symphony*. Composed in 1912 and 1913, this was first performed at the Queen's Hall in London in March 1914.

Although it was succeeded by another seven symphonies, including some of Vaughan Williams's most profound musical utterances, the *London Symphony* retained a special place in its composer's affections. He conducted it many times (as did Henry Wood, the father of the Proms). And for many years after the premiere he went on tinkering with it, cutting some sections and replacing others. He revised the score twice even before its first publication in 1920, and again in 1933. (A recording has only recently been made of the original version, including no less than 'twenty minutes of previously unrecorded music'.)

The published score was dedicated to the memory of Vaughan Williams's younger contemporary and admirer, George Butterworth, who had been killed in action in 1915. Butterworth had been closely involved in the preparation of the symphony; and after the only full score had been sent to Germany just before the war (according to different accounts, either to the publishers Breitkopf and Härtel or to the conductor Fritz Busch), he had organised the recopying of the score from the orchestral parts. But, more than that, Vaughan Williams once wrote that he owed the whole idea of the *London Symphony* to Butterworth, who had said, at the end of a musical evening they had spent together, 'You know, you ought to write a symphony.'

By the composer's own account, this remark spurred him into action: 'I looked out some sketches I had made for what I believe was going to have been a symphonic poem (!) about London and decided to throw it into symphonic form.' The defensive jokiness of the exclamation mark and the phraseology disguise an apparent embarrassment about programme music which persists in the composer's later attitude to the piece. He seems not to have objected to other writers' detailed pictorial interpretations of the work. But his own programme note of 1925 says:

> It has been suggested that this Symphony has been mis-named, it should rather be called 'Symphony by a Londoner'. That is to say it is in no sense descriptive, and though the introduction of the 'Westminster Chimes' in the first movement, the slight reminiscence of the 'Lavender cry' in the slow movement, and the very faint suggestion of mouth organs and mechanical pianos in the Scherzo give it a tinge of 'local colour', yet it is intended to be listened to as 'absolute' music. Hearers may, if they like, localise the various themes and movements, but it is hoped that this is not a necessary part of the music.

Despite this warning (which should surely be taken with a pinch of salt), it is helpful to consider the London of the time of the work, at and just after the end of the Edwardian era. This was the city which Vaughan Williams knew, first as a student at the Royal College of Music, and later as a resident of Cheyne Walk in Chelsea. It was the hub of an Empire, the largest city in the world: a byword for noise and dirt, and the focus of much human misery. Yet it was much more compact, much nearer to true countryside, than today's urban sprawl; and, with its transport still dominated by the river, the rail-way and the horse, it was much quieter than it has become in the age of the internal combustion engine. Vaughan Williams was able to reflect in his symphony both the bustling metropolis and its more contemplative corners, both its industrial horrors and its roots in nature: both Babylon and Jerusalem.

The symphony begins with a slow introduction – founded on a distinctive pattern of rising fourths and seconds – which to an innocent ear might well evoke the peace of the country-side, but which in this context presumably suggests a London scene at a quiet time of day. In fact, its mood is very much that

of Wordsworth's famous sonnet 'Upon Westminster Bridge',
an early-morning idyll which ends:

> Ne'er saw I, never felt, a calm so deep!
> The river glideth at his own sweet will:
> Dear God! The very houses seem asleep
> And all that mighty heart is lying still!

The suspicion that Vaughan Williams may have had this
scene in mind is all but confirmed when he introduces the
sound of Big Ben striking the half-hour in harp harmonics.

The rising figure then leads into the main Allegro, which
begins with a plangent downward chromatic wail. This is the
first of a whole series of thematic ideas, which together suggest not only, as Vaughan Williams wrote, 'the noise and
hurry of London', but also its multiplicity. One of the themes
is perky in character; another blossoms in flowing, radiant
counterpoint; another has a striding bass line in ragtime
rhythms. And this bass line contains within it the rising
fourths and seconds of the introduction, which then return to
crown the long exposition with trumpet fanfares.

The development section traces a descent from the chromatic wail into a region of increasingly deep peace and tranquillity, dominated by the rising intervals of the introduction
and by fragments of folk-like melody. The calm of this passage
spreads into the totally recast recapitulation, which begins with
the chromatic wail pianissimo on flutes and horns, and remains
subdued for some time. But the ragtime melody and other
associated ideas reassert themselves strongly, and the movement ends in a blaze of the home key, G major.

Vaughan Williams did not dissent from a description of the
slow movement as representing 'Bloomsbury Square on a
November afternoon' – again a scene of greater calm than
would be possible in the London of today. In the first section
of the movement, an arching melody – derived, like much of
Vaughan Williams's material, from English folk song, yet
tonally too unstable to be an actual folk song – is introduced
by the cor anglais, and taken up by the strings with increasing

intensity. This melody alternates with passages founded on quietly repeated string chords of C major, like a psalm chant.

A solo viola leads into a middle section, in which local colour is provided not only by the quotations of a Chelsea lavender seller's cry on solo viola and cello, but also by the jingles of a hansom cab. But all sense of place is transcended by two passionate outbursts from the full orchestra – the first brief, but the second sustained at ecstatic length. A brief final section brings back the cor anglais melody and the chanted C major chords, and ends with the solo viola.

The D minor third movement presents a scene – or several scenes – of nocturnal revelry, as if heard from the distance on the Embankment. In form it is a scherzo with two trios: the first led off with ferocious accents on horns and strings; the second beginning with mouth-organ chords in strings and horns, and continuing with a gawky dance tune to a street piano. The real achievement of the movement, however, lies not in the ingenuity of these imitations, but in the way the all-enveloping night is suggested by the quiet scurryings of the Scherzo, and especially by the long slow fade of the coda.

The finale begins with another of the moments of apparently personal expression which give such depth to the symphony, a cry of despair marked 'appassionato', culminating in a falling chromatic phrase related to the wail of the first movement. This gives way to a sombre march in C minor: possibly, as has been suggested, a hunger march; or perhaps the daily trudge of the City workers described by T. S. Eliot in *The Waste Land* only a few years later:

> Under the brown fog of a winter dawn,
> A crowd flowed over London Bridge, so many,
> I had not thought death had undone so many.
> Sighs, short and infrequent, were exhaled,
> And each man fixed his eyes before his feet.

After this, a brief E minor Allegro picks up and develops ideas from the march, along with a ferocious circling figure. The slow march returns, its expression now intensified, to reach a climax on the downward chromatic figure of the introduction. Then comes a tiny cluster of ideas from the first movement, including the wail itself, and harp harmonics once more pick out Big Ben sounding, this time, three quarters of the hour.

This leads to an epilogue, permeated by the rising fourths and seconds of the first-movement introduction. First they underpin rustling figuration in the upper strings and wood-wind; then they launch a quiet string melody; and then they provide the material for a rising solo violin line, before a last G major chord dies into silence.

When the composer's biographer Michael Kennedy asked about the significance of this striking ending, Vaughan Williams referred him to the final chapter of H. G. Wells's novel *Tono-Bungay*, published in 1909. In this, the narrator, passing down the Thames at night towards the open sea, seems to bid farewell not only to London but also to what we, with hindsight, can see as the lost England of before the First World War:

> Light after light goes down. England and the Kingdom, Britain and the Empire, the old prides and the old devotions, glide abeam, astern, sink down upon the horizon, pass – pass. The river passes – London passes, England passes.

© Anthony Burton

❧ *A Pastoral Symphony* (Symphony No. 3) (1921)

1 Molto moderato
2 Lento moderato
3 Moderato pesante
4 Lento

Vaughan Williams was nearly fifty when he composed his *Pastoral Symphony*: it was written mostly in 1921, and first performed in London in January 1922 under Adrian Boult.

Compared to its predecessors, the all-embracing *Sea Symphony* and the vivid *London Symphony*, it marked a new direction in Vaughan Williams's music. But this was part of the continuing evolution of his highly individual musical language, independent of any spirit of the times. The *Pastoral Symphony* has nothing in common with, for example, Walton's *Façade*, which had its first (private) performance two days earlier. If there is a contemporary work with which it has any affinity, it is perhaps the calmest of Sibelius's symphonies, the Sixth, completed in 1923.

The title *Pastoral Symphony* misled many of the work's first listeners into thinking that it was concerned chiefly with the English countryside, as a kind of rural companion piece to the *London Symphony* – a view which Philip Heseltine (alias the composer Peter Warlock) voiced at its most crass when he said that the symphony was 'like a cow looking over a gate'. Certainly the gentle progress of the piece – which its composer described as 'in four movements, all of them slow' – resembles the contours of the English landscapes which Vaughan Williams loved, rather than any more dramatic scenery. But the work owes more to the fields of Flanders, where the composer served with the Royal Army Medical Corps in 1916, bringing back the wounded from the trenches. In 1938, he wrote to Ursula, his future wife, that the symphony was

> . . . really war-time music – a great deal of it incubated when I used to go up night after night with the ambulance waggon at Ecoivres and we went up a steep hill and there was a wonderful Corot-like landscape in the sunset – it's not really lambkins frisking at all as most people take for granted.

Neither is this a folk-song symphony: it contains no quotations of actual folk melodies. But it does demonstrate how much the modality of English folk song had permeated Vaughan Williams's musical language by this time. Almost every theme in the symphony is modally inflected, rather than being firmly in a major or minor key; and changes of mood are conveyed as much by alterations of mode as by shifts of key centre. Nor does Vaughan Williams's use of modes straitjacket him into harmonic blandness: there are some harsh bitonal clashes at points of tension, and complexity is added to the harmonies by the use of streams of parallel triads instead of single lines – as at the opening of the work.

The moderately paced first movement (beginning and ending in G) has the outline of sonata form, with the first subject on cellos and harp against the woodwinds' triads, the second in proliferating woodwind lines at a slightly slower tempo, and the third on cellos and clarinet at a faster tempo, crowned by glowing string chords recalling Vaughan Williams's early *Tallis Fantasia*. The only mild departure from orthodoxy is that the first subject, after forming the basis of much of the development section, including an extended violin solo, is no more than hinted at at the start of the recapitulation; its full, though still varied, restatement is reserved for the coda. All the same, this hardly feels like a conventional sonata movement: its plan is overlaid by a continuous unfolding of the thematic material, in an even flow in which the dynamic level rises only twice even to forte.

The slow second movement, scored for a reduced orchestra with muted strings, is built out of the alternation of two themes, in varied versions: the first the melody played by the horn at the outset, its C major tonality clashing with the supporting F minor chord; the second introduced by flute and solo viola a little later. But the sequence is broken by the intervention of a quiet trumpet cadenza over sustained strings – after which the first theme bursts out in the first fortissimo of the work. Then the final return of the first theme, on solo clarinet, is combined with a shortened restatement of the cadenza, now on solo horn. Vaughan Williams asks for both the trumpet and horn solos to be played on natural instruments or, failing that, without using the valves, so that the prominent sevenths in the melody are heard in their true, un-tempered intonation. The effect is to recall the sound of the military bugle; and indeed the initial rising fifth of both solos is the first interval of the Last Post bugle call. This movement is surely Vaughan Williams's elegy for his many friends and colleagues who did not survive the war.

The third movement (in G minor) is an inspired solution to the problem of how to write a scherzo for an essentially meditative symphony. It begins as a heavy, moderately paced dance, which after some contrasting material accelerates into a more assertive trio; then the trio in turn puts on speed, to culminate in the symphony's first *fff*. With a sudden return to the first tempo, the process begins again, with both scherzo and trio in varied and truncated forms. But then the third, even more foreshortened, statement of the scherzo leads to a scurrying contrapuntal Presto coda – the symphony's only passage of genuinely fast music, and an extraordinary moment of release.

The slow finale begins with a quiet timpani roll on a low A, over which a distant solo voice (soprano or tenor) sings a rhapsodic, wordless modal melody. This recalls the almost unsupported horn and trumpet solos in the second movement; paradoxically, though, the use of the voice seems not to humanise the expression of that movement, but to render it more remote and impersonal. Following this, cor anglais and flute echo a phrase from the vocal solo, while the violins rise into the heights. A phrase from the violins' ascent then becomes the basis of a warmly lyrical paragraph, marked 'Moderato maestoso', which begins on wind and harp and is taken up by the strings. Hugh Ottaway was surely right to hear in this passage 'an inescapable feeling of community' – perhaps suggesting social cohesion as the only possible response to the horrors of war.

The central section of the movement juxtaposes echoes of this episode, more agitated passages of tremolando strings, and a long, calm melody on cellos and then flute overlapping harp figuration. But the climax of the section, and of the whole work, is reached with a restatement of the singer's melody, declaimed by high strings and woodwind in unsupported octaves, and marked '*fff* appassionato' – now surely protest rather than lament. After this the movement retraces its steps: the lyrical paragraph returns, even more purposeful than before; then the violins ascend again into the heights, ending on a high A in octaves. This is sustained while, below it, the distant voice resumes its wordless rhapsody. The values of the community in post-war society have been reasserted; but the need to mourn the war dead remains.

© Anthony Burton

∾ Symphony No. 4 in F minor (1931–4)

1 Allegro
2 Andante moderato
3 Scherzo: Allegro molto –
4 Finale con Epilogo fugato: Allegro molto – con anima

Vaughan Williams, in his sixties, occupied a secure place in British musical life, but not as a purveyor of aggressive modernism: his music was associated with English landscape and traditions, with folk song and hymnody, with evocations of nature and mystical faith. His first three symphonies had each possessed an identifiable subject and poetic focus: *A Sea Symphony* (No. 1), *A London Symphony* (No. 2), *A Pastoral Symphony* (No. 3). The Fourth, premiered at the Queen's Hall, London, in a BBC Symphony Orchestra concert on 10 April 1935 conducted by Sir Adrian Boult, gave its hearers no such clue. It seemed formidably 'abstract' in its processes, concerned with strenuous polyphony and the extended, architectural development of germinal themes. But it also took the audience aback by its uncompromisingly severe expressive stance and abrasive dissonance. One critic wrote that Vaughan Williams had 'abandoned the humanities'; and even so discerning a reviewer as Neville Cardus prophesied that it would be forgotten within twenty years. He was wrong.

In retrospect there had been hints of a growing 'radicalism' in Vaughan Williams's music for some time, in works such as *Sancta civitas*, *Job* and the Piano Concerto. The Fourth Symphony was a logical continuation from these works. Commentators were quick to align it with recent symphonies by Walton and Bax (to whom Vaughan Williams dedicated this work) as an expression of contemporary tensions and anxieties, as the rise of the European dictators began to threaten war. In fact it was largely sketched in 1931–2, before the Nazis came to power in Germany, but right after *Job* and the Piano Concerto. Very likely Vaughan Williams wished to make use of some of the new musical techniques brewing on the Continent, represented by his younger contemporaries Schoenberg, Stravinsky and Hindemith. Nevertheless some reflection on the state of the world (this was still the Depression era) probably found its way into the music. The emotional content may be open to debate, but sheer anger seems a sizeable component of it, mingled with passionate aspiration, depressive elegy and black humour. One of Vaughan Williams's most consistently, indeed obsessively, contrapuntal works, Symphony No. 4 has an almost apocalyptic power.

Two four-note cells or motifs engender much of the Fourth Symphony's material, appearing both in their own right and as components of other themes. One is nearly horizontal, moving within the space of a whole tone, F–E–G flat–F (this is not quite a transposed version of B–A–C–H: by returning to the same pitch with which it began, it has a more closed and obstinate feel). The second is nearly vertical, ascending mainly by fourths and spanning a minor ninth, F–B flat–E flat–G flat (with later extensions and interval changes). Thus melody and harmony are tightly integrated in two dimensions.

The first movement crashes in with a grinding dissonance which immediately resolves on to another. In this wrathful initial tutti the first four-note motif soon appears in unison on strings, woodwind and trumpets, followed at only a few bars' distance by the second, rearing up on trumpets, trombones and tuba. Pulsing horns introduce a wild, impassioned string cantilena, a huge melodic idea to counter the baleful fragments so far heard. The second subject proper is an insistent, forceful idea like a war dance, closely related to the music of Vaughan Williams's 'Masque for Dancing', *Job*. An extremely compressed development is largely concerned with the opening ideas; in the recapitulation, therefore, they are much curtailed and the music moves swiftly to the string cantilena before subsiding to a uneasy, mist-shrouded coda – the sudden quietness is as shocking as all the sound and fury that preceded it – largely assigned to muted, divided strings.

The coda's numbed mood extends into the start of the second (slow) movement, opening out with the 'vertical' motif in wind instruments and proceeding to a doleful violin theme over a pizzicato bass. This is developed in sombre counterpoint, leading to a climactic passage over a marching bass, rounded off by a tranquillo cadence figure in solo flute. The pizzicato bass reappears and the process starts again. As the tension builds up, the 'vertical' motif arises on the brass, creating a harsh climax. The tensions gradually unwind in long cantabile melodic lines; the flute's cadence figure returns and is extended into a melancholic cadenza (with the 'horizontal' motif in muted trombones) descending to a low E.

The third-movement Scherzo has a raffish, devil-may-care energy, its main subject audibly fashioned from the two germinal motifs which are here brought into opposition, with a sense of hand-to-hand combat between them. A dancing second subject combines with a powerfully syncopated accompaniment. A Falstaffian trio is ponderously led off by tuba and bassoons and spreads upwards through the orchestra all the way to the piccolo. The scherzo material returns, after which a brief reminder of the trio leads into a sinister, mysterious transition passage. The syncopated figure turns into a nagging pedal in the bass; the 'horizontal' motif sounds out with increasing anxiety; and the Finale breaks out with an angry descending tune (actually a version of the flute's cadence figure from the slow movement).

This seamless move from Scherzo to Finale is a kind of diabolic inversion of the similar passage in Beethoven's Fifth Symphony. Whereas Beethoven's ascending fanfare introduces a confident march, Vaughan Williams's descending theme gives way to a grotesque 'oompah' bass. An urgent cantabile theme for woodwind is juxtaposed against this, the descending theme splitting into angry two-note figures. In subsequent development the music turns malevolently jazzy, with an irruption of the 'vertical' motif, then subsides to an eerie phantasmal lento for divided strings. The 'horizontal' figure looms threateningly through the murk, and a curtailed recapitulation gets under way, passing the main material in furious review until it breaks up into a fusillade of the spitting two-note figure, like ricocheting shell fire.

Suddenly the 'horizontal' theme sounds out balefully on the trombones, initiating the Epilogo fugato. Here Vaughan Williams puts his material through its most strenuous polyphonic and polyrhythmic paces, the two main motifs augmented and inverted in dissonant, angular, chromatic combat, and using the Finale's themes as countersubjects. At the crown of the process, the movement's initial descending tune makes a ferocious reappearance. It seems to be about to have the last word – but it collides with the grinding dissonances of the symphony's very opening, and the 'vertical' motif brings the work to an explosive and very final cadence.

© Malcolm MacDonald

∾ Symphony No. 5 in D major (1938–43)

1 Preludio: Moderato – Allegro – Tempo 1
2 Scherzo: Presto misterioso
3 Romanza: Lento
4 Passacaglia: Moderato – Allegro – Tempo 1 – Tempo del Preludio

In the Royal Albert Hall on Midsummer Night 1943, Vaughan Williams raised his baton to conduct the London

Philharmonic Orchestra in the first performance of his new Symphony in D. He was over seventy, and many thought that this might be his last major work – a final statement of his thoughts and ideas. With hindsight, we know that there were four more symphonies to come, as different from each other as the first four were from the Fifth. The *Times* music critic welcomed the work: 'A new symphony by Dr Vaughan Williams is an event of major importance . . . it turns its back on the violence of the F minor symphony . . . and shows affinity with *Job* and the settings of the mystical poets.'

Vaughan Williams had begun his Symphony in D in 1938: it was only later referred to as Symphony No. 5. In the original 1943 Proms programme note, Edwin Evans also felt that the new symphony had an affinity with the ballet piece (or 'Masque for Dancing'), *Job*, though he noted, too, that 'the composer has dispensed us from such a quest by stating on his score that "some of the themes are taken from an unfinished opera *The Pilgrim's Progress*"'. Some of the music was indeed used in a radio dramatisation of Bunyan's allegory several months later (the 'Morality', as the composer preferred to call the full stage work, only followed in 1951). Yet, in a note on the manuscript score of the symphony, Vaughan Williams himself maintained that, 'except in the slow movement, the Symphony has no dramatic connection with Bunyan's allegory.'

In 1943, two years after the bombing of Queen's Hall, London was in the middle of the Blitz; but morale was high and the Proms continued in the Albert Hall as usual, a welcome relief from wartime austerity. The Queen and Princess Elizabeth had visited the Proms the night before, and a memorial concert for Rakhmaninov was planned for the following evening. The first four weeks of the season were being given by the London Philharmonic Orchestra, with the BBC Symphony Orchestra due to take over from mid-July. Henry Wood was to share the conducting at each concert with either Basil Cameron or Adrian Boult. At the beginning of the week in which he was to have shared the rostrum with Vaughan

Williams, Wood suffered a mild stroke while conducting Brahms's Second Symphony and was unable to appear. He telegraphed Vaughan Williams to wish him 'all possible good luck', and the rest of the programme was conducted by Basil Cameron.

Jean Pougnet had led the orchestra in the first play-through of the symphony in May at the BBC's Studio 1 at Maida Vale; Ursula Wood (Vaughan Williams's secretary and later his wife) recalled that the LPO took the work to their hearts and played beautifully. Of the Proms performance, she felt that 'the music seemed to many people to bring the peace and blessing for which they longed'. Adrian Boult also heard the performance on that wartime evening. He wrote to Vaughan Williams: 'Its serene loveliness is completely satisfying in these times and shows, as only music can, what we must work for when this madness is over. I look forward . . . to the privilege of doing it myself some time soon.' Ten years later, Boult made a commercial recording of the symphony with the London Philharmonic Orchestra, in the presence of the composer.

At the start of the symphony, low string chords and a horn call suggest that the music has already been going on, unheard; a clash of C (cellos and basses) against D (horns) makes it difficult to decide the real key of the work, and this ambiguity persists. Soon, there is a magical change of key to E major; in the 'Morality' this is heard as Evangelist shows Pilgrim the wicket gate through which he must pass on his journey to the Celestial City. At the climax, the brass restates an earlier theme, and the movement ends quietly with muted horn calls.

The Scherzo has no thematic connection with *The Pilgrim's Progress*, though it has been said to personify Bunyan's 'hobgoblins and foul fiends', and proceeds, jauntily, menacingly and swiftly, with important passages for woodwind, trombones and muted strings. Fleet of foot, with many cross-rhythms, it disappears as quickly and quietly as it began.

The strongest direct link with *Pilgrim* is (as the composer acknowledged) in the slow movement, marked 'Romanza'. The manuscript score originally bore words from Bunyan's book: 'Upon this place stood a cross, and a little below a sepulchre.' The cor anglais theme is heard in the 'Morality' to the words 'He hath given me rest by His sorrow and life by His death.' The animated central section relates to Pilgrim's 'Save me! Save me, Lord! My burden is greater than I can bear.'

The last movement is almost a meditation on what has gone before. The main theme is taken from the scene where Pilgrim receives instructions about his journey from the Interpreter. The middle of the movement is more lively, but in the last pages, thematic fragments from the Preludio are heard, and the final bars fade into a celestial silence that is surely a vision of the world to come.

© John Mayhew

∾ Symphony No. 6 in E minor (1944–7)

1 Allegro –
2 Moderato –
3 Scherzo: Allegro vivace –
4 Epilogue: Moderato

Outside the select band of friends and colleagues who heard Vaughan Williams's Sixth Symphony before its first performance, few people knew what to expect. After the *Sea Symphony*, the *London Symphony* and the *Pastoral Symphony*, the Fourth was aggressive and the Fifth spoke of peace. Was there anything else to say? Here, well into in his seventies, was England's revered senior composer, greatly loved and respected. Perhaps he would be 'slowing up'; perhaps he would be repeating himself; might the Sixth Symphony be a disappointment – bland and unmemorable – or would there be a new message?

When he started writing the symphony in 1944, Vaughan Williams was completing music for several films and a radio play, and he incorporated thematic material from these scores at several points in the new work. The first draft of the symphony finished, he wrote to his friend Roy Douglas, asking him to 'vet' the score and 'wash its face' – euphemisms for editing and making working copies of his sometimes barely legible manuscripts. Then, on a Sunday in the summer of 1946, Michael Mullinar played through the symphony for friends and colleagues at the composer's house in Dorking. Vaughan Williams listened patiently to comments and suggestions.

It took nearly a year for Roy Douglas, in consultation with the composer, to make a full score. He managed about sixteen bars a day, battling through 'clouds of semiquavers, sharps, flats, dots, accents and dynamics' which covered the composer's manuscript pages. At the Royal College of Music in June 1947, Michael Mullinar played the revised work four times for some distinguished musicians. Barbirolli heard the first play-through, then Sargent borrowed the only full score; later in the day, Boult heard the work played twice, propping the score on a large music stand for himself and some colleagues. Boult and the BBC Symphony Orchestra began rehearsals in Studio 1 at Maida Vale in December 1947. Vaughan Williams was there, and took the orchestra through the work a second time before handing back the baton to Boult, who gave its first performance at the Albert Hall on 21 April 1948.

For that first performance, the composer wrote his own programme note: 'This Symphony was begun probably about 1944 and finished in 1947 . . . Each of the first three [movements] has its tail attached to the head of its neighbour.' Not a word in the ensuing notes about a 'programme' – no mention of war, desolate landscapes or nuclear destruction. Indeed, VW made it absolutely clear that no programme was intended or suggested. Wishing to silence the critics who had dubbed the Sixth his 'War Symphony', he confided to Roy Douglas that 'I suppose it never occurs to these people that a man might just want to write a piece of music'. The score bears the dedication 'to Michael Mullinar'.

Following its first, highly successful performance, the work was heard many times; in July 1950 the hundredth performance was given by Barbirolli and the Hallé at the Cheltenham Festival. In London's Kingsway Hall during December 1953, Boult and the London Philharmonic Orchestra made a series of recordings which completed the cycle of symphonies to date – the *Sea Symphony*, the Fourth, Fifth, Sixth, *Sinfonia Antartica* and *The Wasps* incidental music. At the end of four solid days of recording, on Saturday 5 December, Vaughan Williams recorded a short speech, in which he thanked orchestra and conductor for sensitive and beautiful playing. In that speech, which was included on the subsequent LP record, he also praised the 'wonderful feat of endurance to play an absolute pianissimo for three hours on end . . . it was a positive, sensitive pianissimo, full of meaning and tension'.

The meaning and tension are evident, not only in the last movement, but throughout the whole symphony. In the opening Allegro there is a feeling of tense activity, with a gallumphing, march-like tune for wind instruments and a folklike melody for the violins. The movement ends as it began – tense and menacing. A three-note motto pervades the bleak Moderato; the brass sounds a fanfare, and after several climaxes, the cor anglais comments solemnly on this mournful scene.

The Scherzo is based on a series of chords and a scampering passage for wind instruments. The trio has a tune for the saxophone, later taken up mockingly by the orchestra. The Epilogue has proved the least understood of the four movements: its bleakness is unremitting, and the orchestra is instructed to play 'sempre pianissimo e senza crescendo'. Vaughan Williams later reminded a friend that 'I do not believe in meanings and mottoes, as you know, but I think we can get in words nearest to the substance of my last movement in "We are such stuff as dreams are made on, and our little life is rounded with a sleep."' And so Prospero's farewell is Vaughan Williams's message to the listener, as the eerie, uneasy pianissimo dissolves into an even deeper silence.

© John Mayhew

∾ Symphony No. 7, *Sinfonia antartica* (1947–53)

1 Prelude
2 Scherzo
3 Landscape
4 Intermezzo
5 Epilogue

The seventh of Vaughan Williams's nine symphonies, *Sinfonia antartica*, was first performed on 14 January 1953 at a Hallé concert in Manchester, conducted by Sir John Barbirolli, who introduced it to London a week later.

Its origin lay in an invitation to Vaughan Williams in 1947 to compose music for the film *Scott of the Antarctic*. The subject haunted him – he was horrified, for instance, by the amateurish incompetence of Scott's last expedition in 1911–12 – and after the film had been shown in 1948 he began to reshape some of the themes into this symphony. The work is scored for a large orchestra which includes vibraphone, celesta, piano, organ and wind machine, and also uses a small wordless women's chorus and soprano soloist.

The *Antartica* marked a new phase in Vaughan Williams's development, at the age of eighty, but pointers to its power and scale may be found in the music he wrote in 1946 for another film, *The Loves of Joanna Godden*. Even earlier, of course, in 1925, the one-act opera *Riders to the Sea* had demonstrated his mastery of a subject involving conflict between implacable nature and human lives.

Antartica is on a heroic scale. Although there is little conventionally symphonic development of the material, the imaginative use of tone colour and the quality of the themes are strong enough to raise the symphony above graphic pictorialism and to give it genuine tragic stature. Each movement is prefaced by an apposite literary quotation, so that there can be no doubt that this is 'programme music' – and none the worse for that.

1 *Prelude*

> To suffer woes which hope thinks infinite,
> To forgive wrongs darker than death or night,
> To defy power which seems omnipotent,
> Neither to change, nor falter, nor repent:
> This . . . is to be
> Good, great and joyous, beautiful and free,
> This is alone life, joy, empire and victory.
>
> Percy Bysshe Shelley (1792–1822), from *Prometheus Unbound*
> (1820)

The noble, striving theme which opens the symphony is one of Vaughan Williams's finest and most memorable inventions, strikingly successful in its representation of heroic endeavour doomed to failure. It is used first as a majestic introduction, and when it has reached a full close, xylophone and piano provide what the composer called 'a few Antarctic shimmerings' before the soprano and chorus utter their chilling siren song, suggesting at one and the same time hallucinatory visions at the limit of endurance and the 'terror and fascination' of the Polar region, further illustrated by the wind machine. The central section continues the description of Antarctic conditions, with vibraphone chords, runs on the celesta and broken chords on the piano. At a fortissimo climax, there is a sudden halt; flute, clarinets and violins eerily introduce the sound of deep bells – 'supposed in the film to be "menacing"', the composer said – and the return of the voices. Then a trumpet fanfare sounds man's challenge to nature and the battle is joined as the introductory theme returns.

2 *Scherzo*

> There go the ships,
> And there is that Leviathan
> Whom thou hast made to take his pastime therein.
>
> Psalm 104

All the bustle of the start of a voyage opens this movement – horn call, swirling harps and strings, and a trumpet tune harking back to the Scherzo of *A Sea Symphony*. At sea the ships encounter whales (the psalmists' Leviathan) and, on landfall, penguins (scherzando, on trumpets and trombones, forming the trio section). There is no regular return of the scherzo and the movement ends with a soft chord for muted brass and celesta.

3 *Landscape*

> Ye ice falls! Ye that from the mountain's brow
> Adown enormous ravines slope amain –
> Torrents, methinks, that heard a mighty voice,
> And stopped at once amid their maddest plunge!
> Motionless torrents! Silent cataracts!
>
> Samuel Taylor Coleridge (1722–1834), from 'Hymn before Sunrise,
> in the Vale of Chamounix'

In the film the landscape was 'Ice waste – Ross Island'. This movement contains the most remarkable and original music in the symphony, an exploration of sonorities, harsh and glittering, in a manner new to the octogenarian composer. The themes, some apparently related to themes in the Sixth Symphony, are bare and fragmentary: muted horns, percussion icicles, falling thirds in the bass, wailing major seconds on the flutes, all bound together by a slow theme for trombones and tuba in canon with a rising motif for strings and wind. A richer theme on the strings brings a human element into this white world, but the movement goes inexorably towards its astonishing climax, the pealing chords from the organ which represent the 'silent cataracts', the glacier itself. After this imposing outburst the music passes quietly into the fourth movement.

4 *Intermezzo*

> Love, all alike, no season knows, nor clime,
> Nor hours, days, months, which are the rags of time.
>
> John Donne (1572–1631), from 'The Sun Rising'

The solo oboe, supported by harp, brings back lyricism and humanity, its melody recalling Vaughan Williams's themes from much earlier works, but with a disquieting tragic difference because of the flattened inflections. The structure of this movement is distinctly episodic. A reverie, with solo violin, is interrupted by a new version of the introductory theme from the Prelude and the return of the deep bells, followed by a quiet elegy (for Captain Oates, in the film). The oboe theme returns as coda.

5 *Epilogue*

> I do not regret this journey; we took risks, we knew we took them, things have come out against us, therefore we have no cause for complaint.

From the last journal of Captain Scott (1868–1912)

The finale is based chiefly on material from the first movement. A trumpet fanfare, taken up by horns over a gigantic tremolando for the full orchestra, is followed by a defiant march based on the main theme of the Prelude. Soon the Antarctic blizzard – woodwind, brass and piano – intervenes and the march is swept aside by bells, voices and wind machine. The Prelude theme returns like an elegy, but the blizzard and the voices on the wind have the last word.

© Michael Kennedy

∾ Symphony No. 8 in D minor (1956)

1 Fantasia (Variazioni senza Tema)
2 Scherzo alla Marcia (per stromenti a fiato)
3 Cavatina (per stromenti ad arco)
4 Toccata

Each of the nine symphonies of Vaughan Williams explores a different aspect of his musical personality. Together, they form a many-sided world of imagination great enough to transcend musical fashions, to be of importance in musical history, and thus to speak to us today with vitality and meaning.

Vaughan Williams might, like Beethoven, have affectionately described his Eighth as his 'Little' Symphony. It is in some ways more relaxed; its appeal is more direct; the structure is concise, and technically it is a brilliant achievement. The composer was over eighty when he wrote this vigorous-minded and exuberant work.

The novelty, the adventure, lie mainly in its unusual plan and in its power of direct communication. A Schubert-sized orchestra is used, plus a harp or two; and a very large percussion section: five players are needed, and the instruments include vibraphone, xylophone, glockenspiel, tubular bells, and three tuned gongs (as in Puccini's *Turandot*). The use, in the last movement, of 'all the 'phones and spiels known to the composer' (Vaughan Williams's phrase) produces at times almost the effect of a 'Toy Symphony' – certainly a forthright enjoyment of sound for its own sake.

For a work by an allegedly 'unexportable' composer, this symphony has had a remarkable international success. The first performance was in May 1956 in Manchester by the Hallé Orchestra under Barbirolli, and within six months it had been performed in New York, Lille, Brussels, Strasbourg, Zurich, Lisbon, Vienna, Gothenburg and Helsinki. In New York (under Eugene Ormandy) its success was such that their Music Critics' Circle voted it the best symphonic work heard there during that year.

'Symphony in D minor' is a misleading description. It begins in D minor and ends in D major, but the tonality in the course of the work is constantly changing, and very little is in D minor. The first movement has no definite themes as such, but consists of a set of contrasted variations in which the different musical textures are unified by the intervals of a rising fourth and a falling second. Then comes a short, high-spirited Scherzo for wind instruments only, with 'mechanical' counterpoint, some 'oompah' accompaniment, a far-fetched contrasting section, and a truncated recapitulation – pawky VW humour at its most unbuttoned. In complete contrast, the Cavatina, for strings alone, is in the composer's characteristic contemplative style, but with many unexpected touches, and often ambiguous in mood, unquiet beneath the surface.

Many different opinions of the rondo-like finale have been expressed – from curt dismissal as a trivial romp to enthusiastic acceptance as a highly original movement which effectively rounds off what has gone before. The composer saw a 'sinister' element in it; for others the mood is that of Psalm 150 ('Praise him on the well-tuned cymbals . . .'). The title Toccata suggests a virtuoso piece, which it certainly is. Beyond that, listeners must judge for themselves.

© David Cox

William Walton (1902–83)

Born in industrial Lancashire, Walton made an early escape to Oxford, becoming a chorister at Christ Church cathedral, then staying on at Christ Church as an undergraduate. Here he had the good fortune to fall in with the literary Sitwell family (Edith, Sacheverell and Osbert), who supported him for ten years as well as introducing him to leading artists of the day. His *Façade* (1922) – a chic, jazzy entertainment for reciter and ensemble, to texts by Edith – caused a stir. The Viola Concerto (1929) soon followed, as did the cantata *Belshazzar's Feast* (1931), which quickly became a staple diet of choral societies. During the 1940s he produced film scores for, among others, Olivier's *Henry V* and *Hamlet*. Following his marriage in 1949 he and his wife Susana moved to Ischia, off the Naples coast. He also wrote concertos for violin (1939) and cello (1956), and showed a flair for occasional music, displayed in the marches *Crown Imperial* and *Orb and Sceptre* written for the coronations of George VI and Elizabeth II respectively.

❧ Symphony No. 1 in B flat minor (1931–5)

1 Allegro assai
2 Presto, con malizia
3 Andante, con malinconia
4 Maestoso – Brioso ed ardentemente

The first performance of William Walton's finally completed First Symphony, given by the BBC Symphony Orchestra under Hamilton Harty at the Queen's Hall on 6 November 1935, was one of the outstanding British musical successes of the twentieth century. One newspaper carried the headline 'Historic night for British music'. Henry Wood, founding conductor of the Proms, wrote to Walton's publisher: 'What a work, truly marvellous, it was like the world coming to an end, its dramatic power was superb; what orchestration, what vitality and rhythmic invention – no orchestral work has carried me away so much.' The symphony was recorded just five weeks later, and when the composer John Ireland heard the discs he wrote immediately to Walton: 'This is the work of a true Master . . . It has established you as the most vital and original genius in Europe. No-one but a bloody fool could possibly fail to see this.'

With time, some of the praise has toned down a little. But the First Symphony remains the most widely admired of all Walton's works, praised both by die-hard Waltonites, and by those who are more agnostic about his later works. The combination of blazing energy and keen intellectual focus is unique in his output. Such mastery was not achieved without cost. It took Walton four years to complete the symphony. Finishing the finale gave him such agonising difficulties that he eventually allowed the work to be performed without it, as a three-movement torso, in 1934, and there were moments during the composition of the first three movements when he came close to despair.

Part of the problem was the level of expectation the work aroused. After the triumphant premieres of the Viola Concerto (at a 1929 Prom) and the choral and orchestral *Belshazzar's Feast* (1931), Walton found himself under enormous pressure to produce the great modern British symphony. Anxiety made him more acutely self-critical than ever. But there was a more personal dimension. As Walton later told his wife Susana, 'Symphonies are a lot of work to write. Too much. One has to have something really appalling happen to one, that lets loose the fount of inspiration.'

So what were the 'really appalling' circumstances that set Walton's musical imagination working with such concentrated intensity? One answer can be found in the symphony's dedication, 'To the Baroness Imma Doernberg'. The words refer to one of the great loves of Walton's life. His relationship with Imma was one of extremes: passionate, maddening, frustrating, and ultimately – for Walton at least – terribly painful (Imma deserted Walton for a Hungarian doctor in 1933). It was only the advent of a new love affair, with the 'beautiful, intelligent' Alice Wimborne, that gave Walton the strength he needed to complete the symphony. The state of mind Walton described on losing Imma – 'jealousy and hatred all mixed up with love' – can easily be heard in the emotional convulsions of the first and third movements, and in the 'malice' of the second. With all this in mind, modern commentators have tended to dismiss earlier suggestions that Walton may have been responding to the worrying political situation in Europe in the early 1930s. But a letter from Walton to Hamilton Harty in 1933 hints obliquely that the mood of the times also left its imprint on the symphony:

I must say I think it is almost hopeless for anyone to produce anything in any of the arts these days. It is practically impossible to get away from the general feeling of hopelessness and chaos which exists everywhere, however one may try – so you mustn't think I'm an exception, and one capable of compassing all difficulties and producing a masterpiece. But I'm trying my best.

Walton's self-doubt may sometimes be reflected in the emotional tone of the First Symphony, but at the same time the music is remarkable for its superb technical confidence. The beginning is riveting: a pianissimo drum roll, a touch of harmony on horns, a nervous flickering rhythm on strings, and a potently economical motif on oboe – these simple elements are enough to set a mighty current in motion. Eventually, after a tortured slower section, the music builds steadily to a cathartic, wrenchingly dissonant climax, before working through to a savagely triumphant major-key conclusion.

The second movement's rhythmic games (constant teasing alternations between bars of three and five beats) at first seem to offer a kind of relief, but this movement too builds inexorably to a climax of almost frenzied power. Walton hardly needed to add the marking 'con malizia' (with malice) – the music speaks for itself.

If the second movement tells of rage, the emotional territory of the third is one of regret and grief. The lyrical Walton – somewhat reined in during the first two movements – carries the argument here. The lovely, melancholic flute theme at the opening is never heard again in its entirety, but the return of one broken phrase at the very end of the movement, after another cathartic climax, is one of the symphony's most telling masterstrokes.

At first, the resolution and growing upbeat vitality of the finale suggest the beginning of a new story – perhaps a kind of Berliozian 'return to life'. But shades of earlier themes return throughout, especially in the magnificent coda – a paean of triumph, but not unclouded by memories of things past.

© Stephen Johnson

Chronology of works

1768	Haydn	Symphony No. 49 in F minor, 'La passione'
1772	Haydn	Symphony No. 45 in F sharp minor, 'Farewell'
1774	Mozart	Symphony No. 29 in A major, K201
	Mozart	Symphony No. 31 in D major, K297, 'Paris'
	Mozart	Symphony No. 35 in D major, K385, 'Haffner'
	Mozart	Symphony No. 36 in C major, K425, 'Linz'
	Mozart	Symphony No. 38 in D major, K504, 'Prague'
1787	Haydn	Symphony No. 88 in G major
1788	Mozart	Symphony No. 39 in E flat major, K543
	Mozart	Symphony No. 40 in G minor, K550
	Mozart	Symphony No. 41 in C major, K551, 'Jupiter'
1791	Haydn	Symphony No. 96 in D major, 'Miracle'
	Haydn	Symphony No. 99 in E flat major
	Haydn	Symphony No. 100 in G major, 'Military'
	Haydn	Symphony No. 101 in D major, 'Clock'
	Haydn	Symphony No. 103 in E flat major, 'Drumroll'
	Haydn	Symphony No. 104 in D major, 'London'
1799–1802	Beethoven	Symphony No. 2 in D major, Op. 36
1800	Beethoven	Symphony No. 1 in C major, Op. 21
	Beethoven	Symphony No. 3 in E flat major, Op. 55, 'Eroica'
1806	Beethoven	Symphony No. 4 in B flat major, Op. 60
1807–8	Beethoven	Symphony No. 5 in C minor, Op. 67
	Beethoven	Symphony No. 6 in F major, Op. 68, 'Pastoral'
	Beethoven	Symphony No. 7 in A major, Op. 92
	Beethoven	Symphony No. 8 in F major, Op. 93
1816	Schubert	Symphony No. 5 in B flat major
1822	Schubert	Symphony No. 8 in B minor, 'Unfinished'
1823–4	Beethoven	Symphony No. 9 in D minor, Op. 125, 'Choral'
1825–6	Schubert	Symphony No. 9 in C major, 'Great'
1829–42	Mendelssohn	Symphony No. 3 in A minor, Op. 56, 'Scottish'
1830	Berlioz	*Symphonie fantastique*, Op. 14
1833	Mendelssohn	Symphony No. 4 in A major, Op. 90, 'Italian'
1841	Schumann	Symphony No. 1 in B flat major, Op. 38, 'Spring'
	Schumann	Symphony No. 4 in D minor, Op. 120 (revised 1851)
1845–6	Schumann	Symphony No. 2 in C major, Op. 61
1850	Schumann	Symphony No. 3 in E flat major, Op. 97, 'Rhenish'
1862–7	Brahms	Symphony No. 1 in C minor, Op. 68
1872	Tchaikovsky	Symphony No. 2 in C minor, Op. 17
1874	Bruckner	Symphony No. 4 in E flat major, 'Romantic' (revised 1889–90)

1875–6	Bruckner	Symphony No. 5 in B flat major
1877	Brahms	Symphony No. 2 in D major, Op. 73
	Tchaikovsky	Symphony No. 4 in F minor, Op. 36
1881–3	Bruckner	Symphony No. 7 in E major
1883	Brahms	Symphony No. 3 in F major, Op. 90
1884–5	Brahms	Symphony No. 4 in E minor, Op. 98
–1885	Dvořák	Symphony No. 7 in D minor, Op. 70
–1887	Bruckner	Symphony No. 8 in C minor
–1888	Mahler	Symphony No. 1 in D major (revised 1893–6)
1886–8	Franck	Symphony in D minor
	Saint-Saëns	Symphony No. 3 in C minor, Op. 78, 'Organ Sympho
1887	Bruckner	Symphony No. 9 in D minor
1888–94	Mahler	Symphony No. 2 in C minor, 'Resurrection'
	Tchaikovsky	Symphony No. 5 in E minor, Op. 64
1889	Dvořák	Symphony No. 8 in G major, Op. 88
1893	Dvořák	Symphony No. 9 in E minor, Op. 95,
		'From the New World'
	Tchaikovsky	Symphony No. 6 in B minor, Op. 74, 'Pathétique'
1893–6	Mahler	Symphony No. 3 in D minor
1898	Sibelius	Symphony No. 1 in E minor, Op. 39
1899–1900	Mahler	Symphony No. 4 in G major, (revised 1901–1910)
1901–2	Sibelius	Symphony No. 2 in D major, Op. 43
	Mahler	Symphony No. 5 in C sharp minor
1903–4	Mahler	Symphony No. 6 in A minor
–1911	Elgar	Symphony No. 2 in E flat, Op. 63
1904–5	Mahler	Symphony No. 7 in B minor
1906–7	Rakhmaninov	Symphony No. 2 in E minor, Op. 27
	Mahler	Symphony No. 8 in E flat major,
		'Symphony of a Thousand'
1907–8	Elgar	Symphony No. 1 in A flat major, Op. 55
1907	Sibelius	Symphony No. 3 in C major, Op. 52
1909–11	Sibelius	Symphony No. 4 in A minor, Op. 63
1909–10	Mahler	Symphony No. 9 in D major
	Mahler	Symphony No. 10 (performing version 1959–75)
1911–15	R. Strauss	*An Alpine Symphony*, Op. 64
1912–13	V. Williams	*A London Symphony* (Symphony No. 2)
		(revised 1920, 1933)
1914	Nielsen	Symphony No. 4, Op. 29, 'The Inextinguishable'
1915	Sibelius	Symphony No. 5 in E flat major, Op. 82
		(revised 1916, 1919)
1917	Prokofiev	Symphony No. 1 in D major, 'Classical'
1920–2	Nielsen	Symphony No. 5, Op. 50
1921	V. Williams	*A Pastoral Symphony* (Symphony No. 3)
1923	Sibelius	Symphony No. 6 in D minor, Op. 104

1923–5	Shostakovich	Symphony No. 1 in F minor, Op. 10
1924	Sibelius	Symphony No. 7 in C major, Op. 105
1931–5	Walton	Symphony No. 1 in B flat minor
1931–4	V. Williams	Symphony No. 4 in F minor
1932	Elgar	Symphony No. 3 – The Sketches (elaboration 1993–7)
1935–6?	Shostakovich	Symphony No. 4 in C minor, Op. 43
	Rakhmaninov	Symphony No. 3 in A minor, Op. 44
1937	Shostakovich	Symphony No. 5 in D minor, Op. 47
1938–9	Harris	Symphony No. 3, In One Movement
1938–43	V. Williams	Symphony No. 5 in D major
1939	Britten	*Sinfonia da Requiem*, Op. 20
	Stravinsky	Symphony in C
1942–5	Stravinsky	Symphony in Three Movements
1943	Shostakovich	Symphony No. 8 in C minor, Op. 65
1944	V. Williams	Symphony No. 6 in E minor
	Prokofiev	Symphony No. 5 in B flat major, Op. 100
1944–6	Copland	Symphony No. 3
1946–8	Messiaen	*Turangalîla Symphony*
1953	Shostakovich	Symphony No. 10 in E minor, Op. 93
	V. Williams	Symphony No. 7, *Sinfonia antartica*
1956	V. Williams	Symphony No. 8 in D minor
1957	Shostakovich	Symphony No. 11 in G minor, Op. 103, 'The Year 1905'
1971	Shostakovich	Symphony No. 15 in A major, Op. 141